Conversations with Kenelm

Essays on the Theology of the *Commedia*

John Took

Professor of Dante Studies
UCL

UCL
Arts & Humanities Publications
2013

]u[

ubiquity press
London

Published by
Ubiquity Press Ltd.
Gordon House
29 Gordon Square
London WC1H 0PP
www.ubiquitypress.com

and

The Faculty of Arts and Humanities
University College London
Gower Street, London WC1E 6BT

Text © John Took 2013

First published 2013

Cover illustration: Dante, *Paradiso X*, depicting twelve teachers of wisdom led by Thomas Aquinas; MS Thott 411.2.
By kind permission of the Royal Library of Copenhagen.

Printed in the UK by Lightning Source Ltd.

ISBN: 978-1-909188-00-6

DOI: http://dx.doi.org/10.5334/baa

This work is licensed under the Creative Commons Attribution 3.0 Unported License. To view a copy of this license, visit http://creativecommons.org/licenses/by/3.0/ or send a letter to Creative Commons, 444 Castro Street, Suite 900, Mountain View, California, 94041, USA. This licence allows for copying any part of the work for personal and commercial use, providing author attribution is clearly stated.

Suggested citation:
Took, J. 2013 *Conversations with Kenelm*. London: University College London Arts & Humanities Publications / Ubiquity Press. DOI: http://dx.doi.org/10.5334/baa

To read the online open access version of this book, either visit http://dx.doi.org/10.5334/baa or scan this QR code with your mobile device:

For Paul

... e 'l padre dice al figlio 'amor mio' (*Convivio* III.xi.16)

Contents

Foreword   i

I   Between Philology and Friendship: Dante and Aquinas Revisited   1
1. Preliminary considerations: Dante, Aquinas and intimations of otherness. 2. Patterns of deconstruction and reconstruction: Nardi, Gilson and Foster. 3. An alternative proposal: modes of reading and reception. 4. Dante and the theological project: theology and the crisis of existence. 5. Conclusion: philology, friendship and the common proclamation.

II   The Twin Peaks of Dante's Theology in the *Paradiso*   49
1. Introduction: preliminary emphases – being, affectivity and a reconfiguration of the theological issue. 2. Atonement theology I: Anselm and the Christ event as a matter of reparation. 3. Atonement theology II: Dante and the Christ event as a matter of re-potentiation. 4. Election theology I: Thomas, implicit faith and salvation *in casu*. 5. Election theology II: Dante, explicit faith and the love-susceptibility of the Godhead.

III   Dante and the Modalities of Grace   81
1. Preliminary considerations: Singleton, Singletonians, and patterns of grace-theological consciousness. 2. Dante and the revised geometry of grace awareness. 3. Dante and the modalities of grace: grace as a principle of encouragement (being under the aspect of fortitude) – grace as a principle of emancipation (being under the aspect of freedom) – grace as a principle of ecstasy (being under the aspect of rejoicing). 4. Conclusion: grace as but love by another name.

IV   Events and Their Inner Life: an Essay in Actual Eschatology   105
1. Preliminary considerations: patterns of eschatological awareness in Dante. 2. Axes of concern: the triumph of the *innermost* over the *aftermost* (the cases of Francesca da Rimini, Pier della Vigna and Guido da Montefeltro). 3. Conclusion: eschatology, immanence and the power to terrify.

V   Two Dantes or One? An Essay in Transparency and Theatricality   121
1. Introduction: *ego, alter ego* and the problem of authorial intentionality – a preliminary response. 2. Piety, Peripateticism and sin as unreason: 'The Theology of the *Inferno*'. 3. Irreconcilability in the depths: 'The Two Dantes'. 4. Two Dantes or one?: dimensionality, decorum and the comprehensive geometry of the text.

VI   Complementarity and Coalescence:
Dante and the Sociology of Authentic Being   139
1. Introduction: the social dimension of the *Inferno* and a moment of misgiving. 2. The New Testament perspective: Pauline and Johannine collectivity. 3. The sociology of estrangement: self-denial and social denial. 4. The sociology of emergence: co-presence, co-immanence and the revised dimensionality of being.

VII   Dante and the Protestant Principle   155
1. Introduction: Protestantism and the protestant principle – preliminary considerations. 2. The Dantean protest: patterns of sacramentalism (Dante, grace and the historical encounter) and superintendence (Dante, episcopacy and self-episcopacy). 3. Conclusion: ecclesiality, existentiality and the whereabouts of the Dantean protest.

VIII   The Courage of the *Commedia*   171
1. Paul Tillich, *The Courage To Be*, and species of ontological anxiety: the anxiety of death and fate – the anxiety of guilt and condemnation – the anxiety of meaninglessness. 2. A further distinction: the *courage to be as part* and the *courage to be as oneself* – Dante and the *courage to be as part* (*civitas*, *imperium* and *ecclesia*). 3. Dante and the *courage to be as oneself*: the moment of acknowledgement (*Inferno*), the moment of alignment (*Purgatorio*), and the moment of actualization (*Paradiso*). 4. Conclusion: the courage of the pilgrim and the courage of the poet.

Afterword   191

Index of names   195

Foreword

> Indi, come orologio che ne chiami
> ne l'ora che la sposa di Dio surge
> a mattinar lo sposo perché l'ami,
> che l'una parte e l'altra tira e urge,
> tin tin sonando con sì dolce nota,
> che 'l ben disposto spirto d'amor turge;
> così vid' ïo la gloriosa rota
> muoversi e render voce a voce in tempra
> e in dolcezza ch'esser non pò nota
> se non colà dove gioir s'insempra.
>
> (*Par.* X.139-48)[1]

My first encounter with Kenelm Foster was in the depths of the Cambridge winter. The snow lay round about, and I had come to Blackfriars as a doctoral student just starting out and seeking advice on the usefulness or otherwise of comparing Dante and the second-generation Thomist

---

[1] Then, like a clock which calls us at the hour when the bride of God rises to sing her matins to her bridegroom, that he may love her, in which one part draws or drives the other, sounding *ting! ting!* with notes so sweet that the well-disposed spirit swells with love, so did I see the glorious wheel move and render voice to voice with harmony and sweetness that cannot be known except there where joy is everlasting. Principal editions: for the *Commedia*, ed. G. Petrocchi, *La Commedia secondo l'antica vulgata*, 4 vols (Milan and Verona: Mondadori, 1966-67); for the *Vita Nuova*, ed. D. De Robertis in *Opere minori*, 2 vols (Milan and Naples: Ricciardi, 1984), vol. 1, part 1, pp. 1-247; for the *Rime*, ed. G. Contini, 2nd edn (Turin: Einaudi, 1965), and in *Opere minori*, 2 vols (Milan and Naples: Ricciardi, 1984), vol. 1, part 1, pp. 249-552 ; for the *De vulgari eloquentia*, ed. P. V. Mengaldo in *Opere minori* (Milan and Naples: Ricciardi, 1979), vol. 2, pp. 3-237; for the *Convivio*, ed. C. Vasoli and D. De Robertis in *Opere minori* (Milan and Naples: Ricciardi, 1988), vol 1, part 2; for the *Monarchia*, ed. P. G. Ricci (Milan: Mondadori, 1965) and P. Shaw (ed. and trans.) (Cambridge: Cambridge University Press, 1995); for the *Epistole*, A. Frugoni and G. Brugnoli in *Opere minori* (Milan and Naples: Ricciardi, 1979), vol. 2, pp. 505-643. Translations (slightly amended): for the *Commedia*, *The Divine Comedy*, C. S. Singleton (Princeton: Princeton University Press, 1973-1980); for the *Convivio*, C. Ryan, *Dante. The Banquet* (Saratoga (Calif.): Anma Libri, 1989); for the *Monarchia*, P. Shaw cit. I am grateful to Princeton University Press for permission to quote from the Singleton translation.

John of Paris in the area of political thought. I knocked, the door opened, and there he was, spectacularly dishevelled but at once notable for his sparkling Thomist eyes, eyes accustomed to seeing into the nature of things and determining their specificity. Not quite sure what to say or how to get started, he ushered me into his study, found me somewhere to sit among the piles of books competing for space on his floor, enquired of me whether I was up to speed with the *Mittelalterliches Geistesleben* of Grabmann, and straightaway fell into a gentle state of abstraction. But the best was yet to come, for having looked over my plan and commented in a preliminary way on its viability, he led me through to the kitchen, sat me down at a large oval table with those brothers recently returned from the town, from the garden and from the chapel, took his place at the table – but at a chair's remove from me – and once again retreated into the stillness of his own inner world. The silence, I remember, seemed interminable. I coughed, rearranged myself on my seat, and eyed one by one the kindly faces of the brethren, the modest fair on the table, the bereft state of the room in which we were sitting, Kenelm himself in his egg-stained abstraction, and the world-weary chair between us confirming in its inbetweenness his, for the moment at least, total unreachability. But then all of a sudden, and as if summoned from deep within himself by an ancient comforter and companion, he lent over the empty chair, cocked his ear in an attitude of attentiveness, and whispered gently, 'I wonder what Brother Thomas would have to say about that'; for there in the chair between us *was* Brother Thomas, less than discernible, certainly, to the naked eye, but very definitely there, and perfectly prepared, as Brother Thomas always had been for Kenelm, to resolve the passing doubt and to assuage the passing anxiety. I was – and still am – impressed, for in my part of the Church there is nothing quite like it. For while in my part of the Church we revere our heroes – Luther, Calvin, Cranmer, Kierkegaard, Barth, Tillich and the cloud of Protestant witnesses generally, rarely do we lean over the chair to engage them in quite the same way and with quite the same degree of affection. We admire them, listen to them and learn from them, but we are not, somehow, quite so deeply in love with them. But there, ready and waiting for Kenelm, was Thomas, friend, fellow traveller, counsellor, and party to an intimate colloquium of the spirit. All would now be well.

The essays gathered together in this volume are not so much in commemoration of Kenelm Foster as in conversation with him, in the kind of conversation going on between those standing within the theological circle but inclined to deconstruct and reconstruct the argument according to the properties of formation and temperament. The first of them, entitled

'Between Philology and Friendship: Dante and Aquinas Revisited' and taking up afresh a question addressed in their time by Bruno Nardi, Etienne Gilson and Kenelm Foster himself, seeks to develop that question in terms, not only, nor even primarily, of the *what* of Dante's reading of the Thomist text, but of the *how* of that reading, of his capacity for finding there – as often as not over against its declared or otherwise evident intention – grounds for encouragement in respect of his own leading emphases. The relationship, then, is a complex one, otherness at the level of ideas being taken up in a kind of spiritual collegiality, in a species of *inmeing* and *inyouing* (the 'intuare' and 'inmiare' of *Par.* IX.81) tending, not only to transcend it, but to authorize it as the means to a more complete humanity.

The second essay, entitled 'The Twin Peaks of Dante's Theology in the *Paradiso*', turns on those instances of the text bearing witness to his readiness, not merely to restate, but to reshape the theological issue in the interests of something more persuasive, more accountable to its innermost – which for Dante means its innermost *affective* – reasons. On the one hand, then, there is his theology of atonement in Canto VII of the *Paradiso*, where propitiation at once gives way to potentiation as a means of seeing and understanding the life, death and resurrection of the Christ, to a sense of these things as a matter of God's confirming man afresh in respect of his power to significant self-affirmation. On the other hand, there is his theology of salvation in Cantos XIX and XX of the same canticle, where, starting with the predicament of those unfortunate enough to be born either before or beyond the Christian dispensation and with the apparent injustice, therefore, of their reprobation, Dante settles at last on a sense, not of God's impassivity as regards antique righteousness, but of his willingness to be persuaded by it. True, this is righteousness as engendered, sustained and perfected by grace; but, for all that, it *is* righteousness, Dante's logical and lexical preferences – his developing the issue in terms of the love whereby love itself is vanquished – constituting, if only for an instant, a shaking of the theological foundations.

The third essay, entitled 'Dante and the Modalities of Grace', takes its cue from the discussion generated by Antonio Mastrobuono's book *Dante's Journey of Sanctification* on the relationship of nature and grace in Dante and Thomas. Where, then, Singleton had been inclined to see in the Virgilian phase of the *Commedia* (i.e. in just about the whole of the first two canticles of the poem) a preparation for the influx or incomingness of grace as mediated by Beatrice, Mastrobuono insisted on the status of this too as a product of grace, there being no movement of the spirit into God other than by way of his facilitating that movement in the first place.

The thesis is unexceptionable, both operative and co-operative grace (the latter more prominent as an object of contemplation in Dante) entering as of the essence into the moral and theological structure both of the *Inferno* and of the *Purgatorio*, my own contribution to the discussion, therefore, proceeding by way, less of the priority, than of the practicality of grace – of grace as present to the individual under the aspect (*a*) of *encouragement*, (*b*) of *emancipation*, and (*c*) of *ecstatic affirmation*. It is, in other words, by grace that the anxious subject is strengthened in respect of the task in hand (grace as encouragement), that he is freed from the tyranny of his own leading but self-consciously inauthentic preferences (grace as emancipation), and that he emerges at last into the immediate presence of God in the ineffability of that presence (grace as ecstatic affirmation), this, therefore, constituting an essay, less in the *what* or the *why*, than in the *how* of grace in the moment of its verification.

The fourth essay, taking its cue as far as the title is concerned – 'Events and Their Inner Life: an Essay in Actual Eschatology' – from another pivotal moment of Dante scholarship in the English-speaking world (from Alan Charity's book on events and their afterlife in Dante),[2] sets out to explore on the basis of three episodes in particular of the *Inferno* the whereabouts of the ἔσχατος as the 'last thing' in human experience, the 'last thing', however, amounting for Dante, not only to the *aftermost* truth of human experience on the plane of the horizontal, but to the *innermost* truth of that experience on the plane of the vertical, herein, in its capacity for rising up from the depths to confront self in its destitution, lying its power to terrify.

The fifth essay, entitled 'Two Dantes or One? An Essay in Transparency and Theatricality', addresses Kenelm's sense of the *Commedia* as but further evidence of the tension in Dante between the pagan and the Christian components of his spirituality and of his failure to dispel this tension. The argument, eloquently set out in the twilight pages of his volume *The Two Dantes* of 1977, is, as always in Kenelm, as searching as it is seasoned, but it is not unanswerable; for over against everything in the poem making for tension and instability there are forces at work making for consistency and resolution, namely the kind of *transparency* whereby every surface inflexion of the spirit is brought home at last to its theological substance, and the kind of *theatricality* whereby, distributed as it is among the players, the restive voice is at once neutralized as a principle of disruption.

The sixth essay, entitled 'Complementarity and Coalescence: Dante and the Sociology of Authentic Being', touches on one of the most

---

[2] A. C. Charity, *Events and Their Afterlife. The Dialectics of Christian Typology in the Bible and Dante* (Cambridge: Cambridge University Press, 1966).

radiant emphases of Dante's mature spirituality, his sense, not only of the contiguity or *alongsideness*, but of the co-immanence or *indwellingness* of self and of the other-than-self in circumstances of consummate being. If, then, as the first-person articulation of the *Commedia* suggests, there is a sense in which the individual stands alone in respect of what matters alone, in respect of his destiny as a creature of eschatological accountability, then that, within the economy of the whole, is nonetheless qualified by a sense of the presence to self of the next man as a parameter of ontological awareness, as that whereby he both *is* and knows himself in the fullness of his own humanity.

The last two essays, entitled 'Dante and the Protestant Principle' and 'The Courage of the *Commedia*', take their cue from positions in the great German-American theologian Paul Tillich, who understood with perfect precision what is going on in Dante as the leading representative in the European Middle Ages of (as Tillich himself used to say) the existential point of view in theology, of theology as deriving its significance in human experience from its being unfolded across the problematics of existence as verified by the subject of that existence.[3] The first of them, entitled 'Dante and the Protestant Principle', has as I shall stress again nearer the time nothing whatever to do with fashioning from him a protestant spirit in any prototypical or otherwise historically anachronistic sense of the term, since for all his misgiving at the level of practicality, his is a spirit of reform contained by an untroubled sense of what the Church is in its apostolicity, its catholicity and its sacramentality. It has, however, everything to do with seeing in him, and especially in the mature spirituality of the *Commedia*, a desire to rethink accredited positions in the areas of soteriology and of election theology in the name and for the sake of their agapeic substance. On the one hand, then, there is his sense of the salvific significance, not only of the ecclesiastical encounter in particular, but of the historical and cultural encounter in general, while on the other there is his no less developed sense of episcopacy as a matter ultimately of *self*-episcopacy, of the soul's at last knowing itself in the autonomy of self, in the power of self to self-governance. And it is the courageousness of this, the element of heroism attendant upon the notion of self in its power to self-governance, that comes into focus in the final essay entitled

---

[3] Paul Tillich, *The Courage To Be* (London: Collins, 1962; originally 1952), pp. 128-29: 'The greatest poetic expression of the Existentialist point of view in the Middle Ages is Dante's *Divina Commedia*. It remains, like the religious depth psychology of the monastics, within the framework of the scholastic ontology. But within these limits it enters the deepest places of human self-destruction and despair as well as the highest places of courage and salvation, and gives in poetic symbols an all-embracing existential doctrine of man.'

'The Courage of the *Commedia*'; for if as Tillich maintains the courage of the Middle Ages was by and large the *courage to be as part* (which as far as Dante is concerned would mean the courage to affirm self by way of the Church, of the Empire, and of the city as instruments of divine purposefulness in the world), then we need also to acknowledge how it is that Dante's is a taking up of the *courage to be as part* in the *courage to be as oneself*, in the affirmation of self from out of its proper capacity for self-confrontation, for self-reconfiguration and for self-transcendence as constituting between them the infernal, the purgatorial and the paradisal moments of the soul's journey into God. For all his commitment, in other words, to the indispensability of the great institutions of medieval life as features of the soteriological scheme generally, there can be no question in Dante of resolving self in the other-than-self as the way of properly human being and becoming, in anything other than the power of the individual to moral and ontological self-determination.

In a celebratory moment of the *Paradiso*, Dante has Thomas go round the circle of sage spirits identifying each in turn in point of proper calling and confirming how it is that self is everywhere present to the other-than-self as a co-efficient of being in the endless and endlessly varied instantiation of that being. The image, at once perfectly Dantean and perfectly resplendent, underlies and informs these conversations of mine with Kenelm; for if in reading and rereading the cherished text, I have from time to time felt the need to enter a qualification, it is a matter here, as in the high consistory of paradise, of otherness as both contained and as authorized by sameness, as conditioned and set free by it for a life of its own. Never, in other words, is it a question in what follows of the stark alternativism of the *sed contra*, but instead a matter of formed friendship, of the kind of friendship which, conceived in love, makes for a sweet choreography of the spirit.

John Took,
Easter 2012

Between Philology and Friendship: Dante and Aquinas Revisited

> "Dio vede tutto, e tuo veder s'inluia",
> diss' io, "beato spirto, sì che nulla
> voglia di sé a te puot' esser fuia.
>   Dunque la voce tua, che 'l ciel trastulla
> sempre col canto di quei fuochi pii
> che di sei ali facen la coculla,
>   perché non satisface a' miei disii?
> Già non attendere' io tua dimanda,
> s'io m'intuassi, come tu t'inmii".
>
> (*Par.* IX.73-81)[1]

1. Preliminary considerations: Dante, Aquinas and intimations of otherness. 2. Patterns of deconstruction and reconstruction: Nardi, Gilson and Foster. 3. An alternative proposal: modes of reading and reception. 4. Dante and the theological project: theology and the crisis of existence. 5. Conclusion: philology, friendship and the common proclamation.

Perhaps the single most important accomplishment of twentieth-century Dante scholarship – certainly in the area of philosophy and theology – was the separating out of Dantean and Thomist spirituality, a process which, though coloured by the properties of personality, culminated by virtue of the energy and erudition of those party to it in a fresh sense both of what Dante owed to Thomas as more than ordinarily accomplished in the ways of Christian-theological intelligence and of what made of him his own man, a Christian thinker quite other in kind than Aquinas. Approaches to the issue were as many and varied as those who cared to address it, but for the moment we may settle for just three, the first two to an extent mutually dependent, the third presupposing them both, but each

---

[1] "God sees all, and into him your vision sinks, blessed spirit", I said, "so that no wish may steal itself from you. Why then does your voice, which ever gladdens heaven – together with the singing of those devout fires that make themselves a cowl with the six wings – not satisfy my longings? Surely I should not wait for your request were I in you even as you are in me."

committed to the business of disentanglement, of marking the difference between one species of Christian spirituality and another. First, then, there was Bruno Nardi with his at times abrasive sense, not only of the otherness of Dantean and Thomist positions in the areas of cosmology and metaphysics, but of the often more Albertan than Thomist complexion of Dante's thinking in these and related areas of concern. Then there was Etienne Gilson, who, while himself an occasionally militant spirit, was notable above all for his patient account of what he saw as, vis-à-vis that of Thomas, the more differentiated character of Dantean teleology, its tendency towards a more phased or periodic account of human experience in its positive unfolding. And finally there was Kenelm Foster, who, as one authorized by profession to pronounce in this matter, made it his business, not only to confirm Dante's admiration and indeed love for Thomas in the twofold piety and precision of his mind, but to stress as a matter both of temperamental and of methodological difference the depth of their divergence in the areas particularly of anthropology, epistemology and creation theology. Well before the end of the century, then, the myth of Dante's Thomism, at least in its more indiscriminate reaches, had as a result of these and of similar interventions been put to rest and the way opened up for a more responsible account of Dante's relationship with one of the most cherished of his *auctores*.[2]

---

[2] P. H. Wicksteed, *Dante and Aquinas* (London: Dent and New York: Dutton, 1913, with a facsimile reprint Honolulu (Hawaii): University Press of the Pacific, 2002); G. Busnelli, *Cosmogonia e antropogenesi secondo Dante Alighieri e le sue fonti* (Rome: Civiltà cattolica, 1922, with a review by Nardi in the *Giornale storico della letteratura italiana* 81 (1923), 307-34 and reproduced in his *Saggi di filosofia dantesca* (note 3 below), pp. 341-80); V. Vettori, 'S. Tommaso e Dante oggi', in *Tommaso d'Aquino nella storia del pensiero* (Naples: Edizioni Domenicane Italiane, 1976), vol. 2 (*Dal medioevo ad oggi*), pp. 149-51; M. Corti, *Dante a un nuovo crocevia* (Florence: Sansoni, 1982); eadem, *La felicità mentale: nuove prospettive per Cavalcanti e Dante* (Turin: Einaudi, 1983); E. Stump, 'Dante's Hell, Aquinas' Moral Theory, and the Love of God', *Canadian Journal of Philosophy* 16 (1986), 2, 181-98; B. Panvini, 'La concezione tomistica della grazia nella *Divina Commedia*', in *Letture classensi* 17 (Ravenna: Longo, 1988), pp. 69-85; L. M. La Favia, 'Thomas Aquinas and Siger of Brabant in Dante's *Paradiso*', in *Lectura Dantis Newberryana II (Chicago, Illinois, 1985-1987)*, ed. P. Cherchi and A. C. Mastrobuono (Evanston, Ill.: Northwestern University Press, 1990), pp. 147-72; A. C. Mastrobuono, *Dante's Journey of Sanctification* (Washington DC: Gateway, 1990); R. D. Crouse, 'Dante as Philosopher. Christian Aristotelianism', *Dionysius* 16 (1998), 141-56; M. Cogan, *The Design in the Wax. The Structure of the* Divine Comedy *and its Meaning* (Notre Dame and London: University of Notre Dame Press, 1999); A. A. Iannucci, 'Dante's Theological Canon in the *Commedia*', *Italian Quarterly* 37 (2000), 51-56; idem, 'Tommaso e il canone teologico in Dante', in *La Ciociaria tra letteratura e cinema. Atti del Convegno di Studi, Ripi 17-20 gennaio 2002*, ed. F. Zangrilli (Pesaro: Metauro, 2002), pp. 317-26; A. Gagliardi, 'Dante fra Sigieri e Tommaso', in *Tommaso d'Aquino e Averroè. La visione di Dio* (Soveria Mannelli: Rubbettino, 2002), pp. 273-94; W. Metz, 'Das Weltgericht bei Dante in Differenz zu Thomas von Aquin', in

2. Bruno Nardi's critique of the Thomist gloss on Dante rests upon an incomparable familiarity with medieval philosophy in its central emphases and endless by-ways.³ Committed as he was to an interpretation of the text in terms of the variety of its sources and allegiances in the areas both of

Ende und Vollendung. Eschatologische Perspektiven im Mittelalter, ed. J. A. Aertsen and M. Pickavé (Berlin and New York: Gruyter, 2002), pp. 626-37; G. Mazzotta, 'The Heaven of the Sun: Dante between Aquinas and Bonaventure', in *Dante for the New Millennium*, ed. T. Barolini and H. W. Storey (New York: Fordham University Press, 2003), pp. 152-68; F. Adorno, 'Dante (1265-1321), tra San Tommaso (1225/26-1274) e San Bonaventura (1221-1274)', in *Filosofi d'oggi per Dante*, ed. N. Ancarani, *Letture classensi* 32-34 (Ravenna: Longo, 2005), pp. 13-22.

³ On Nardi as a *dantista*, T. Gregory, 'Bruno Nardi', *Giornale critico della filosofia italiana* 22 (1968), 469-501 (also, with G. Petrocchi, 'Ricordo di Bruno Nardi', in *L'Alighieri. Rassegna bibliografica dantesca* 20 (1979), 1, 3-16, and, with P. Mazzantini (eds), Gli scritti di Bruno Nardi', in *'Lecturae' ed altri studi danteschi* (Florence: Le Lettere, 1990), pp. 285-312); E. Garin, 'Ricordo di Bruno Nardi (1884-1968)', *Studi danteschi* 45 (1969), 5-28; C. Vasoli, 'Bruno Nardi dantista', in *Letteratura italiana: I critici*, vol. 3 (Milan: Marzorati, 1970), pp. 2023-51; idem, 'Bruno Nardi e il "restauro" della filosofia di Dante', *Letteratura e filologia tra Svizzera e Italia. Studi in onore di Guglielmo Gorni*, 3 vols, ed. M. A. Terzoli et al. (Rome: Edizioni di Storia e Letteratura, 2010), vol. 1 (*Dante: la Commedia e altro*), pp. 57-73; A. Schiaffini, 'Bruno Nardi filologo e scrittore', in *Italiano antico e moderno*, ed. T. De Mauro and P. Mazzantini (Milan and Naples: Ricciardi, 1975), pp. 331-39; A. Vallone, *Storia della critica dantesca dal XIV al XX secolo*, 2 vols (Milan: Vallardi, 1981), vol. 2, pp. 890-93; idem, 'Bruno Nardi "lettore" di Dante con Appendice di lettere inedite', in *Profili e problemi del dantismo* (Naples: Liguori, 1985), pp. 355-420; F. Mazzoni, 'Bruno Nardi dantista', in *L'Alighieri. Rassegna bibliografica dantesca* 23 (1982), 2, 8-28; T. Nardi, 'Dal carteggio di Bruno Nardi', in *La Società Dantesca Italiana 1888-1988 (Atti del Convegno Internazionale, Firenze 24-26 novembre 1988*, ed. R. Abardo (Milan and Naples: Ricciardi, 1995), pp. 89-97; G. M. Cao, 'Appunti storiografici in margine al carteggio Gilson-Nardi', in *Giornale critico della filosofia italiana*, 6th series, 21 (2001), 137-70; O. Capitani, 'Bruno Nardi e il percorso dantesco dal *Convivio* alla *Commedia*', in *Medievistica e medievisti nel secondo Novecento* (Spoleto: Centro Italiano di Studi sull'Alto Medioevo, 2003), pp. 239-62 (originally the introduction to the second edn of *Dal Convivio alla Commedia* (Rome: Istituto Italiano per il Medio Evo, 1992), pp. 5-29). Nardi himself on Dante and Thomas, 'Intorno al tomismo di Dante e alla quistione di Sigieri', *Giornale Dantesco* 22 (1914), 182-97; 'Il tomismo di Dante e il P. Busnelli S.J.', *Giornale storico della letteratura italiana* 81 (1923), 307-34 (a review of G. Busnelli, *Cosmogonia e antropogenesi secondo Dante Alighieri e le sue fonti* (note 2 above), also in *Saggi di filosofia dantesca*, 2nd edn (Florence: La Nuova Italia, 1967), pp. 341-80); *Dante e la cultura medievale* (Bari: Laterza, 1942, in a new edn by P. Mazzantini with an introduction by T. Gregory (Rome and Bari: Laterza, 1983)); review of F. Orestano, 'Dante e "il buon frate Tommaso"' (*Sophia* 9 (1941), 1-19), *Studi danteschi* 26 (1942), 148-60; *Nel mondo di Dante* (Rome: Edizioni di Storia e Letteratura, 1944); *Dal 'Convivio' alla 'Commedia': sei saggi danteschi* (Rome: Nella sede dell'Istituto, 1960; in a new edn with a preface by O. Capitani (Rome: Istituto Storico Italiano per il Medio Evo, 1992)); *Saggi e note di critica dantesca* (Milan: Ricciardi, 1966); *'Lecturae' e altri studi danteschi*, ed. R. Abardo (Florence: Le Lettere, 1990). For a general bibliography, *Saggi sulla cultura veneta del Quattro e Cinquecento*, ed. P. Mazzantini (Padua: Antenore, 1971), pp. ix-xlix.

philosophy and of theology, he was never less than impatient (*a*) with too ready a referral of Dante to Aquinas as in any sense paramount among his authorities, (*b*) with instances of intertextuality reducible to the mere τόποι of scholastic discourse, and (*c*) with the least hint of carelessness in respect of the precise form of the source text, be it Thomist or otherwise, and thus as regards its precise meaning. Exemplary in respect of the first of these is the following passage on Busnelli's alignment of Thomas and Dante in the field of general cosmology, this, Nardi thinks, being but another instance of his at-all-costs attempt, if not to reconcile the unreconcilable exactly, then to extract from the text a meaning other than that evidently intended by the author: 'il passo della stessa opera [*Contra gentiles*], II.30, tende a dimostrare che le cose create possono dirsi assolutamente necessarie per rapporto ai principii prossimi di cui risultano. Così, per il fatto che gli esseri del mondo inferiore son costituiti di materia e di forma, e siccome la loro materia è in potenza a ricevere forme contrarie, essi sono necessariamente corruttibili. Al contrario, poiché la forma è atto e non potenza, quando essa sussiste senza materia, come nelle intelligenze separate, oppure esaurisce tutta la potenza della materia, com'è il caso dei corpi celesti, è necessariamente incorruttibile. Io chiedo al Busnelli che cosa ha che fare questo discorso col passo in cui Dante afferma, con alcuni vecchi Dottori scolastici, che "Dio in principio creò tre cose": la pura forma (le intelligenze), la materia informe (soggetto dei quattro elementi) e il composto indissolubile di materia e di forma (i cieli)!'[4] In fact, the issue may be more delicate than Nardi supposed, for

---

[4] The passage drawn from the same work (*ScG* II.xxx) sets out to show how things which are created might be said to be absolutely necessary as regards the proximate principles from which they flow. So, by virtue of the fact that beings here below are made up of form and matter, and that their matter is in potential to receiving other forms, they are necessarily corruptible. Since form, by contrast, is act rather than potency, whenever it subsists immaterially (as in the separate substances), or when it exhausts the whole potentiality of matter (as with the heavenly bodies), it is necessarily incorruptible. I therefore ask of Busnelli what all this has to do with the passage in which, with some of the old scholastic doctors, Dante affirms that "God in the beginning created three things", pure form (the Intelligences), uninformed matter (the subject of the four elements), and the indissoluble amalgamation of matter and form (the heavens)! (*Saggi di filosofia dantesca* (note 3 above), p. 343). For the triple procession of pure form, pure matter and their amalgamation in the superlunary world from the Godhead, *Par.* XXIX.10-36. Thomas, in the passage indicated (*ScG* II.xxx.9-11), has 'Ex his autem principiis, secundum quod sunt essendi principia, tripliciter sumitur necessitas absoluta in rebus. Uno quidem modo, per ordinem ad esse eius cuius sunt. Et quia materia, secundum id quod est, ens in potentia est; quod autem potest esse, potest etiam et non esse: ex ordine materiae necessario res aliquae corruptibiles existunt; sicut animal quia ex contrariis compositum est, et ignis quia eius materia est contrariorum susceptiva. Forma autem, secundum id quod est, actus est: et per eam res actu existunt. Unde ex ipsa provenit necessitas ad esse in quibusdam.

as often as not when it comes to Dante and his *auctores* it is a question, not so much of the *what*, as of the *how* of his reading, of what, over and beyond (or even over and against) the author's original intention, he chooses to find there – at which point reading shades off into reception as the nub of the issue. For Nardi, however, this is not the point, for at the level of authorial intention they are simply not talking about the same thing. And that is not all, for even when they *are* talking about the same thing, it often comes down, Nardi thinks, to the mere commonplaces of the scholastic mind, these, therefore, as a means of identifying patterns of allegiance and of antagonism, making for something less than good scholarship; so, for example, on Dante's supposed recourse to the *Contra gentiles* in the areas of creation theology and of astral determinism, these remarks, peremptory as ever, on the unexceptionality of it all: 'il passo della stessa somma *Contra gent.*, II.19, e gli altri affini, in cui è detto che la creazione è passaggio istantaneo dal non essere all'essere, simile al diffondersi della luce, secondo la fisica antica, racchiude un concetto comune fra gli Scolastici ... la citazione di San Tommaso, ov'è detto che i cieli influiscono colla luce e col moto, è superflua. Si tratta di un luogo comune.'[5] Here,

Quod contingit vel quia res illae sunt formae non in materia: et sic non inest ei potentia ad non esse, sed per suam formam semper sunt in virtute essendi; sicut est in substantiis separatis. Vel quia formae earum sua perfectione adaequant totam potentiam materiae, ut sic non remaneat potentia ad aliam formam, nec per consequens ad non esse: sicut est in corporibus caelestibus. In quibus vero forma non complet totam potentiam materiae, remanet adhuc in materia potentia ad aliam formam. Et ideo non est in eis necessitas essendi, sed virtus essendi consequitur in eis victoriam formae super materia: ut patet in elementis et elementatis. Forma enim elementi non attingit materiam secundum totum eius posse: non enim fit susceptiva formae elementi unius nisi per hoc quod subiicitur alteri parti contrarietatis. Forma vero mixti attingit materiam secundum quod disponitur per determinatum modum mixtionis. Idem autem subiectum oportet esse contrariorum et mediorum omnium, quae sunt ex commixtione extremorum. Unde manifestum est quod omnia quae vel contrarium habent vel ex contrariis sunt, corruptibilia sunt. Quae autem huiusmodi non sunt, sempiterna sunt: nisi per accidens corrumpantur, sicut formae quae non subsistunt sed esse earum est per hoc quod insunt materiae.'

[5] the passage from the selfsame *Summa contra gentiles* (II.19), and others like it, where – somewhat after the manner of the diffusion of light in ancient physics – it is said that creation is a matter of the immediate passage from non-being to being, embodies a notion common among the scholastics ... the quotation from Saint Thomas, where it is said that the heavens exercise their influence by their light and their movement, is superfluous, for this is a mere commonplace (*Saggi di filosofia dantesca* (note 3 above), pp. 343 and 353). Spirited in this respect, p. 354: 'Il ravvicinare, quindi, questa dottrina antica alle dottrine dei moderni astronomi, sull'azione che certi corpi celesti esercitano sulla terra, è una specie di concordismo molto simile a quello biblico dell'abate Moigno; meglio ancora, una tardiva e inaspettata difesa dei dilemmi di Don Ferrante.' Thomas, at II.xix.6, has 'Relinquitur igitur quod creatio sit in instanti. Unde simul aliquid, dum creatur, creatum est: sicut simul illuminatur et illuminatum est.'

then, it is a question of discernment, of the kind of sixth sense whereby those genuinely expert in these things pick up on the significant instance. And finally, there is Nardi's impatience at the philological level, where anything less than scrupulous attention to editorial exactness spells disaster for exact understanding. Exemplary in this sense is the following passage on the difference between seminal reason as a property of matter and the virtual presence of the idea to the Creator as its author and origin, where Busnelli, addressing a passage in the Dantean *Quaestio* but misled as to punctuation, is said by Nardi to confuse the issue:

> per dimostrarmi che Dante nega nella materia le *rationes seminales*, il Busnelli mi cita questo passo della *Quaestio*, XVIII, 46:
>
> Cum omnes forme, que sunt in potentia materie idealiter, sint in actu in Motore celi ...
>
> A p. 16, n. 1, il Busnelli aveva dichiarato di riferirsi, per le citazioni di Dante, al testo critico della Società Dantesca. Ora invece, zitto zitto, senza darne avviso al lettore, mi trasporta, come fanno altre edizioni, la virgola che nel testo critico è, con ragione, dopo la parola *materie*, e non dopo *idealiter*, e così mi cambia tutto il senso del passo citato. È vero che il Busnelli potrebbe farsi forte di altre edizioni. Ma egli avrebbe torto. Prima di tutto, perché il passo della *Quaestio* va messo in relazione coi versi 127-138 del canto II e coi versi 67-69 del canto XIII del *Paradiso*. Poi per un'altra ragione: il passo d'Averroè, citato da Dante, non si trova nel *De substantia orbis*, ma nel commento alla *Metafisica*, e suona così:
>
> Omnes proportiones et formae sunt in potentia in prima materia et in actu in primo Motore.
>
> L'*idealiter* non c'è; ma Dante, che cita a senso, senza avere il testo sotto gli occhi, l'ha aggiunto per render meglio il significato. Anche Tommaso cita questo passo, nel II delle *Sentenze*, per provare l'esistenza delle *idee* in Dio.[6]

---

[6] for the purposes of convincing me how it is that Dante denies the presence in matter of seminal reasons, Busnelli cites the passage from the *Quaestio* at XVIII, 46: "Since all forms, which are ideally present in matter potentially, are in act in the mover of the heavens ...". On p. 16 at note 1, Busnelli had made it plain that, when it comes to quoting Dante, he had used the critical text of the Società Dantesca. Now, however, without so much as a word, he follows other editions in relocating the comma which, in the critical text, and with good reason, is put, not after 'idealiter', but after 'materie', thus changing the entire sense of the quotation. True, Busnelli could well draw comfort in this from the other editions, but he would be wrong in doing so, above all because the passage from the *Quaestio* needs to be set alongside lines 127-38 of Canto II of the *Paradiso* and

Unmistakable here is the note of philosophical and philological triumphalism never far beneath the surface in Nardi as one exceptionally competent in the field; but never even so is there any attempt in his work to minimize, still less to spirit away, Thomas's presence to Dante as to the fore among his *auctores*, as tending to shape the notional or expressive instance. On the contrary, he has by his own admission no axe to grind, no 'mulino antitomistico' where Dante is concerned,[7] for, Thomas, certainly, is there, if as but one of those from whom Dante derived comfort in respect of this or that inflexion of the spirit: 'Né tomista, né antitomista, Dante prende il materiale della sua informazione filosofica con largo spirito eclettico, nel ricco arsenale della Scolastica, senza esclusione di scuole; e quel materiale poi rifonde nel crogiuolo della sua mente, collo sforzo della riflessione personale, in quell'ardente crogiuolo da cui escono, temprati di pensiero filosofico, i fantasmi della più alta poesia'.[8] The 'fantasmi della più alta poesia' element in this way of putting it, touching as it does upon the power of poetry properly or at least persuasively to signify in the area of theology, raises as many issues as it resolves, but in respect of what matters here – namely the nature of Dante's dealings with his *auctores* in general and with Thomas in particular – the formula is unexceptionable.

Etienne Gilson, whose work as a historian of medieval thought consistently, though not uncritically, complements that of Nardi, is similarly preoccupied by the problem of over-interpretation, by the need come what may to accredit Dante by way of Aquinas, an issue he pursues, however, by way pre-eminently of otherness and eccentricity, of what from a strictly Thomist point of view amounts to too ready an inclination in Dante to interrupt the continuity of human activity in time and eternity in favour of moral and intellectual finalities open to accomplishment here and now.[9] The

---

lines 67-69 of Canto XIII. And that's not all, for the Averroes passage cited by Dante is not, in fact, in the *De substantia orbis*, but in the commentary on the *Metaphysics*, and runs thus: "All proportions and forms are in potential in prime matter and in act in the first mover." There is no 'idealiter' here, Dante, citing according to his sense of the passage and without the text to hand, adding it all the better to bring out its meaning. Thomas too cites this passage in Book II of the *Sentences* for the purpose of proving the existence of *ideas* in God (*Saggi di filosofia* (note 3 above), p. 347).

[7] Ibid., p. 379: 'Il Parodi, in un benevolo cenno di coserelle mie, mi accusa garbatamente di tirare l'acqua, trattando della filosofia di Dante, al mio "mulino antitomistico".'

[8] Neither for Thomas nor against Thomas, Dante proceeds on an ample eclectic basis to gather up all he needs by way of philosophical substance and inspiration from the rich arsenal of scholasticism, excluding as he does so no tradition; and all this he refashions by way of his own personal reflection in the crucible of his mind, the crucible from which proceed, philosophically tempered, the most exalted flights of poetic imagination (ibid., pp. 379-80).

[9] On Gilson as a *dantista*, *Etienne Gilson's letters to Bruno Nardi*, ed. P. Dronke (Tavarnuzze (Florence): Galluzzo, 1998); S. Toussaint, 'Dante tra neoscolastica e teologia poetica:

pattern is indeed a recognizable one, Dante's, in respect both of cognition and of appetition, being a tendency to interrupt the flow of human experience under the aspect both of time alone and of time and eternity taken together in favour of its successive instants, of points of arrival along the way; so, for example, as regards cognition, these lines from Book IV of the *Convivio* (xiii.1-2) with their sense of human intellection as but a movement from one peak of understanding to the next:

> A la questione rispondendo, dico che propriamente crescere lo desiderio de la scienza dire non si può, avvegna che, come detto è, per alcuno modo si dilati. Ché quello che propriamente cresce, sempre è uno: lo desiderio de la scienza non è sempre uno, ma è molti, e finito l'uno, viene l'altro; sì che, propriamente parlando, non è crescere lo suo dilatare, ma successione di picciola cosa in grande cosa. Che se io desidero di sapere li principii de le cose naturali, incontanente che io so questi, è compiuto e terminato questo desiderio. E se poi io desidero di sapere che cosa e com'è ciascuno di questi principii, questo è un altro desiderio nuovo, né per l'avvenimento di questo non mi si toglie la perfezione a la quale mi condusse l'altro; e questo cotale dilatare non è cagione d'imperfezione, ma di perfezione maggiore. Quello veramente de la ricchezza è propriamente crescere, ché è sempre pur uno, sì che nulla successione quivi si vede, e per nullo termine e per nulla perfezione.[10]

Curtius, Maritain, Maurras, Gilson', in *Dante e la cultura del suo tempo. Dante e le culture dei confini. Atti del Convegno Internazionale di Studi Danteschi, Gorizia, ottobre 1997* (Gorizia: Società Dante Alighieri (Fondazione Cassa di Risparmio di Gorizia), 1999), pp. 81-90; C. Marabelli, 'Etienne Gilson e Dante', in *Medievali e medievisti. Saggi su aspetti del Medioevo teologico e della sua interpretazione* (Milan: Jaca Book, 2000), pp. 243-48. On Gilson generally, L. K. Shook, *Etienne Gilson* (Toronto: Pontifical Institute of Mediaeval Studies, 1984). In Gilson himself, *Dante and Philosophy*, trans. D. Moore (New York: Harper and Row, 1963; originally *Dante et la philosophie*, Paris: Vrin, 1939; in Italian, *Dante e la filosofia*, ed. C. Marabelli, (Milan: Jaca Book, 1987)); 'Dante's Notion of a Shade: *Purgatorio* XXV', *Medieval Studies* 29 (1967), 14-42 (also in *Dante. The Critical Complex*, 8 vols, ed. R. Lansing (New York and London: Routledge, 2003), vol. 3, pp. 340-58); 'Dante's *Mirabile Visione*', *Cornell Library Journal* 5 (1968), 1-17; *Dante et Béatrice: études dantesques* (Paris: Vrin, 1974), with an Italian translation ed. B. Garavelli (Milan: Medusa, 2004); 'Dante, la filosofia e la politica', *Cultura e libri* 57 (1990), 56-60; 'Dante's Place in History', in *Critical Essays on Dante*, ed. G. Mazzotta (Boston: G. K. Hall, 1991), pp. 119-39. On Thomas, and apart from *Le Thomisme: introduction à la philosophie de saint Thomas d'Aquin* (5th and 6th edn Paris: Vrin, 1947 and 1965 respectively; originally 1919) and its many reprints both of the original and in translation, *The Elements of Christian Philosophy* (New York: Doubleday, 1960). For a general bibliography, *Etienne Gilson: a bibliography / une bibliographie* (*The Etienne Gilson Series*, 3), ed. M. McGrath (Toronto: Pontifical Institute of Medieval Studies, 1982).

[10] My response to the difficulty is as follows. The desire for knowledge cannot be said to grow in the strict sense, although, as I have shown, it broadens out in a certain way. Whatever grows in the strict sense always remains a single entity. The desire for knowledge does not remain a single entity. It is multiple, and when one desire is satisfied

while as regards appetition, these from Book III (xv.7-10) designed to secure in the wake of a now soaring spirituality a species of philosophical wisdom, and thus of philosophical happiness, proportionate to those 'many men and women in this language of ours burdened by domestic and civic care' but anxious in respect of their proper humanity, of what it might mean *to be* as a creature of adult accountability:

> Veramente può qui alcuno forte dubitare come ciò sia, che la sapienza possa fare l'uomo beato, non potendo a lui perfettamente certe cose mostrare; con ciò sia cosa che 'l naturale desiderio sia a l'uomo di sapere, e sanza compiere lo desiderio beato essere non possa. A ciò si può chiaramente rispondere che lo desiderio naturale in ciascuna cosa è misurato secondo la possibilitade de la cosa desiderante: altrimenti andrebbe in contrario di sé medesimo, che impossibile è; e la Natura l'avrebbe fatto indarno, che è anche impossibile. In contrario andrebbe: ché, desiderando la sua perfezione, desiderrebbe la sua imperfezione; imperò che desiderrebbe sé sempre desiderare e non compiere mai suo desiderio (e in questo errore cade l'avaro maladetto, e non s'accorge che desidera sé sempre desiderare, andando dietro al numero impossibile a giungere). Avrebbelo anco la Natura fatto indarno, però che non sarebbe ad alcuno fine ordinato. E però l'umano desiderio è misurato in questa vita a quella scienza che qui avere si può, e quello punto non passa se non per errore, lo quale è di fuori di naturale intenzione. E così è misurato ne la natura angelica, e terminato, in quanto, in quella sapienza che la natura di ciascuno può apprendere. E questa è la ragione per che li Santi non hanno tra loro invidia, però che ciascuno aggiugne lo fine del suo desiderio, lo quale desiderio è con la bontà de la natura misurato. Onde, con ciò sia cosa che conoscere di Dio e di certe altre cose quello esse sono non sia possibile a la nostra natura, quello da noi naturalmente non è desiderato di sapere. E per questo è la dubitazione soluta.[11]

another comes into being, so that, in the broadening out of the desire for knowledge, growth, strictly speaking, does not occur; rather, what happens is that something small is successively replaced by something large. For instance, if I desire to know the constitutive principles of physical objects, this desire is fulfilled and brought to completion as soon as I know what these principles are. If I then desire to know with respect to each of these principles how it is composed, and what are its sources, this is another and distinct desire. Further, the occurrence of this new desire does not deprive me of the perfection gained through fulfilling the first desire. Such broadening out does not cause imperfection. In the case of the desire for riches, by contrast, what occurs is growth in the strict sense, since the desire always remains one and the same thing: one entity is replaced by another, since nothing comes to completion and no perfection is attained.

[11] However, at this point a person may seriously wonder how it can be that wisdom can make man happy, if it cannot perfectly show certain things to him, since the natural desire of man is to know, and he cannot be happy unless that desire is satisfied. To this, the clear answer can be given that the natural desire in everything is in accordance with the

Throughout, then, the pattern is the same, Dante, with respect both to knowing and to willing, being inclined to construe these things successionally or in terms of an ideal progression from one qualitatively distinct moment to the next. Gilson, however, pursues the idea on the basis, not of these, but of two other passages pointing in the same direction, namely *Conv.* II.xiv.14-18 as touching on ethics rather than metaphysics as (theology apart) the human science *par excellence*, and *Mon.* III.xvi.7-8 as touching on the complementarity of philosophy and theology as the means respectively to mortal and immortal happiness, each of these passages, he thinks, testifying to this same preoccupation, less with understanding in the round, than with the completeness of the cognitive instance. First, then, on ethics as the ground of human happiness this side of death, the *Convivio* passage, secure in its sense of moral science as the architectonic or organizational science in human experience and of the authorization of this position both in Thomas and in the Philosopher:

> Lo Cielo cristallino, che per Primo Mobile dinanzi è contato, ha comparazione assai manifesta a la Morale Filosofia; ché Morale Filosofia, secondo che dice Tommaso sopra lo secondo de l'Etica, ordina noi a l'altre scienze. Che, sì come dice lo Filosofo nel quinto de l'Etica, 'la giustizia legale ordina la scienze ad apprendere, e comanda, perché non siano abbandonate, quelle essere apprese e ammaestrate'; e così lo detto cielo ordina col suo movimento la cotidiana revoluzione

capacity of the thing which desires; otherwise the thing would strive in a fashion contrary to its own being, which is impossible; and Nature would have made it in vain, which is also impossible. It would strive in a self-contrary fashion, for in desiring its own perfection it would desire its own imperfection, because it would desire always to be desiring and never to satisfy its own desire (which is the error into which the accursed miser falls: he does not recognize that he desires always to be desiring, in striving after a number impossible to reach). Also, Nature would have made it in vain, because it would not be directed to any end. Human desire, consequently, is measured in this life in accordance with that knowledge which can be gained here, and never passes that point except in error, which is something foreign to the intention of nature. In the angelic nature desire is likewise measured, and is limited precisely to that wisdom which the nature of each is capable of apprehending. It is for this reason, too, that the saints do not envy each other, for each attains the end of his own desire, and this desire is commensurate with the quality of his goodness. Since, then, it is impossible for our nature to know of God what He is (the same holds true of certain other things), this is not something which we naturally desire to know. In this way the difficulty is resolved. For the 'many men and women in this language of ours' element of the argument, *Conv.* I.ix.5 and i.4: 'e questi nobili sono principi, baroni, cavalieri, e molt'altra nobile gente, non solamente maschi ma femmine, che sono molti e molte in questa lingua, volgari, e non litterati ... Di fuori da l'uomo possono essere similemente due cagioni intese, l'una de le quali è induttrice di necessitade, l'altra di pigrizia. La prima è la cura familiare e civile, la quale convenevolmente a sé tiene de li uomini lo maggior numero, sì che in ozio di speculazione esser non possono.'

di tutti li altri, per la quale ogni die tutti quelli ricevono [e mandano] qua giù la vertude di tutte le loro parti. Che se la revoluzione di questo non ordinasse ciò, poco di loro vertude qua giù verrebbe o di loro vista. Onde ponemo che possibile fosse questo nono cielo non muovere, la terza parte del cielo sarebbe ancora non veduta in ciascun luogo de la terra; e Saturno sarebbe quattordici anni e mezzo a ciascuno luogo de la terra celato, e Giove sei anni quasi si celerebbe, e Marte uno anno quasi, e lo Sole centottantadue dì e quattordici ore (dico dì, cioè tanto tempo quanto misurano cotanti dì), e Venere e Mercurio quasi come lo Sole si celerebbe e mosterrebbe, e la Luna per tempo di quattordici dì e mezzo, starebbe ascosa ad ogni gente. E da vero non sarebbe qua giù generazione né vita d'animale o di piante: notte non sarebbe né die, né settimana né mese né anno, ma tutto l'universo sarebbe disordinato, e lo movimento de li altri sarebbe indarno. E non altrimenti, cessando la Morale Filosofia, l'altre scienze sarebbero celate alcuno tempo, e non sarebbe generazione né vita di felicitade, e indarno sarebbero scritte e per antico trovate. Per che assai è manifesto, questo cielo [in] sé avere a la Morale Filosofia comparazione.[12]

[12] The crystalline heaven, described as the first moving body in the account given above, is quite clearly similar to moral philosophy, because, as Thomas says in his commentary on the second book of the *Ethics*, moral philosophy directs us towards the other sciences. For, as the Philosopher states in the fifth book of the *Ethics*, "civic justice directs that the sciences be learned in due order, and, to ensure that they never be abandoned, commands that they be both learned and taught"; similarly the heaven just mentioned directs with its movement the daily revolution of all the others, by which means all those heavens every day receive and communicate to our world below the power invested in their every part, for if the revolution of this heaven did not direct this, little of their power would come down to our world below, and we would have little sight of them. Consequently, in the hypothetical case that this ninth heaven did not move, a third of the heaven of the stars would not yet have been seen from any place on earth; Saturn would be hidden from every place on earth for fourteen and a half years; Jupiter would be hidden for almost six years, Mars for almost a year, the Sun for one hundred and eighty two days days and fourteen hours. Venus and Mercury would be hidden and be visible for much the same time as the Sun, and the Moon would remain concealed from all mankind for fourteen and a half days. And indeed in this world below, plant and animal life would neither be generated nor continue; there would be neither night nor day, no weeks, months or years, and in fact the whole universe would be thrown into disorder, and the movement of other heavens would be in vain. In the same way, should moral philosophy disappear, the other sciences would be hidden for some time, the life of happiness would neither be generated nor continue, and it would have been in vain that the sciences were discovered in ancient times and committed to writing. It is quite clear, then, that this heaven has a similarity to moral philosophy. Thomas (*In eth.* II, lect. 1, note 1), tracing the structure of the second book of the *Ethics*, has 'Prima autem pars dividitur in partes duas: in prima determinat de virtutibus moralibus. In secunda de intellectualibus, in sexto libro, ibi; quia autem existimus prius dicentes et cetera. Et ratio ordinis est, quia virtutes morales sunt magis notae, et per eas disponimur ad intellectuales.' For Thomas on *iustitia legalis* and the common good, V, lect. 3, but the form of Dante's argument suggests I, lect. 2, n. 9:

Gilson, alarmed by Dante's commitment to ethics pure and simple – to ethics as untouched by theology – as the ground of human well-being here and now, lets it pass for the moment, contenting himself instead with some remarks relative to his, Thomistically speaking, no less strange promotion of ethics over metaphysics in the order of scientific excellence: 'at the risk', he says, 'of slightly stretching Dante's thought, but with the object of bringing out what seems to me the idea which a great number of passages suggest, I am going to say, in definitely stating that the formula is not his, that metaphysics as conceived by Dante remains *in itself* the loftiest and most perfect of the sciences, but that it is not so *as far as we are concerned*'.[13] But by the time we reach the *Monarchia* he is more resolute, more intent on pointing up the damage done to the fabric of Christian wisdom, and thus of Christendom itself, by what amounts to Dante's effrontery at this point, to his indifference to the seamlessness of it all. The offending text reads thus:

> Duos igitur fines providentia illa inenarrabilis homini proposuit intendendos: beatitudinem scilicet huius vite, que in operatione proprie virtutis consistit et per terrestrem paradisum figuratur; et beatitudinem vite ecterne, que consistit in fruitione divini aspectus ad quam propria virtus ascendere non potest, nisi lumine divino adiuta, que per paradisum celestem intelligi datur. Ad has quidem beatitudines, velut ad diversas conclusiones, per diversa media venire oportet. Nam ad primam per phylosophica documenta venimus, dummodo illa sequamur secundum virtutes morales et intellectuales operando; ad secundam vero per documenta spiritualia que humanam rationem transcendunt, dummodo illa sequamur secundum virtutes theologicas operando, fidem spem scilicet et karitatem.[14]

'Sed scientiae speculativae praecipit civilis solum quantum ad usum, non autem quantum ad determinationem operis; ordinat enim politica, quod aliqui doceant vel addiscant geometriam. Huiusmodi enim actus inquantum sunt voluntarii pertinent ad materiam moralem et sunt ordinabiles ad finem humanae vitae. Non autem praecipit politicus geometrae quid de triangulo concludat, hoc enim non subiacet humanae voluntati, nec est ordinabile humanae vitae, sed dependet ex ipsa rerum ratione. Et ideo dicit, quod politica praeordinat quas disciplinarum debitum est esse in civitatibus, scilicet tam practicarum quam speculativarum, et quis quam debeat addiscere, et usque ad quod tempus.' Also note 11: 'Et dicit quod, cum politica, quae practica est, utatur reliquis practicis disciplinis, sicut secundo dictum est, et cum ipsa legem ponat quid oporteat operari et a quibus abstinere, ut primo dictum est, consequens est quod finis huius tamquam architectonicae complectitur, idest subse continet fines aliarum scientiarum practicarum.'

[13] *Dante and Philosophy* cit. (note 9 above), p. 122 (italics original).

[14] Ineffable providence has thus set before us two goals to aim at; i.e. happiness in this life, which consists in the exercise of our own powers and is figured in the earthly paradise; and happiness in the eternal life, which consists in the enjoyment of the vision of God (to which our own powers cannot raise us except with the help of God's light)

– at which point Gilson, a shade rhetorically (for neither 'shattering' nor 'striking' forms part either of Dante's logic or of his lexis in this final chapter of the *Monarchia*), notes that, just as by way of his separating out Church and Empire Dante splits the Christian world into two camps, so also, by way of separating out philosophy and theology, he 'completely shatters the unity of Christian wisdom, the unifying principle and the bond of Christendom. In each of these vital matters this alleged Thomist struck a mortal blow at the doctrine of St Thomas Aquinas'.[15] Rhetoric aside, however, the formula is again unexceptionable; for though, as Gilson insists, there is hardly sufficient here to align him with the more radical philosophical spirits of his time, with those committed to the notion of a double order of truth in the world, there is more than enough to mark him out from Thomas and from the rhythm of specifically Thomist spirituality, from a way of seeing and understanding the human situation attuned to ulteriority rather than to periodicity as the means of its interpretation.

Temperamentally as well as by profession Kenelm Foster lived in the company of one whom he believed to be incomparably gifted in point both of holiness and of erudition, of one who offered a perfect example of how to be a Christian in – as Kenelm himself used to say – the Dominican way of being a Christian.[16] And this, he thought, this special combination of

and which is signified by the heavenly paradise. Now these two kinds of happiness must be reached by different means, as representing different ends. For we attain the first through the teachings of philosophy, provided that we follow them putting into practice the moral and intellectual virtues; whereas we attain the second through spiritual teachings which transcend human reason, provided that we follow them putting into practice the theological virtues, namely faith, hope and charity.

[15] *Dante and Philosophy* cit. (note 9 above), p. 212.

[16] K. Foster, O.P., *The Mind in Love*, Aquinas Society of London, Aquinas paper no. 25 (London: Blackfriars, 1956); *God's Tree: Essays on Dante and Other Matters* (London: Blackfriars, 1957), with, at pp. 141-49, an essay entitled 'The Tact of St Thomas'; 'Religion and Philosophy in Dante', in *The Mind of Dante* (Cambridge: Cambridge University Press, 1965), pp. 47-78 (subsequently in *Dante. The Critical Complex*, 8 vols, ed. R. Lansing (New York and London: Routledge, 2003), vol. 6, pp. 113-44); 'Tommaso d'Aquino', in the *Enciclopedia dantesca*, 6 vols (Rome: Istituto della Enciclopedia Italiana, 1970-76), vol. 5, pp. 626-49; *Dante e San Tommaso* (Rome: Casa di Dante, 1975; lecture of 17 November, 1974 at the Casa di Dante in Rome); *The Two Dantes and Other Studies* (London: Darton, Longman and Todd, 1977), with, at pp. 56-65, 'St Thomas and Dante'; '*Purgatorio* XXII', in *Cambridge Readings in Dante's Comedy*, ed. K. Foster and P. Boyde (Cambridge: Cambridge University Press, 1981), pp. 138-54; 'Dante's Idea of Purgatory, with Special Reference to *Purgatorio* XXI.58-66', in *Dies Illa. Death in the Middle Ages (Proceedings of the 1983 Manchester Colloquium)*, ed. J. H. M. Taylor (Liverpool: Cairns, 1984), pp. 97-106; 'Dante and Two Friars: *Paradiso* XI-XII', *New Blackfriars* 66 (1985), 480-96 (and, in a revised form, as 'Gli elogi danteschi di san Francesco e di san Domenico', in *Dante e il francescanesimo (Lectura Dantis Metelliana)* (Cava di Tirreni: Avagliano, 1987), pp. 229-49). Also (ed. and trans.), *The Life of Saint Thomas Aquinas: Biographical Documents*

piety and precision, was what Dante too saw in him. What Dante saw in Thomas, Kenelm thought, was the power to structured consciousness, to an orderly expression of the idea in all the complexity of the idea; so, for example, on intellectual discretion and, implicitly, Thomas as exemplary in this area, this passage from the *Convivio* at IV.viii.1: 'Lo più bello ramo che de la radice razionale consurga si è la discrezione. Ché, sì come dice Tommaso sopra lo prologo de l'Etica, "conoscere l'ordine d'una cosa ad altra è proprio atto di ragione", e è questa discrezione',[17] a passage which, taken together with the 'infiammata cortesia / di fra Tommaso e 'l discreto latino' moment of *Par*. XII.143-44,[18] determines the shape and substance of the 'Con questa distinzion prendi 'l mio detto' sequence of *Paradiso* XIII as a hymn to the properties of the Thomist mind in act:

> Non ho parlato sì, che tu non posse
> ben veder ch'el fu re, che chiese senno
> acciò che re sufficïente fosse;
> non per sapere il numero in che enno
> li motor di qua sù, o se *necesse*
> con contingente mai *necesse* fenno;
> non *si est dare primum motum esse*,
> o se del mezzo cerchio far si puote
> trïangol sì ch'un retto non avesse.
> Onde, se ciò ch'io dissi e questo note,
> regal prudenza è quel vedere impari
> in che lo stral di mia intenzion percuote;
> e se al "surse" drizzi li occhi chiari,
> vedrai aver solamente respetto
> ai regi, che son molti, e ' buon son rari.
> Con questa distinzion prendi 'l mio detto;

(London: Longmans, 1959), and, with P. Boyde, *Dante's Lyric Poetry*, 2 vols (Oxford: Clarendon Press, 1967). C. Ryan, 'Kenelm Foster on Dante', *New Blackfriars* 59 (1978), 187-92; M. Roddewig, 'In memorian Pater Kenelm Foster, O.P. (26.12.1910-6.2.1986)', in *Mitteilungsblatt der deutschen Dante Gesellschaft* (1986), 20; P. Boitani, 'Kenelm Foster: la mente innamorata', in *Dante e la Bibbia. Atti del convegno internazionale promosso da 'Biblia', Firenze, 26-28 settembre 1986*, ed. G. Barblan (Florence: Olschki, 1988), pp. 63-66; W. Wilson, 'Kenelm Foster', *Lectura Dantis* 8 (1991), 20-22.

[17] The fairest branch that springs from the root of reason is discretion, for, as Thomas says, commenting on the prologue to the *Ethics*, "To know how one thing is related to another is the distinctive act of reason", this being precisely what discretion is. Aquinas, *In Eth*. I. i, note 1: 'Sicut philosophus dicit in principio metaphysicae, sapientis est ordinare. Cuius ratio est, quia sapientia est potissima perfectio rationis, cuius proprium est cognoscere ordinem. Nam etsi vires sensitivae cognoscant res aliquas absolute, ordinem tamen unius rei ad aliam cognoscere est solius intellectus aut rationis'; *ScG* I.i.2, etc.

[18] the glowing courtesy and the well-judged discourse of Brother Thomas ...

> e così puote star con quel che credi
> del primo padre e del nostro Diletto.
>   E questo ti sia sempre piombo a' piedi,
> per farti mover lento com' uom lasso
> e al sì e al no che tu non vedi:
>   ché quelli è tra li stolti bene a basso,
> che sanza distinzione afferma e nega
> ne l'un così come ne l'altro passo;
>   perch' elli 'ncontra che più volte piega
> l'oppinïon corrente in falsa parte,
> e poi l'affetto l'intelletto lega.
>   Vie più che 'ndarno da riva si parte,
> perché non torna tal qual e' si move,
> chi pesca per lo vero e non ha l'arte.
>
> (*Par.* XIII.94-123)[19]

Thomas, then, for Dante, was a guide to the refined utterance, a mentor in the ways and means of truth under the aspect of articulation: 'Di qui, per concludere, la pressante raccomandazione suaccennata a chiunque si metta a "pescare per il vero", d'imparare con cura "l'arte" di pensare, per conoscere dove affermare e dove dubitare, prima di pronunciarsi su materie difficili. L'Aquinate dantesco è un educatore.'[20] At the same time, however, there is discernible here a pattern of divergence, an independence of spirit and of leading emphasis in just about every area of concern. Cosmologically, then, there is little in Aquinas to encourage Dante in his – from a Thomist point

---

[19] I have not so spoken that you cannot plainly see that he was a king, who asked for wisdom, in order that he might be a worthy king; not to know the number of the mover spirits here above, nor if *necesse* with a contingent ever made *necesse*; nor *si est dare primum motum esse*; nor if in a semicircle a triangle can be so constructed that it shall have no right angle. Wherefore, if you note this along with what I said, kingly prudence is that peerless vision on which the arrow of my intention strikes. And if to 'rose' you turn your discerning eyes, you will see it has respect only to kings – who are many and the good are rare. Take my words with this distinction, and they can stand thus with what you believe of the first father and of our beloved. And let this ever be as lead to your feet, to make you slow, like a weary man, in moving either to the yes or the no which you see not; for he is right low down among the fools, alike in the one and in the other case, who affirms or denies without distinguishing; because it happens that oftentimes hasty opinion inclines to the wrong side, and then fondness for it binds the intellect. Far worse than in vain does he leave the shore (since he returns not as he puts forth) who fishes for the truth and has not the art.

[20] Hence, to conclude, the above advice to anyone about to 'go fishing for the truth' to the effect that he should master carefully the 'art' of thinking, of knowing when to affirm and when to hold back, before pronouncing on difficult matters. Dante's Aquinas, in short, is an educator (*Dante e San Tommaso*, note 16 above, p. 19).

of view – extravagant commitment to secondary causality as the means of divine purposefulness in the world,[21] while metaphysically Dante reflects but faintly Thomas's preoccupation with the Pentateuchal I AM as a basis for something approaching a revolution in respect of every kind of ancient essentialism, every antique preference for *whatness* as distinct from *thereness* as an object of concern.[22] And what applies in the area of cosmology and metaphysics applies also in that of anthropology and psychology; for if Dante's is a sense of the rational soul as the entelechy or formal principle

---

[21] *Conv.* III.vi.5: 'e però che Dio è universalissima cagione di tutte le cose, conoscendo lui, tutte le cose conosce in sé, secondo lo modo de la Intelligenza. Per che tutte le Intelligenze conoscono la forma umana, in quanto ella è per intenzione regolata ne la divina mente; e massimamente conoscono quella le Intelligenze motrici, però che sono spezialissime cagioni di quella e d'ogni forma generale, e conoscono quella perfettissima, tanto quanto essere puote, sì come loro regola ed essemplo'; *Par.* II.121-23: 'Questi organi del mondo così vanno, / come tu vedi omai, di grado in grado, / che di sù prendono e di sotto fanno'; VII.130-38: 'Li angeli, frate, e 'l paese sincero / nel qual tu se', dir si posson creati, / sì come sono, in loro essere intero; / ma li alimenti che tu hai nomati / e quelle cose che di lor si fanno / da creata virtù sono informati. / Creata fu la materia ch'elli hanno; / creata fu la virtù informante / in queste stelle che 'ntorno a lor vanno.' Thomas, *ScG* III.lxvi.6: 'Secundum ordinem causarum est ordo effectuum. Primum autem in omnibus effectibus est esse: nam omnia alia sunt quaedam determinationes ipsius. Igitur esse est proprius effectus primi agentis, et omnia alia agunt ipsum inquantum agunt in virtute primi agentis. Secunda autem agentia, quae sunt quasi particulantes et determinantes actionem primi agentis, agunt sicut proprios effectus alias perfectiones, quae determinant esse'; *ST* Ia.65.4 resp.: 'Et ideo, cum simile fiat a suo simili, non est quaerenda causa formarum corporalium aliqua forma immaterialis; sed aliquod compositum, secundum quod hic ignis generatur ab hoc igne. Sic igitur formae corporales causantur, non quasi influxae ab aliqua immateriali forma, sed quasi materia reducta de potentia in actum ab aliquo agente composito', etc. A. Mellone, O.F.M., *La dottrina di Dante Alighieri sulla prima creazione* (Salerno: Convento S. Maria degli Angeli, 1950, and in *Saggi e letture dantesche. Lectura Dantis Metelliana* (Angri (Salerno): Editrice Gaia, 2005), pp. 21-87); idem, 'Emanatismo neoplatonico di Dante per le citazioni del *Liber de Causis*', *Divus Thomas* 54 (1951), 205-12; idem, 'Il concorso delle creature nella produzione delle cose secondo Dante', *Divus Thomas* 56 (1953), 273-86, and in *Saggi e letture dantesche* cit., pp. 89-110; idem, 'Il canto XXIX del *Paradiso*', in *Nuove letture dantesche* (Casa di Dante, Roma), 7 (Florence: Le Monnier, 1974), 193-213 (subsequently in *Saggi e letture dantesche* cit., pp. 157-74, with the title 'Il canto XXIX del *Paradiso*. (Una lezione di angelologia)'); B. Nardi, 'Il canto XXIX del *Paradiso*', *Convivium* 24 (1956), 294-302; S. Bemrose, *Dante's Angelic Intelligences. Their Importance in the Cosmos and in Pre-Christian Religion* (Rome: Edizioni di Storia e Letteratura, 1983).

[22] K. Foster, O.P., *Dante e San Tommaso* cit. (note 16 above), p. 11, with reference both to Thomas (*ST* Ia 3.4; *ScG* I.xxii and xxviii, etc.) and E. Gilson (*Le Thomisme* (note 9 above), pp. 44-58, 515-18): 'A simile conclusione ci porterebbe, io credo, un accurato confronto ... fra lo scarso uso che fa Dante del termine "esse", o "essere", in senso filosofico, e l'uso diffusissimo e personalissimo che ne fa Tommaso – al segno che questo dell'"esse", ossia dell'"actus essendi", può chiamarsi il vero e proprio concetto chiave della sua metafisica, quello per cui (secondo Tommaso) meglio si coglie e si misura e la realtà intrinseca di ogni cosa ed i suoi rapporti con Dio, il quale appunto è l'"ipsum esse subsistens", e perciò l'unica sorgente dello "esse" di qualsiasi cosa.'

of the psychosomatic whole in man, then the *Convivio* testifies on more than one occasion to something closer to the pneumatic, to a sense of the soul as a spiritual entity captive *pro tempore* to the flesh;[23] and if Dante's is a sense of the empirical and abstractive mechanism of properly human intellection, he, unlike Thomas, is inclined to opt for the possible rather than for the active intellect as the principle of specifically human being.[24] Clearly, the argument requires – and in Kenelm always enjoys – careful statement, Dante's, again, being a virtually unqualified admiration for Thomas as the embodiment of Christian-theological wisdom and sanctity ('nel santo dottore il genio di Dante percepiva e ammirava qualcosa di ben altrimenti personale e profondo; voglio dire, una certa combinazione d'intelligenza e di santità, tal che le stesse sue qualità di forza e di finezza intellettuale fossero insieme riflesso e espressione di probità morale');[25] but for all that,

---

[23] *Conv.* III.ii.14: 'però che l'anima è tanto in quella sovrana potenza nobilitata e dinudata da materia, che la divina luce, come in angelo, raggia in quella'; vii.5 'Così la bontà di Dio è ricevuta altrimenti da le sustanze separate, cioè da li Angeli, che sono sanza grossezza di materia, quasi diafani per la purità de la loro forma, e altrimenti da l'anima umana, che, avvegna che da una parte sia da materia libera, da un'altra è impedita, sì come l'uomo ch'è tutto ne l'acqua fuor del capo, del quale non si può dire che tutto sia ne l'acqua né tutto fuor da quella; e altrimenti da li animali, la cui anima tutta in materia è compresa, ma alquanto è nobilitata; e altrimenti da le piante, e altrimenti da le minere; e altrimenti da la terra che da li altri [elementi], però che è materialissima, e però remotissima e improporzionalissima a la prima simplicissima e nobilissima vertude, che sola è intellettuale, cioè Dio', etc. Aquinas, by contrast, *ScG* II.lxviii (a chapter variously interesting from the point of view of the *Convivio*): 'Si enim substantia intellectualis non unitur corpori solum ut motor, ut Plato posuit, neque continuatur ei solum per phantasmata, ut dixit Averroes, sed ut forma; neque tamen intellectus quo homo intelligit, est praeparatio in humana natura, ut dixit Alexander; neque complexio, ut Galenus; neque harmonia, ut Empedocles; neque corpus, vel sensus, vel imaginatio, ut antiqui dixerunt: relinquitur quod anima humana sit intellectualis substantia corpori unita ut forma' (2); *ST* Ia.76.1 resp. etc.

[24] *Mon.* I.iii.6-7: 'sed esse apprehensivum per intellectum possibilem ... Patet igitur quod ultimum de potentia ipsius humanitatis est potentia sive virtus intellectiva', *à propos* of which K. Foster, O.P., *Dante e San Tommaso* (note 16 above), pp. 10-11: 'E mi sembra molto significativo che quando Dante vuol dare, nella *Monarchia*, una definizione precisa dell'agire umano in quanto tale, tira in campo solo lo "intellectus possibilis", asserendo che il "constitutivum spetiei" dell'uomo è "esse apprehensivum per intellectum possibilem" – formula inconcepibile in bocca a sanTommaso, ma a cui avrebbe potuto sottoscrivere benissimo un filosofo così lontano dal tomismo come fu, ad esempio, il francescano inglese Roger Bacon. Insomma, l'assenza totale d'"intellectus agens" dal lessico di Dante è argomento piuttosto forte contro il suo tomismo.' Aquinas, *ScG* II.lxxvi.20: 'Operatio autem propria hominis est intelligere: cuius primum principium est intellectus agens, qui facit species intelligibiles, a quibus patitur quodammodo intellectus possibilis, qui factus in actu, movet voluntatem'; *ST* Ia.79.3, etc.

[25] in the saintly doctor Dante in his wisdom saw and admired something far more personal and profound, by which I mean a certain combination of intelligence and

there is no disguising the otherness of Dante's thinking with respect to the *ipse dixit* of the master, his willingness for the sake of an alternative spirituality to embrace the alternative solution.

3. By the time, then, of Kenelm Foster's initiative the myth of Dante's Thomism — certainly if by this we mean anything approaching a sense of his systematic espousal of Thomist positions in key areas of moral-philosophical, natural-philosophical and theological concern — had been laid. Fashioned by a desire to claim the text for Thomas and for Thomism as normative in the area of Christian-theological understanding, it had gradually been dismantled in favour of something closer to contrast than to continuity as the hallmark of a relationship nonetheless decisive for Dante's emergence as a philosophical and theological spirit. But for all the power and persuasiveness of the argument so far, there is still a way to go; for to live with the question of Dante and Aquinas is to be impressed by two things: (*a*) by the way in which it stands to be proposed in terms, not so much of the *what*, as of the *how* of Dante's reading of Thomas, not so much of the *substance* as of the *psychology* of that reading, and (*b*) by the notion that, mediated as it is by the problematics of existence as verified by the subject of that existence, Dante's, vis-à-vis that of Aquinas, is a revised sense of the theological project in its essential shape and structure. As far, then, as the first of these things is concerned we may begin by saying that, in a manner apt to defy the mathematics of the case — just five references in all, four in the *Convivio* and one in the *Monarchia*[26] — Thomas

---

holiness, such that these selfsame qualities of strength and intellectual finesse were in one and the same moment a reflection and an expression of moral integrity (*Dante e San Tommaso*, note 16 above, p. 17).

[26] *Conv.* IV.xv.12: 'Ché, secondo la malizia de l'anima, tre orribili infermitadi ne la mente de li uomini ho vedute. L'una è di naturale jattanza causata: ché sono molti tanto presuntuosi, che si credono tutto sapere, e per questo le non certe cose affermano per certe; lo qual vizio Tullio massimamente abomina nel primo de li Offici e Tommaso nel suo Contra-li-Gentili, dicendo: "Sono molti tanto di suo ingegno presuntuosi, che credono col suo intelletto poter misurare tutte le cose, estimando tutto vero quello che a loro pare, falso quello che a loro non pare"' (*ScG* I.v.4: 'Sunt enim quidam tantum de suo ingenio praesumentes ut totam rerum naturam se reputent suo intellectu posse metiri, aestimantes scilicet totum esse verum quod eis videtur et falsum quod eis non videtur'); *Conv.* IV.xxx.3: 'Dico adunque: *Contra-li-erranti mia*. Questo *Contra-li-erranti* è tutto una parte, e è nome d'esta canzone, tolto per essemplo del buono frate Tommaso d'Aquino, che a un suo libro, che fece a confusione di tutti quelli che disviano da nostra Fede, puose nome Contra li Gentili'; *Mon.* II.iv.1: 'sicut dicit Thomas in tertio suo *contra Gentiles*, miraculum est quod preter ordinem in rebus comuniter institutum divinitus fit' (*ScG* III. xcix.2: 'Potest autem Deus praeter hunc ordinem facere: ut scilicet ipse effectum aliquem in inferioribus operetur, nihil ad hoc agente superiori agente'). For the commentary on the *Ethics*, *Conv.* II.xiv.14: 'Lo Cielo cristallino, che per Primo Mobile dinanzi è contato,

is everywhere discernible as that whereby Dante feels able to settle on the exact notional and expressive solution. Instances abound, but to take first the least complicated of them there is, for example, the 'oportet igitur ultimum finem universi esse bonum intellectus' of *ScG* I.i.4[27] for the 'ben de l'intelletto' of *Inf.* III.18 at the heart of his anthropology and ethic;[28] or the 'ut ex hoc ad divinum amorem inflammarentur' of *ScG* IV.lv.13[29] for the 'Questo decreto, frate, sta sepulto / a li occhi di ciascuno il cui ingegno / ne la fiamma d'amor non è adulto' of *Par.* VII.58-60 at the heart of his soteriology;[30] or the 'si aliquis non videret solem et lunam et alia astra' of *ScG* II.xcii.9[31] for the 'amor che move il sole e l'altre stelle' of *Par.* XXXIII.145 at the heart of his affective theology.[32] Everywhere the pattern is the same, for everywhere it is a question of Thomas's functioning, not merely as a master or mentor, but as a friend or fellow traveller, as one co-involved at the point of precise understanding and exact expression. And what applies at the level of the merely phrasal, clausular or otherwise minimal syntactic unit applies also at the level of

ha comparazione assai manifesta a la Morale Filosofia; ché Morale Filosofia, secondo che dice Tommaso sopra lo secondo de l'Etica, ordina noi a l'altre scienze' (*In eth.* I, lect. 2, note 7: 'Optimus finis pertinet ad principalissimam scientiam, et maxime architectonicam. Et hoc patet ex his, quae supra praemissa sunt. Dictum est enim quod sub scientia vel arte quae est de fine continentur illae quae sunt circa ea quae sunt ad finem. Et sic oportet quod ultimus finis pertineat ad scientiam principalissimam, tamquam de principalissimo fine existentem, et maxime architectonicae, tamquam praecipienti aliis quid oporteat facere. Sed civilis scientia videtur esse talis, scilicet principalissima, et maxime architectonica. Ergo ad eam pertinet considerare optimum finem'); *Conv.* IV.viii.1: 'Lo più bello ramo che de la radice razionale consurga si è la discrezione. Ché, sì come dice Tommaso sopra il prologo de l'Etica, "conoscere l'ordine d'una cosa ad altra è proprio atto di ragione", e è questa discrezione' (*In eth.* I, lect. 1, note 1: 'Sicut philosophus dicit in principio metaphysicae, sapientis est ordinare. Cuius ratio est, quia sapientia est potissima perfectio rationis, cuius proprium est cognoscere ordinem ...').

[27] the ultimate end of the universe must therefore be the good of the intellect ...; cf. the 'bonum igitur intellectus etiam in cognitione mali consistit' of I.lxxi.4 and the 'nam verum est bonum intellectus et finis ipsius' of II.lxxxiv.4.

[28] [We have come to the place where you will see the wretched people who have lost] the good of the intellect.

[29] [First, indeed, because it was necessary for men to know the beneficence of the Incarnation] so as to be thereby inflamed in the divine love.

[30] This decree, brother, is buried from the eyes of everyone whose understanding is not matured within love's flame.

[31] [In the same way, a person who had not seen] the sun or the moon or the other stars [and had heard that they were incorruptible bodies, might call them by the names of these corruptible bodies ...].

[32] [Here power failed the lofty phantasy; but already my desire and my will were revolved, like a wheel that is evenly moved, by the] love which moves the sun and the other stars.

the period as a whole, where again the original utterance is on hand, not so much to determine the Dantean initiative in its precise notional and linguistic complexion, as to free the reader for an independent movement of the mind; so, for example, in respect of these lines (1-12) from *Purgatorio* IV on the psychology of layered consciousness, on the binding and loosing of the soul in circumstances of intense concentration:

> Quando per dilettanze o ver per doglie,
> che alcuna virtù nostra comprenda,
> l'anima bene ad essa si raccoglie,
>   par ch'a nulla potenza più intenda;
> e questo è contra quello error che crede
> ch'un'anima sovr' altra in noi s'accenda.
>   E però, quando s'ode cosa o vede
> che tegna forte a sé l'anima volta,
> vassene 'l tempo e l'uom non se n'avvede;
>   ch'altra potenza è quella che l'ascolta,
> e altra è quella c'ha l'anima intera:
> questa è quasi legata e quella è sciolta.[33]

this passage from the *Contra gentiles* at II.lviii.10 on the referability of every movement of the mind to one and the same intellectual principle, to the rational soul as one and undivided in essence and operation:

> Videmus autem quod diversae actiones animae impediunt se: cum enim una est intensa, altera remittitur. Oportet igitur quod istae actiones, et vires quae sunt earum proxima principia, reducantur in unum principium ... quae est anima. Relinquitur igitur quod omnes actiones animae quae sunt in nobis, ab anima una procedunt. Et sic non sunt in nobis plures animae.[34]

Here, certainly, it is a question of reading, reception and the subtle psychology thereof, for if on the one hand there is enough in Dante by way

---

[33] When through impression of pleasure or of pain, which some one of our faculties receives, the soul is entirely centred thereon, it seems that it gives heed to no other of its powers; and this is contrary to that error which holds that one soul above the other is kindled within us; and therefore when aught is heard or seen which holds the soul strongly bent to it, the time passes away and we perceive it not, for one faculty is that which notes it, and another that which possesses the entire soul, the latter as it were bound, the former free.

[34] Now we observe that the diverse actions of the soul hinder one another, for when one is intense another is remiss. Therefore, these actions and powers that are proximate principles must be referred to one principle ... which is the soul. It follows, then, that all the actions of the soul which are in us proceed from the one soul. Thus, there are not several souls in us.

of *sameness* to suggest an element of positive borrowing (the 'questo è contra quello error che crede / ch'un'anima sovr' altra in noi s'accenda' of lines 5 and 6 for Thomas's 'Et sic non sunt in nobis plures animae', or the 'altra potenza è quella che l'ascolta, / e altra è quella c'ha l'anima intera' of lines 10 and 11 for Thomas's 'cum enim una est intensa, altera remittitur'), there is at the same time sufficient by way of *otherness* – Dante's proposal of the question in terms of distraction and temporality, of the waylaying of self by its own passing preoccupations – to confirm something more refined than this, namely, the function of the original utterance as a means of emancipation, as that whereby, far from being constrained by the text, the spirit is empowered in respect of a discourse uniquely and unmistakably its own. And what applies to this passage from the early part of the *Purgatorio* applies also to the love-meditation in the central part of the canticle, where again it is a question, less of authorization, than of formed friendship, of companionship as the means of laying hold of the idea and thus of self itself in its now – for the moment at least – settled disposition. The question here is one of astral determinism, of the role of the stars in making us what we are. If, then, as Dante is willing to allow, the stars do indeed have some part to play in the shaping of self, this can only ever be preliminary, their role being at best dispositive, a matter of readying the soul for the task of free moral choice; for man as man, he believes, is moved, not so much by those forces ranged over against him, be they ever so exalted, as by free will as that whereby he most commends himself to God (the 'e quel ch'e' più apprezza' of *Par.* V.21),[35] his, therefore, being a nobler species of subjection, the kind of subjection amounting to perfect freedom. The key lines (XVI.58-84) run as follows:

> "Lo mondo è ben così tutto diserto
> d'ogne virtute, come tu mi sone,
> e di malizia gravido e coverto;
>   ma priego che m'addite la cagione,
> sì ch'i' la veggia e ch'i' la mostri altrui;
> ché nel cielo uno, e un qua giù la pone".
>   Alto sospir, che duolo strinse in "uhi!",
> mise fuor prima; e poi cominciò: "Frate,
> lo mondo è cieco, e tu vien ben da lui.
>   Voi che vivete ogne cagion recate
> pur suso al cielo, pur come se tutto
> movesse seco di necessitate.
>   Se così fosse, in voi fora distrutto
> libero arbitrio, e non fora giustizia

---

[35] and that which he most prizes ...

> per ben letizia, e per male aver lutto.
>   Lo cielo i vostri movimenti inizia;
> non dico tutti, ma, posto ch'i' 'l dica,
> lume v'è dato a bene e a malizia,
>   e libero voler; che, se fatica
> ne le prime battaglie col ciel dura,
> poi vince tutto, se ben si notrica.
>   A maggior forza e a miglior natura
> liberi soggiacete; e quella cria
> la mente in voi, che 'l ciel non ha in sua cura.
>   Però, se 'l mondo presente disvia,
> in voi è la cagione, in voi sì cheggia;
> e io te ne sarò or vera spia."[36]

relative to which we may note the following extracts from the *Contra gentiles* at III.lxxxv.11 and 19-20:

> Frustra etiam darentur leges et praecepta vivendi, si homo suarum electionum dominus non esset. Frustra etiam adhiberentur poenae et praemia bonis aut malis, ex quo non est in nobis haec vel illa eligere. His autem desinentibus, statim socialis vita corrumpitur. Non igitur homo est sic secundum ordinem providentiae institutus ut electiones eius ex motibus caelestium corporum proveniant ... Sciendum tamen est quod, licet corpora caelestia non sint directe causa electionum nostrarum quasi directe in voluntates nostras imprimentia, indirecte tamen ex eis aliqua occasio nostris electionibus praestatur, secundum quod habent impressionem super corpora ... Manifestum autem est, et experimento cognitum, quod tales occasiones, sive sint exteriores sive sint interiores, non sunt causa necessaria electionis: cum homo per rationem possit eis resistere vel obedire ... quia scilicet impressio

---

[36] "The world is indeed as utterly deserted by every virtue as you declare to me, and pregnant and overspread with iniquity, but I beg you to point out to me the cause, so that I may see it and show it to men, for one places it in the heavens and another here below." He first heaved a deep sigh which grief wrung into an "Ah me!", and then began, "Brother, the world is blind, and truly you come from it! You who are living refer every cause upward to the heavens alone, as if they of necessity moved all things with them. If this were so, free will would be destroyed in you, and there would be no justice in happiness for good or grief for evil. The heavens initiate your movements – I do not say all of them, but given for the moment that that is what I am saying, a light is given you to know good and evil, and free will, which if it endure fatigue in its first battles with the heavens, afterwards, if it is well nurtured, it conquers completely. You lie subject, in your freedom, to a greater power and to a better nature, and that creates the mind in you which the heavens have not in their charge. Therefore if the present world goes astray, in you is the cause and in you let it be sought; and I shall now bear you true testimony in this."

stellarum in pluribus sortitur effectum, qui non resistunt inclinationi quae est ex corpore; non autem semper in hoc vel in illo, qui forte per rationem naturali inclinationi resistit.[37]

Again, there is plenty here to sustain the critic in the more routine aspects of his calling, in the pinning down of Dante to his sources: Thomas's 'frustra etiam adhiberentur poenae et praemia bonis aut malis, ex quo non est in nobis haec vel illa eligere' for Dante's 'non fora giustizia / per ben letizia, e per male aver lutto', or Thomas's 'licet corpora caelestia non sint directe causa electionum nostrarum quasi directe in voluntates nostras imprimentia' for Dante's 'Lo cielo i vostri movimenti inizia; / non dico tutti ...', or Thomas's 'cum homo per rationem possit eis resistere vel obedire' for Dante's 'lume v'è dato a bene e a malizia, / libero voler'. But here too there is sufficient by way of difference – by way of Dante's reconfiguration and indeed re-substantiation of the text in point both of emphasis (the 'A maggior forza e a miglior natura / liberi soggiacete' moment of lines 79-81) and of expressivity (the 'duolo strinse in "uhi!"' moment of lines 64-66) – to encourage him in a sense of something at once more subtle and sublime than this, namely in a sense of the text as a principle of deliverance, as that whereby the receptive spirit is made equal at last to the matter in hand.

As a third example of textuality under the aspect of friendship we may take Dante's account in the *Paradiso* of the role of providence both in fashioning personality and in ensuring its proper functionality as an instrument of God's purposes in the world. If, then, nature, in the sense of *natura naturans*, does a good job in perpetuating the species, it is down to providence as operative through the stars that the individual is confirmed (*a*) in the fullness of his individuality, and (*b*) in his status as a means of divine intentionality:

---

[37] Besides, it would be useless for laws and rules of living to be promulgated if man were not master of his own choices. Useless, too, would be the employment of punishments and rewards for good or evil deeds, in regard to which it is not in our power to choose one or the other. In fact, if these things disappear, social life is at once corrupted. Therefore, man is not so established by the order of providence that his choices originate from the motions of the celestial bodies ... Yet we should note that, though celestial bodies are not directly the cause of our choices, in the sense of directly making impressions on our wills, some occasion for our choices may be indirectly offered by them, because they do make an impression on bodies ... Moreover, it is plain and well known by experience that such occasions, whether they are external or internal, are not the necessary cause of choice, since man is able, on the basis of reason, either to resist or obey them. But there are many who follow natural impulses, while but few, the wise only, do not take these occasions of acting badly and of following those natural impulses.

> Ond' elli ancora: "Or dì: sarebbe il peggio
> per l'omo in terra, se non fosse cive?"
> "Sì", rispuos' io; "e qui ragion non cheggio".
> E puot' elli esser, se giù non si vive
> diversamente per diversi offici?
> Non, se 'l maestro vostro ben vi scrive".
> Sì venne deducendo infino a quici;
> poscia conchiuse: "Dunque esser diverse
> convien di vostri effetti le radici:
> per ch'un nasce Solone e altro Serse,
> altro Melchisedèch e altro quello
> che, volando per l'aere, il figlio perse.
> La circular natura, ch'è suggello
> a la cera mortal, fa ben sua arte,
> ma non distingue l'un da l'altro ostello.
> Quinci addivien ch'Esaù si diparte
> per seme da Iacòb; e vien Quirino
> da sì vil padre, che si rende a Marte.
> Natura generata il suo cammino
> simil farebbe sempre a' generanti,
> se non vincesse il proveder divino".
>
> (*Par.* VIII.115-35)[38]

Here as before, the line is perfectly Dantean, perfectly secure in point both of substance and of expression. Wanting for nothing, it proceeds with superlative assurance to address a complex issue – the interplay of providence and of personality within the economy of the whole – by way of a series of propositions (socio-political, world-historical and theological) as robust in conception as they are in articulation. But for all that, the Thomist text is once again everywhere to hand as that whereby the hitherto anxious spirit comes home to itself on the plane of understanding:

> Sicut supra ostensum est, divina providentia ad omnia singularia
>   se extendit, etiam minima. Quibuscumque igitur sunt aliquae

---

[38] Whereupon he again, "Now say, would it be worse for man on earth if he were not a citizen?" "Yes", I replied, "and here I ask for no proof." "And can that be, unless men below live in diverse ways for diverse duties? Not if your master writes well of this for you." Thus he came deducing as far as here, then he concluded, "Therefore the roots of your works must needs be diverse, so that one is born Solon and another Xerxes, one Melchizedek and another he who flew through the air and lost his son. Circling nature, which is a seal on the mortal wax, performs its art well, but does not distinguish one house from another. Whence it happens that Esau differs in the seed from Jacob, and Quirinus comes from so base a father that he is ascribed to Mars. The begotten nature would always make its course like its begetters, did not divine provision overrule."

actiones praeter inclinationem speciei, oportet quod per divinam providentiam regulentur in suis actibus praeter directionem quae pertinet ad speciem. Sed in rationali creatura apparent multae actiones ad quas non sufficit inclinatio speciei: cuius signum est quod non similes sunt in omnibus, sed variae in diversis. Oportet igitur quod rationalis creatura dirigatur a Deo ad suos actus non solum secundum speciem, sed etiam secundum individuum.Item. Deus unicuique naturae providet secundum ipsius capacitatem: tales enim singulas creaturas condidit quales aptas esse cognovit ut per suam gubernationem pervenirent ad finem. Sola autem creatura rationalis est capax directionis qua dirigitur ad suos actus non solum secundum speciem, sed etiam secundum individuum: habet enim intellectum et rationem, unde percipere possit quomodo diversimode sit aliquid bonum vel malum secundum quod congruit diversis individuis, temporibus et locis. Sola igitur creatura rationalis dirigitur a Deo ad suos actus non solum secundum speciem, sed etiam secundum individuum.

(*ScG* III.cxiii.3-4)[39]

Here again, everything is ready and waiting, the authoritative text reaching out to shape and substantiate the argument: the co-subsistence of specificity and singularity as properties of human being under the aspect of time and space; time and space themselves as the arena of properly human being and becoming; selfhood and the uniqueness thereof as the means of divine purposefulness in the world, of God's carrying out the cosmic plan. Dante, then, could not but have been impressed. Everything is there, everything one could possibly wish for when it comes to human

---

[39] Besides, as we showed above, divine providence extends to all singular things, even to the least. In the case of those beings, then, whose actions take place apart from the inclination appropriate to their species, it is necessary for them to be regulated in their acts by divine providence, over and above the direction which pertains to the species. But many actions are evident, in the case of the rational creature, for which the inclination of the species is not enough. The mark of this is that such actions are not alike in all, but differ in various cases. Therefore, the rational creature must be directed by God in his acts, not only specifically, but also individually. Moreover, God takes care of each nature according to its capacity; indeed, he created singular creatures of such kinds that he knew were suited to achieving the end under his governance. Now, only the rational creature is capable of this direction, whereby his actions are guided, not only specifically, but also individually. For he possesses understanding and reason, and consequently he can grasp in what different ways a thing may be good or bad, depending on its suitability for various individuals, times and places. Therefore, only the rational creature is directed in his acts by God, individually as well as specifically. III. cxxxiv.2: 'Haec autem distributio diversorum officiorum in diversas personas fit divina providentia, secundum quod quidam inclinantur magis ad hoc officium quam ad alia', etc.

and divine intentionality and their coalescence *in re*. But for all the decisiveness of the archetypal text, it is a question here, less of authority, than of alongsidedness, of how it is that, from out of the garner both of his goodness and of his generosity, one man furnishes another with the means of orderly intellection and thus of orderly actualization. The text, in other words, functions as great texts always do, as that whereby those shaped by them at last stand securely in their own presence, thereafter to rejoice in their indebtedness to everyone and no-one.

But with this we are still in the foothills when it comes to Dante, Aquinas and the relationship between them; for companionship as a cause for celebration in circumstances of sameness, of a common mind among those party to it, comes most completely into its own in circumstances of otherness, of an alternative way of seeing, setting up and resolving the matter to hand. Yet here too, in circumstances of otherness amounting to out and out opposition, Thomas is once again on hand to assist in determining the key emphasis. Take, for example, the case of *Conv.* III. xv.8-10, a passage designed to stave off a collapse of the whole project in consequence of its now well-nigh impossibly contradictory character. The problem is readily stated, for having in the first treatise of the book committed himself to the possibility of a species of philosophical happiness appropriate to men and women bowed down by civic and domestic care and thus without the leisure for speculation,[40] and having in the third treatise secured the notion of philosophy as the love of wisdom first and foremost in the mind of God,[41] Dante is suddenly struck by the implications of the position he has now reached for the viability of his undertaking generally in the *Convivio*; for if philosophy is first and foremost the love of wisdom in the mind of God, then what use philosophy to the man in the street, to those looking for something more pragmatic, more medium term? Happily, a solution is to hand, Dante's, in this twilight phase of

---

[40] *Conv.* I.ix.5 and i.4: 'Ché la bontà de l'animo, la quale questo servigio attende, è in coloro che per malvagia disusanza del mondo hanno lasciata la litteratura a coloro che l'hanno fatta di donna meretrice; e questi nobili sono principi, baroni, cavalieri, e molt'altra nobile gente, *non solamente maschi ma femmine, che sono molti e molte in questa lingua, volgari, e non litterati* ... Di fuori da l'uomo possono essere similemente due cagioni intese, l'una de le quali è induttrice di necessitade, l'altra di pigrizia. *La prima è la cura familiare e civile, la quale convenevolmente a sé tiene de li uomini lo maggior numero, sì che in ozio di speculazione esser non possono*'.

[41] *Conv.* III.xii.12-13: 'Ché se a memoria si reduce ciò che detto è di sopra, filosofia è uno amoroso uso di sapienza, lo quale massimamente è in Dio, però che in lui è somma sapienza e sommo amore e sommo atto; che non può essere altrove, se non in quanto da esso procede. È adunque la divina filosofia de la divina essenza, però che in esso non può essere cosa a la sua essenza aggiunta; ed è nobilissima, però che nobilissima è la essenza divina; ed è in lui per modo perfetto e vero, quasi per etterno matrimonio.'

Convivio III, being a sense of our wanting to know here and now only what it is possible for us to know here and now, anything other than this, any overshooting of the mark, being both misconceived and unnatural:

> A ciò si può chiaramente rispondere che lo desiderio naturale in ciascuna cosa è misurato secondo la possibilitade de la cosa desiderante: altrimenti andrebbe in contrario di sé medesimo, che impossibile è; e la Natura l'avrebbe fatto indarno, che è anche impossibile. In contrario andrebbe: ché, desiderando la sua perfezione, desiderrebbe la sua imperfezione; imperò che desiderrebbe sé sempre desiderare e non compiere mai suo desiderio ... Avrebbelo anco la Natura fatto indarno, però che non sarebbe ad alcuno fine ordinato. E però l'umano desiderio è misurato in questa vita a quella scienza che qui avere si può, e quello punto non passa se non per errore, lo quale è di fuori di naturale intenzione ... Onde, con ciò sia cosa che conoscere di Dio e di certe altre cose quello esse sono non sia possibile a la nostra natura, quello da noi naturalmente non è desiderato di sapere. E per questo è la dubitazione soluta.[42]

That he has now contradicted just about everything he has said and is about to say in the *Convivio* relative to man's desire for God as the beginning and end of all desiring goes without saying,[43] the

---

[42] To this the clear answer can be given that the natural desire in everything is in accordance with the capacity of the thing which desires; otherwise the thing would strive in a fashion contrary to its own being, which is impossible; and nature would have made it in vain, which is also impossible. It would strive in a self-contrary fashion, for in desiring its own perfection it would desire its own imperfection, because it would desire always to be desiring and never to satisfy its own desire ... Also, Nature would have made it in vain, because it would not be directed to any end. Human desire, consequently, is measured in this life in accordance with that knowledge which can be gained here, and never passes that point except in error, which is something foreign to the intention of nature ... Since, then, it is impossible for our nature to know of God what he is (the same holds true of certain other things), this is not something which we naturally desire to know. In this way the difficulty is resolved.

[43] *Conv.* III.ii.7: 'E però che naturalissimo è in Dio volere essere – però che, sì come ne lo allegato libro si legge, "prima cosa è l'essere, e anzi a quello nulla è" –, l'anima umana essere vuole naturalmente con tutto desiderio; e però che 'l suo essere dipende da Dio e per quello si conserva, naturalmente disia e vuole essere a Dio unita per lo suo essere fortificare'; IV.xii.14: 'E la ragione è questa: che lo sommo desiderio di ciascuna cosa, e prima da la natura dato, è lo ritornare a lo suo principio. E però che Dio è principio de le nostre anime e fattore di quelle simili a sé (sì come è scritto: "Facciamo l'uomo ad imagine e similitudine nostra"), essa anima massimamente desidera di tornare a quello.' In the *Commedia*, *Purg.* XVII.127-29: 'Ciascun confusamente un bene apprende / nel qual si queti l'animo, e disira; / per che di giugner lui ciascun contende'; *Par.* II.19-21: 'La concreata e perpetüa sete / del deïforme regno cen portava / veloci quasi come 'l ciel vedete'; VII. 142-44: 'ma vostra vita sanza mezzo spira / la somma beninanza, e la innamora / di sé sì che poi

peremptoriness of it all – the 'A ciò si può chiaramente rispondere' with which the passage begins and the 'E per questo è la dubitazione soluta' with which it ends – testifying to his discomfiture at this point. And that he has also now contradicted everything Aquinas has to say on this matter also goes without saying, Thomas's, albeit with some qualifications along the way, being a sense of man's desire even now, this side of death, to know God as the final cause of his every yearning. But for all that, it is once again Aquinas who, from out of the apologetic abundance of the *Contra gentiles*, is on hand to furnish, if not the solution exactly, then its essential ingredients, the parts necessary for its hasty assembly:

> Vanum enim est quod est ad finem quem non potest consequi. Cum igitur finis hominis sit felicitas, in quam tendit naturale ipsius desiderium, non potest poni felicitas hominis in eo ad quod homo pervenire non potest: alioquin sequeretur quod homo esset in vanum, et naturale eius desiderium esset inane, quod est impossibile.
>
> (*ScG* III.xliv.2)[44]

Now Thomas, possessed as he is of a sense of the ultimately uninterrupted teleology of human desiring, has as we have said no interest in the kind of periodization Dante has in mind here, his point in this passage being simply that what we cannot know in this life we shall know in the next:

> Adhuc. Impossibile est naturale desiderium esse inane: natura enim nihil facit frustra. Esset autem inane desiderium naturae si nunquam posset impleri. Est igitur implebile desiderium naturale hominis. Non

---

sempre la disira.' Thomas, *ScG* III.l.7: 'Nos autem, quantumcumque sciamus Deum esse ... non quiescimus desiderio, sed adhuc desideramus eum per essentiam suam cognoscere'; *ST* Ia.44.4 ad 3: 'omnia appetunt Deum ut finem, appetendo quodcumque bonum, sive appetitu intelligibili, sive sensibili, sive naturali, qui est sine cognitione, quia nihil habet rationem boni et appetibilis, nisi secundum quod participat Dei similitudinem', etc.

[44] Indeed, a thing is futile which exists for an end which it cannot attain. So, since the end of man is felicity, to which his natural desire tends, it is not possible for the felicity of man to be placed in something than man cannot achieve. Otherwise, it would follow that man is a futile being, and his natural desire would be incapable of fulfilment, which is impossible. For Dante himself on the nature and function of the *Contra gentiles* as an apologetic undertaking, *Conv.* IV.xxx.3: 'Dico adunque: *Contra-li-erranti mia*. Questo *Contra-li-erranti* è tutto una parte, e è nome d'esta canzone, tolto per essemplo del buono frate Tommaso d'Aquino, che a un suo libro, che fece a confusione di tutti quelli che disviano da nostra Fede, puose nome Contra-li-Gentili.'

autem in hac vita, ut ostensum est. Oportet igitur quod impleatur post hanc vitam. Est igitur felicitas ultima hominis post hanc vitam.

(ibid. III.xlviii.12)[45]

But that, crystal clear as it is in the text, is not what Dante saw there, or at any rate what he chose to see there; for what Dante saw there was a means of confirming that there must after all be a satisfactory point of arrival on the plane of seeing and understanding *here and now*, anything short of this making a mockery of the whole thing. Viewed, in other words, through the eyes of one disposed from deep within himself to rejoice in the realizability of the human project under certain at least of its aspects in the historical order, the *Contra gentiles*, with its talk of the futility of it all short of a positive outcome (the 'alioquin sequeretur quod homo esset in vanum' of the III.xliv.2 passage), was just what he needed, a means of saving both himself and his current project.

As a further example of Thomas's coming to Dante's aid in the moment of his setting off in a fresh direction, we may take the question of secondary causality, the role of the separate substances within the general scheme of things. Dante's position in this matter – not, in fact, a comfortable one – involves a combination of the creationist proper and of the processionist; for though pure form, pure matter and their amalgamation in the heavenly bodies (to which for the sake of completeness we should add the rational soul in man) are understood by him to be the immediate product of divine creativity,[46] form, even in its first instantiation as the intelligible and operative principle of a thing, is referred to the separate substances by which those same bodies appear to be animated.[47] Everything that *is*, in

---

[45] Again, it is impossible for natural desire to be unfulfilled, since "nature does nothing in vain" [*De caelo* ii.11; 291b13]. Now, natural desire would be in vain if it could never be fulfilled. Therefore, man's natural desire is capable of fulfilment, but not in this life, as we have shown. So it must be fulfilled after this life. Therefore, man's ultimate felicity comes after this life.

[46] *Par.* XXIX.13-36, with *Purg.* XXV.67-75 and *Conv.* IV.xxi.4-5 on God's in-breathing of the rational soul into the vegetative and sensitive soul generated *ex materia*. S. Bemrose, '"Come d'animal divegna fante": the Animation of the Human Embryo in Dante', in *The Human Embryo. Aristotle and the Arabic and European Traditions*, ed. G. R. Dunstan (Exeter: Exeter University Press, 1990), pp. 123-35.

[47] *Par.* II.139-41: 'Virtù diversa fa diversa lega / col prezïoso corpo ch'ella avviva, / nel qual, sì come vita in voi, si lega.' D. O'Keeffe, 'Dante's Theory of Creation', *Revue néo-scolastique*, 26 (1924), 45-64; B. Nardi, *Nel mondo di Dante* (note 3 above), pp. 307-13; idem, 'Dante e Pietro d'Abano', in *Saggi di filosofia dantesca* (note 3 above), pp. 40-62 (especially pp. 42-45); A. Mellone, O.F.M., *La dottrina di Dante Alighieri sulla prima creazione*, 'Emanatismo neoplatonico di Dante per le citazioni del *Liber de Causis*?', and 'Il concorso delle creature nella produzione delle cose secondo Dante' (note 21 above); idem, ad voc. 'Creazione', in the *Enciclopedia dantesca*, 6 vols (Rome: Istituto dell'Enciclopedia Italiana, 1970-78),

other words, in the sublunary world (the rational soul of man apart) receives its substantial form – that by virtue of which it is what it is and does what it does – from the Intelligences, Dante's being in this sense a firm commitment in the areas both of creation theology and of general cosmology to the role of intermediate causality in the universe:

> Tu dici: "Io veggio l'acqua, io veggio il foco,
> l'aere e la terra e tutte lor misture
> venire a corruzione, e durar poco;
>   e queste cose pur furon creature;
> per che, se ciò ch'è detto è stato vero,
> esser dovrien da corruzion sicure".
>   Li angeli, frate, e 'l paese sincero
> nel qual tu se', dir si posson creati,
> sì come sono, in loro essere intero;
>   ma li alimenti che tu hai nomati
> e quelle cose che di lor si fanno
> da creata virtù sono informati.
>   Creata fu la materia ch'elli hanno;
> creata fu la virtù informante
> in queste stelle che 'ntorno a lor vanno.
>   L'anima d'ogne bruto e de le piante
> di complession potenzïata tira
> lo raggio e 'l moto de le luci sante;
>   ma vostra vita sanza mezzo spira
> la somma beninanza, e la innamora
> di sé sì che poi sempre la disira.
>
> (*Par.* VII.124-44)[48]

vol. 2, pp. 251-53; J. A. Mazzeo, 'The Analogy of Creation', *Speculum* 32 (1957), 706-21; E. Moore, 'Dante's Theory of Creation', in *Studies in Dante*, Fourth Series, edited and with new introductory matter by C. Hardie (Oxford: Clarendon Press, 1968; originally 1917), pp. 134-65; S. Bemrose, *Dante's Angelic Intelligences: Their Importance in the Cosmos and in Pre-Christian Religion* (note 21 above), pp. 90-113. On the animation of the stars, *Par.* II.139-41: 'Virtù diversa fa diversa lega / col prezïoso corpo ch'ella avviva, / nel qual, sì come vita in voi, si lega.' Thomas (reporting Aristotle) has: 'Est igitur caelum compositum, secundum opinionem Aristotelis, ex anima intellectuali et corpore. Et hoc significat in II de anima [ii.3; 414b19], ubi dicit quod "quibusdam inest intellectivum et intellectus: ut hominibus, et si aliquid huiusmodi est alterum, aut honorabilius", scilicet caelum' (*ScG* II.lxx.4, though cf. 8: 'Hoc autem quod dictum est de animatione caeli, non diximus quasi asserendo secundum fidei doctrinam, ad quam nihil pertinet sive sic sive aliter dicatur. Unde Augustinus, in libro Enchiridion [I.lviii, ult.], dicit: "nec illud quidem certum habeo, utrum ad eandem societatem, scilicet Angelorum, pertineant sol et luna et cuncta sidera: quamvis nonnullis lucida esse corpora, non cum sensu vel intelligentia, videantur"').

[48] You say, "I see water, I see fire and air and earth, and all their mixtures come to corruption and endure but little, and yet these things were created things; so that, if

Now here, as Kenelm Foster was quick to affirm,[49] Thomas is unambiguous, his, both in and beyond the *Contra gentiles*, being an equally firm sense of form in its preliminary manifestation as the immediate product of divine creativity, of the original and abiding *let it be* whereby something is brought forth from nothing, to suppose otherwise being to countenance the notion of pure subsistent matter:

> Prima inductio formarum in materia non potest esse ab aliquo agente per motum tantum: omnis enim motus ad formam est ex forma determinata in formam determinatam; quia materia non potest esse absque omni forma, et sic praesupponitur aliqua forma in materia. Sed omne agens ad formam solam materialem oportet quod sit agens per motum: cum enim formae materiales non sint per se subsistentes, sed earum esse sit inesse materiae, non possunt produci in esse nisi vel per creationem totius compositi, vel per transmutationem materiae ad talem vel talem formam. Impossibile est igitur quod prima inductio formarum in materia sit ab aliquo creante formam tantum: sed ab eo qui est creator totius compositi.
>
> (*ScG* II.xliii.5)[50]

what I have said to you be true, they ought to be secure against corruption". The angels, brother, and the pure country in which you are, may be said to be created even as they are, in their entire being; but the elements which you have named, and all things that are compounded of them, are informed by created power. Created was the matter that is in them, created was the informing virtue in these stars that wheel about them. The soul of every beast and of the plants is drawn from a compound potentiated by the shining and motion of the holy lights; but your life the supreme beneficence breathes forth without intermediary, and so enamours it of itself that it desires it ever after.

[49] *Dante e San Tommaso* (note 16 above), pp. 12-16.

[50] The first induction of forms into matter cannot have originated from an agent acting by means of movement only. All motion directed to a form is from a determinate form toward a determinate form, for matter cannot exist in the absence of all form; the existence of some form in matter is presupposed. But every agent whose action is directed only toward material forms is necessarily an agent that acts by means of motion. For, since material forms are not self-subsistent, and since, in their case, to be is to be in matter, there are but two possible ways in which they can be brought into being: either by the creation of the whole composite, or by the transmutation of matter to this or that form. The first induction of forms into matter, therefore, cannot possibly be from an agent that creates the form alone; rather, this is the work of him who is the creator of the whole composite. Similarly, *ST* Ia.65.4 resp.: 'opinio fuit quorundam quod omnes formae corporales deriventur a substantiis spiritualibus quas Angelos dicimus. Et hoc quidem dupliciter aliqui posuerunt. Plato enim posuit formas quae sunt in materia corporali, derivari et formari a formis sine materia subsistentibus, per modum participationis cuiusdam. Ponebat enim hominem quendam immaterialiter subsistentem, et similiter equum, et sic de aliis, ex quibus constituuntur haec singularia sensibilia, secundum quod in materia corporali remanet quaedam impressio ab illis formis separatis, per modum assimilationis cuiusdam, quam participationem vocabat. Et secundum ordinem

The position, then, is clear: no secondary causality at the point of inception. Subsequently, yes, for secondary causality is everywhere present to being as part of its fundamental mechanism, but at the point of inception, no.[51] But that is not what Dante found in the text; for, sensitive as

---

formarum ponebant Platonici ordinem substantiarum separatarum, puta quod una substantia separata est quae est equus, quae est causa omnium equorum; supra quam est quaedam vita separata, quam dicebant per se vitam et causam omnis vitae; et ulterius quandam quam nominabant ipsum esse, et causam omnis esse. Avicenna vero et quidam alii non posuerunt formas rerum corporalium in materia per se subsistere, sed solum in intellectu. A formis ergo in intellectu creaturarum spiritualium existentibus (quas quidem ipsi intelligentias, nos autem Angelos dicimus), dicebant procedere omnes formas quae sunt in materia corporali, sicut a formis quae sunt in mente artificis, procedunt formae artificiatorum ... Omnes autem hae opiniones ex una radice processisse videntur. Quaerebant enim causam formarum, ac si ipsae formae fierent secundum seipsas. Sed sicut probat Aristoteles in VII Metaphys., id quod proprie fit, est compositum, formae autem corruptibilium rerum habent ut aliquando sint, aliquando non sint, absque hoc quod ipsae generentur aut corrumpantur, sed compositis generatis aut corruptis, quia etiam formae non habent esse, sed composita habent esse per eas, sic enim alicui competit fieri, sicut et esse. Et ideo, cum simile fiat a suo simili, non est quaerenda causa formarum corporalium aliqua forma immaterialis; sed aliquod compositum, secundum quod hic ignis generatur ab hoc igne. Sic igitur formae corporales causantur, non quasi influxae ab aliqua immateriali forma, sed quasi materia reducta de potentia in actum ab aliquo agente composito. Sed quia agens compositum, quod est corpus, movetur a substantia spirituali creata, ut Augustinus dicit III de Trin.; sequitur ulterius quod etiam formae corporales a substantiis spiritualibus deriventur, non tanquam influentibus formas, sed tanquam moventibus ad formas. Ulterius autem reducuntur in Deum, sicut in primam causam, etiam species angelici intellectus, quae sunt quaedam seminales rationes corporalium formarum. In prima autem corporalis creaturae productione non consideratur aliqua transmutatio de potentia in actum. Et ideo formae corporales quas in prima productione corpora habuerunt, sunt immediate a Deo productae, cui soli ad nutum obedit materia, tanquam propriae causae.'

[51] *ScG* III.ciii.3 (over against Avicenna's sense of material agency as merely dispositive with respect to separate agency): 'Haec autem positio satis consona est aliis suis positionibus. Ponit enim [i.e. Avicenna] quod omnes formae substantiales effluunt in haec inferiora a substantia separata; et quod corporalia agentia non sunt nisi disponentia materiam ad suscipiendam impressionem agentis separati. Quod quidem non est verum secundum Aristotelis doctrinam, qui probat in VII Metaphys., quod formae quae sunt in materia, non sunt a formis separatis, sed a formis quae sunt in materia; sic enim invenietur similitudo inter faciens et factum'; *ST* Ia 110.2 resp.: 'Respondeo dicendum quod Platonici posuerunt formas quae sunt in materia, causari ex immaterialibus formis, quia formas materiales ponebant esse participationes quasdam immaterialium formarum. Et hos, quantum ad aliquid, secutus est Avicenna, qui posuit omnes formas quae sunt in materia, procedere a conceptione intelligentiae, et quod agentia corporalia sunt solum disponentia ad formas. Qui in hoc videntur fuisse decepti, quia existimaverunt formam quasi aliquid per se factum, ut sic ab aliquo formali principio procederet. Sed sicut philosophus probat in VII Metaphys., hoc quod proprie fit, est compositum, hoc enim proprie est quasi subsistens. Forma autem non dicitur ens quasi ipsa sit, sed sicut quo aliquid est, et sic per consequens nec forma proprie fit; eius enim est fieri, cuius est esse, cum fieri nihil aliud sit quam via in esse. Manifestum est autem quod factum est simile facienti, quia omne agens

he must have been to Thomas's general position, he nonetheless discovered as he read on into Book III of the *Contra gentiles* what seemed to him to be an exemplary account, if not of the generation, then of the transmission of form, even in its primary instantiation, by the separate substances. In this, he was mistaken, for Thomas, again, will have none of it. But read in a certain way and with a dash of enthusiasm, the text does indeed hold out possibilities, namely a sense (*a*) of form as pre-existent in the intellect of 'some substance or substances' ('in intellectu alicuius substantiae, vel aliquarum'); (*b*) of form in matter as proceeding from form without matter ('formae quae sunt in materia, venerunt a formis quae sunt sine materia); (*c*) of form generally as a product of movement in the heavens ('et causantes formas inferiores per motum caeli'); (*d*) of the Intelligences as directive ('sicut directa in finem a substantia intelligente'); and (*e*) of form as proceeding from natural – in the sense of 'natured' or created – bodies ('ex moventibus naturalibus'). Thus everything once again is to hand, Thomas, never less than careful in the area of secondary causality, appearing to authorize the alternative emphasis:

> Si autem corpus caeleste a substantia intellectuali movetur, ut ostensum est; motus autem corporis caelestis ordinatur ad generationem in inferioribus: necesse est quod generationes et motus istorum inferiorum procedant ex intentione substantiae intelligentis. In idem enim fertur intentio principalis agentis, et instrumenti. Caelum autem est causa inferiorum motuum secundum suum motum, quo movetur a substantia intellectuali. Sequitur ergo quod sit sicut instrumentum intellectualis substantiae. Sunt igitur formae et motus inferiorum corporum a substantia intellectuali causatae et intentae sicut a principali agente, a corpore vero caelesti sicut ab instrumento.
>
> Oportet autem quod species eorum quae causantur et intenduntur ab intellectuali agente, praeexistant in intellectu ipsius: sicut formae artificiatorum praeexistunt in intellectu artificis, et ex eis deriventur in effectus. Omnes igitur formae quae sunt in istis inferioribus, et omnes motus, derivantur a formis intellectualibus quae sunt in intellectu alicuius substantiae, vel aliquarum. Et propter hoc dicit Boetius, in libro de Trin., quod "formae quae sunt in materia, venerunt a formis quae sunt sine materia". Et quantum ad hoc verificatur dictum Platonis, quod formae separatae sunt principia formarum quae sunt in materia: licet Plato posuerit eas per se subsistentes, et

agit sibi simile. Et ideo id quod facit res naturales, habet similitudinem cum composito, vel quia est compositum, sicut ignis generat ignem; vel quia totum compositum, et quantum ad materiam et quantum ad formam, est in virtute ipsius; quod est proprium Dei. Sic igitur omnis informatio materiae vel est a Deo immediate, vel ab aliquo agente corporali; non autem immediate ab Angelo', etc.

causantes immediate formas sensibilium; nos vero ponamus eas in intellectu existentes, et causantes formas inferiores per motum caeli.

Quia vero omne quod movetur ab aliquo per se, non secundum accidens, dirigitur ab eo in finem sui motus; corpus autem caeleste movetur a substantia intellectuali; corpus autem caeleste causat per sui motum omnes motus in istis inferioribus: necessarium est quod corpus caeleste dirigatur in finem sui motus per substantiam intellectualem, et per consequens omnia inferiora corpora in proprios fines.

Sic igitur non est difficile videre qualiter naturalia corpora cognitione carentia moveantur et agant propter finem. Tendunt enim in finem sicut directa in finem a substantia intelligente, per modum quo sagitta tendit ad signum directa a sagittante. Sicut enim sagitta consequitur inclinationem ad finem determinatum ex impulsione sagittantis, ita corpora naturalia consequuntur inclinationem in fines naturales ex moventibus naturalibus, ex quibus sortiuntur suas formas et virtutes et motus.

(*ScG* III.xxiv.1-4)[52]

---

[52] Now, if a celestial body is moved by intellectual substance, as we have shown, and if the motion of a celestial body is ordered to generation in the realm of things here below, it must be that the processes of generation and the motions of these lower things start from the intention of an intelligent substance. For the intention of the principal agent and that of the instrument are directed toward the same thing. Now, the heaven is the cause of the movements of inferior bodies, by virtue of its own motion in which it is moved by an intellectual substance. It follows, then, that the heavenly body is like an instrument for intellectual substance. Therefore, the forms and movements of lower bodies are caused by intellectual substance which intends them as a principal agent, while the celestial body is like an instrument.

It must be, then, that the species of things caused and intended by the intellectual agent exist beforehand in his intellect, as the forms of artifacts pre-exist in the intellect of the artist and are projected from there into their products. So, all the forms that are in these lower substances, and all their motions, are derived from the intellectual forms which are in the intellect of some substance or substances. Consequently, Boethius says in his book, *The Trinity*, that "forms which are in matter have come from forms which are without matter". And on this point, Plato's statement is verified, that forms separated from matter are the principles of forms that are in it. Although Plato claimed that they subsist in themselves and immediately cause the forms of sensible things, we assert that they exist in an intellect and cause lower forms through the motion of the heavens.

Since everything that is moved directly and not merely accidentally by another being is directed by that being to the end of its motion, and since the celestial body is moved by an intellectual substance, and, moreover, the celestial body causes, through its own motion, all the motions in these lower things, the celestial body must be directed to the end of its motion by an intellectual substance, and so must all lower bodies be directed to their own ends.

So, then, it is not difficult to see how natural bodies, devoid of knowledge, are moved and perform actions for an end. They tend to the end as things directed to that end by

Here too, then, the text functions, not as a source, but as a stimulus, as apt from out of its particular kind of spaciousness to quicken the independent initiative.

As a final instance of this same process, of the tendency of the Thomist text to function in Dante as a principle of emancipation, we may take the case of his embryology, his account of the genesis of the rational soul as the formal principle of specifically human being and doing,[53] for here too Dante is both with Thomas and against him. He is *with* him in so far as for Thomas too the rational soul in man is understood to come from beyond, to be infused into the psychosomatic totality *ab extra*. He is *against* him in so far as his – Dante's – is a transformational or evolutionary account of the soul in its vegetative and sensitive aspects, an account envisaging a series of mutations at the level of form until at last the soul generated *ex materia* is ready for the in-breathing of its rational component by God. The key passage here, *Purg.* XXV.52-60, reads as follows:

> Anima fatta la virtute attiva
> qual d'una pianta, in tanto differente,
> che questa è in via e quella è già a riva,
>   tanto ovra poi, che già si move e sente,
> come spungo marino; e indi imprende
> ad organar le posse ond' è semente.
>   Or si spiega, figliuolo, or si distende
> la virtù ch'è dal cor del generante,
> dove natura a tutte membra intende.[54]

an intellectual substance, in the way that an arrow tends toward the target when it has been aimed by the archer. Just as the arrow attains its inclination to a definite end from the archer's act of shooting it, so do natural bodies attain their inclination to natural ends, from natural movers; from which movers they also receive their forms, powers, and motions.

[53] B. Nardi, *Sigieri di Brabante nella Divina Commedia e le fonti della filosofia di Dante* (Spianate (Pescia): Presso l'Autore, 1912; four articles published originally in the *Rivista di filosofia neo-scolastica* in 1911 and 1912; pp. 43-52; idem, 'Intorno al tomismo di Dante e alla quistione di Sigieri' (note 3 above); idem, 'Noterelle polemiche di filosofia dantesca', *Nuovo giornale dantesco* I (1917), 123-29; idem, 'Sull'origine dell'anima umana', in *Dante e la cultura medievale* (Bari: Laterza, 1949), pp. 260-83; idem, 'La formazione dell'anima umana secondo Dante', in *Studi di filosofia medievale* (Rome: Edizioni di Storia e di Letteratura, 1960, with an anastatic reprint in 1979), pp. 9-68 (with 'L'anima umana secondo Sigieri' at pp. 151-161); idem, 'Il tomismo di Dante e il p. Busnelli, S. J.', in *Saggi di filosofia dantesca* (note 3 above), pp. 341-80 (especially pp. 359 ff.); S. Bemrose, '"Come d'animal divegna fante": the Animation of the Human Embryo in Dante' (note 46 above).

[54] The active virtue having become a soul, like that of a plant (but different in so far as this is on the way, and that has already arrived), so works then that now it moves and feels, like a sea-fungus; then it proceeds to develop organs for the power of which it is the germ. Now, my son, expands, now distends, the virtue which proceeds from the

For Thomas, this is out of the question, for form, he believes, is impatient of gradual implementation or of affirmation by degrees, a position secure both in the *Contra gentiles* and in the *Summa theologiae*.⁵⁵ Rather, the question stands for him to be set up substitutionally rather than transformationally, the sensitive and the rational each alike taking the place of its predecessor as distinct from constituting the term of its development. Here too, however, it is Thomas who, for all his rejection of anything resembling a gradualistic account of the psychogenetic issue in man, provides Dante with what he needs for his own solution, the passage from Canto XXV cited a moment ago not only reflecting but invoking Thomist ways of thinking and speaking:

heart of the begetter, where nature makes provision for all the members. With a slight redistribution of emphases, *Conv*. IV.xxi.4-5: 'E però dico che quando l'umano seme cade nel suo recettaculo, cioè ne la matrice, esso porta seco la vertù de l'anima generativa e la vertù del cielo e la vertù de li elementi legati, cioè la complessione; e matura e dispone la materia a la vertù formativa, la quale diede l'anima del generante; e la vertù formativa prepara li organi a la vertù celestiale, che produce de la potenza del seme l'anima in vita. La quale, incontanente produtta, riceve da la vertù del motore del cielo lo intelletto possibile; lo quale potenzialmente in sé adduce tutte le forme universali, secondo che sono nel suo produttore, e tanto meno quanto più dilungato da la prima Intelligenza è.'

⁵⁵ *ScG* II.lxxxix.6: 'Secundum enim hanc positionem, sequeretur quod aliqua virtus eadem numero nunc esset anima vegetabilis tantum, et postmodum anima sensitiva: et sic ipsa forma substantialis continue magis ac magis perficeretur. Et ulterius sequeretur quod non simul, sed successive educeretur forma substantialis de potentia in actum. Et ulterius quod generatio esset motus continuus, sicut et alteratio. Quae omnia sunt impossibilia in natura'; *ST* Ia.118.2 ad 2: 'Dicunt ergo quidam quod supra animam vegetabilem quae primo inerat, supervenit alia anima, quae est sensitiva; et supra illam iterum alia, quae est intellectiva. Et sic sunt in homine tres animae, quarum una est in potentia ad aliam. Quod supra improbatum est. Et ideo alii dicunt quod illa eadem anima quae primo fuit vegetativa tantum, postmodum, per actionem virtutis quae est in semine, perducitur ad hoc quod fiat etiam sensitiva; et tandem perducitur ad hoc ut ipsa eadem fiat intellectiva, non quidem per virtutem activam seminis, sed per virtutem superioris agentis, scilicet Dei deforis illustrantis. Et propter hoc dicit philosophus quod intellectus venit ab extrinseco. Sed hoc stare non potest. Primo quidem, quia nulla forma substantialis recipit magis et minus; sed superadditio maioris perfectionis facit aliam speciem, sicut additio unitatis facit aliam speciem in numeris. Non est autem possibile ut una et eadem forma numero sit diversarum specierum. Secundo, quia sequeretur quod generatio animalis esset motus continuus, paulatim procedens de imperfecto ad perfectum; sicut accidit in alteratione. Tertio, quia sequeretur quod generatio hominis aut animalis non sit generatio simpliciter, quia subiectum eius esset ens actu. Si enim a principio in materia prolis est anima vegetabilis, et postmodum usque ad perfectum paulatim perducitur; erit semper additio perfectionis sequentis sine corruptione perfectionis praecedentis. Quod est contra rationem generationis simpliciter. Quarto, quia aut id quod causatur ex actione Dei, est aliquid subsistens, et ita oportet quod sit aliud per essentiam a forma praeexistente, quae non erat subsistens; et sic redibit opinio ponentium plures animas in corpore. Aut non est aliquid subsistens, sed quaedam perfectio animae praeexistentis, et sic ex necessitate sequitur quod anima intellectiva corrumpatur, corrupto corpore; quod est impossibile'; II *Sent*. 18.2.1 resp., etc.

etsi a principio decisionis in semine non sit anima actu, sed virtute, propter deficientiam organorum; tamen ipsammet virtutem seminis, quod est corpus organizabile, etsi non organizatum, esse proportionaliter semini animam in potentia, sed non actu; et quia vita plantae pauciora requirit organa quam vita animalis, primo semine sufficienter ad vitam plantae organizato, ipsam praedictam virtutem fieri animam vegetabilem; deinde, organis magis perfectis et multiplicatis, eandem perduci ut sit anima sensitiva; ulterius autem, forma organorum perfecta, eandem animam fieri rationalem, non quidem per actionem virtutis seminis, sed ex influxu exterioris agentis, propter quod suspicantur Aristotelem dixisse *intellectum ab extrinseco esse*, in libro de generatione animalium.

(*ScG* II.lxxxix.6)[56]

Here too, therefore, everything is ready and waiting: Thomas's 'vita plantae pauciora' for Dante's 'qual d'una pianta'; Thomas's 'in semine non sit anima actu ... semini animam in potentia' for Dante's 'le posse ond' è semente'; Thomas's 'organa quam vita animalis ... ad vitam plantae organizato ... forma organorum perfecta' for Dante's 'ad organar le posse'. True, there are other possibilities, Dante's proposal of this matter in terms of a series of inchoative instants – of the vegetative as embryonic in respect of the sensitive and of the sensitive as embryonic in respect of the rational – looking very much like Albert's in the *De natura et origine animae* (I.v):

---

[56] From the moment of severance the soul is not present in the semen actually but virtually, because of the lack of organs; and yet this very power of the semen – itself a body potentially endowed with organs though actually without them – is, proportionately to the semen, a potential but not an actual soul. Moreover, since plant life requires fewer organs than animal life, from the moment that the organic development of the semen suffices for plant life, the aforesaid seminal power becomes a vegetative soul; and later, the organs having been perfected and multiplied still more, the same power is raised to the level of a sensitive soul; and finally, with the perfecting of the organs' form, the same soul becomes rational, not, indeed, by the action of that seminal power, but through the influx of an external agent. And for this reason the proponents of the theory suppose Aristotle to have said in the *De generatione animalium* [ii.3; 736b28] that "the intellect is from without". Cf. III.xxii.7: 'In actibus autem formarum gradus quidam inveniuntur. Nam materia prima est in potentia primo ad formam elementi. Sub forma vero elementi existens est in potentia ad formam mixti: propter quod elementa sunt materia mixti. Sub forma autem mixti considerata, est in potentia ad animam vegetabilem: nam talis corporis anima actus est. Itemque anima vegetabilis est potentia ad sensitivam; sensitiva vero ad intellectivam. Quod processus generationis ostendit: primo enim in generatione est fetus vivens vita plantae, postmodum vero vita animalis, demum vero vita hominis. Post hanc autem formam non invenitur in generabilibus et corruptibilibus posterior forma et dignior. Ultimus igitur finis generationis totius est anima humana, et in hanc tendit materia sicut in ultimam formam. Sunt ergo elementa propter corpora mixta; haec vero propter viventia; in quibus plantae sunt propter animalia; animalia vero propter hominem. Homo igitur est finis totius generationis.'

Oportet autem scire, quod, sicut in aliis, ita etiam in homine inchoatio vegetativi est in materia et in esse primo substantiae animandae, et inchoatio sensibilis est in vegetativo, et inchoatio rationalis in sensitivo est ... Ostensum est etiam per ante dicta, quod substantia illa quae est anima hominis partim est ab intrinseco et partim ab extrinseco ingrediens: quia licet vegetativum et sensitivum in homine de materia educantur mediante virtute formativa, quae est in gutta matris et patris, tamen haec formativa non educeret eas hoc modo prout sunt potentiae rationalis et intellectualis formae et substantiae, nisi secundum quod ipsa formativa movetur informata ab intellectu universaliter movente in opere generationis; et ideo complementum ultimum quod est intellectualis formae et substantiae non per instrumentum neque ex materia, sed per lucem suam influit intellectus primae causae purus et immixtus.[57]

But for all its status as exemplary in respect of the transformational as opposed to the substitutional, there can be no privileging of the *De*

---

[57] What we have to understand is that, in man as in other things, the beginning of the vegetative is in matter itself, in the original being of the substance to be quickened, and the beginning of the sensitive in the vegetative, and the beginning of the rational in the sensitive ... It has already been demonstrated in the aforesaid that the substance that is the human soul comes partly from within and partly from beyond; for although the vegetative and the sensitive are brought forth from matter by way of the formative virtue, which is in the fluids of the mother and the father, nonetheless this formative virtue would not bring them forth such that they were powers of the rational soul and of an intellectual form and substance were not that same formative virtue itself moved and informed by the universal intellect at work in the process of generation. Therefore, the point of arrival, which is an intellectual form and substance, is accomplished, not instrumentally or by way of matter, but through an influx of the pure and uncontaminated light of the divine mind as its first cause (text in B. Nardi, 'Alcuni luoghi di Alberto Magno e di Dante', in *Saggi di filosofia dantesca* (note 3 above), pp. 63-72 at p. 71). Thomas, preparatory to rejecting this position, summarises thus in the *De pot.* at 3.9 ad 9: 'Unde alii dicunt, quod anima vegetabilis est in potentia ad animam sensibilem et sensibilis est actus eius; unde anima vegetabilis quae primo est in semine, per actionem naturae perducitur ad complementum animae sensibilis; et ulterius anima rationalis est actus et complementum animae sensibilis; unde anima sensibilis perducitur ad suum complementum, scilicet ad animam rationalem, non per actionem generantis sed per actum creantis; et sic dicunt quod ipsa rationalis anima in homine partim est ab intrinseco, scilicet quantum ad naturam intellectualem; et partim ab extrinseco, quantum ad naturam vegetabilem et sensibilem. Sed hoc nullo modo potest stare: quia vel hoc ita intelligitur quod natura intellectualis sit alia anima a vegetabili et sensibili, et sic redit in idem cum secunda opinione: vel intelligitur ita quod ex istis tribus naturis constituatur substantia animae in qua natura intellectualis erit ut formale, et natura sensibilis et vegetabilis erit ut materiale. Ex quo sequitur quod cum natura sensibilis et vegetabilis sint corruptibiles, utpote de materia eductae, substantia animae humanae non possit esse perpetua. Sequitur idem etiam inconveniens quod inductum est contra primam, scilicet quod forma substantialis successive educatur in actum.'

natura et origine animae over the *Contra gentiles* as the key text here, the difficulty of the Albertan line in both its lexical and syntactical choices ('inchoatio vegetativi ... substantiae animandae ... nisi secundum quod ipsa formativa movetur informata ab intellectu movente ... complementum ultimum') tending to confirm over against the conceptual and expressive congeniality of the Thomist text the remoteness of the former as Dante's 'control', as his vademecum in the area of psychogenesis. On the contrary, his chosen companion, guide and counsellor remains the *Contra gentiles*, a text which, in its commitment to the sorting and sifting of competing emphases (for that is the business of apologetics), provides him with just what he needs in his determination to look the other way.

4. Dante's celebration of Aquinas as spokesman for the sage spirits in paradise testifies to what he saw and most appreciated in him, namely, his poise as a philosophical spirit, his mastery of the Aristotelian text, and, as informing the entire undertaking, the piety of it all, the transparency of the Thomist utterance to something other and greater than itself. But for all his admiration and affection for Thomas as master of the syllogistic statement, as incomparable in his sense of what Aristotle was and of why Aristotle matters, and as secure in his understanding of what it is to live humbly in Christ, Dante's was an alternative sense of the theological project, of what theology is and of how it stands to be done; for the theological project in Dante stands to be proposed by way, not so much of the *propositional* as of the *predicamental*, of the crisis of existence into which the contents of propositional awareness enter as a principle of resurrection, as that whereby the soul lays hold at last of its proper inheritance. Now this, as a way of describing the situation in Dante, needs careful statement, since for all his starting out from the crisis of existence as the *across which* of theological awareness and as the whereabouts of its verification, there can be no referral of the essential to the existential component of his spirituality as to its point of departure, for it is the essential component of that spirituality which, as the *prius* of everything coming next by way both of the substance and of the phenomenology of the moral and religious life (both of the *what* and of the *how* of that life), determines the shape and substance of the existential crisis in the first place. On the one hand, then, we have the dogmatic moment of the text, the moment which, turning as it does upon creation as a matter of the love-overflowing of the Godhead, upon the catastrophe of Eden as a matter of perverse willing, and upon the Christ event as a matter of moral and ontological re-potentiation, constitutes, not only the *prius*, but the *encompassing* of the crisis engendered by the forces of reckless selfhood, by the standing of self over against self in

the forum of conscience; so, for example, on the first of these things, on creation as but the love-extrinsication of the Godhead and on this as the ground in man of the immortality, of the freedom and of the Godlikeness properly his from the outset, these lines (13-18 and 64-75) from Cantos XXIX and VII of the *Paradiso*:

> Non per aver a sé di bene acquisto,
> ch'esser non può, ma perché suo splendore
> potesse, risplendendo, dir *"Subsisto"*,
>   in sua etternità di tempo fore,
> fuor d'ogne altro comprender, come i piacque,
> s'aperse in nuovi amor l'etterno amore.
>   ...
>   La divina bontà, che da sé sperne
> ogne livore, ardendo in sé, sfavilla
> sì che dispiega le bellezze etterne.
>   Ciò che da lei sanza mezzo distilla
> non ha poi fine, perché non si move
> la sua imprenta quand' ella sigilla.
>   Ciò che da essa sanza mezzo piove
> libero è tutto, perché non soggiace
> a la virtute de le cose nove.
>   Più l'è conforme, e però più le piace;
> ché l'ardor santo ch'ogne cosa raggia,
> ne la più somigliante è più vivace.[58]

while on the second of them, on the impudence of Eden as man's response to the love-overflowing of the Godhead thus understood, these (lines 22-30 and 115-17) from Canto XXIX of the *Purgatorio* and Canto XXVI of the *Paradiso*:

> E una melodia dolce correva
> per l'aere luminoso; onde buon zelo
> mi fé riprender l'ardimento d'Eva,
>   che là dove ubidia la terra e 'l cielo,

---

[58] Not for gain of good unto himself, which cannot be, but that his splendour might, in resplendence, say *"Subsisto"* – in his eternity beyond time, beyond every other bound, as it pleased him, the eternal love opened in new loves ... The divine goodness, which spurns all envy from itself, burning within itself so sparkles that it displays the eternal beauties. That which derives immediately from it therefore has no end, because when it seals, its imprint may never be removed. That which rains down from it immediately is wholly free, because it is not subject to the power of the new things. It is the most conformed to it and therefore pleases it the most; for the holy ardour, which irradiates everything is most living in what is most like itself.

femmina, sola e pur testé formata,
non sofferse di star sotto alcun velo;
  sotto 'l qual se divota fosse stata,
avrei quelle ineffabili delizie
sentite prima e più lunga fïata.
...
  Or, figluol mio, non il gustar del legno
fu per sé la cagion di tanto essilio,
  ma solamente il trapassar del segno.[59]

and on the third of them, on the Father's work in the Son as a matter of God's renewing man in his power to moral and eschatological self-determination, these (lines 106-20) from, again, Canto VII of the *Paradiso*:

Ma perché l'ovra tanto è più gradita
da l'operante, quanto più appresenta
  de la bontà del core ond' ell' è uscita,
la divina bontà che 'l mondo imprenta,

---

[59] And a sweet melody ran through the luminous air; wherefore good zeal made me reprove Eve's daring, that, there where earth and heaven were obedient, a woman, alone and but then formed, did not bear to remain under any veil, under which, if she had been devout, I should have tasted those ineffable delights before, and for a longer time ... Now know, my son, that the tasting of the tree was not in itself the cause of so long an exile, but solely the overpassing of the bound. Cf. *Par.* XXXII. 121-23: 'colui che da sinistra le s'aggiusta / è il padre per lo cui ardito gusto / l'umana specie tanto amaro gusta.' N. Borsellino, 'Notizie sull'Eden (*Paradiso* XXVI)', *Lettere Italiane* 41 (1989), 3, 321-33 (and in *Sipario dantesco. Sei scenari della Commedia* (Rome: Salerno, 1991), pp. 88-101); L. Cardellino, 'Struttura del poema e senso del viaggio. Eden: peccato originale e umiltà', in *Autocritica infernale* (Milan: Jaca Book,1992), pp. 25-51; C. A. Mangieri, 'L'Eden dantesco: allegorismo e significazione', *Italian Quarterly* 41, 161-62 (2004), 5-53; W. W. Marshall, 'Dante and the Doctrine of Original Sin. A Theological Gloss on *Purgatorio* XVI, 80-105 and *Paradiso* XXVII, 121-41', *Dante. Rivista internazionale di studi su Dante Alighieri* 3 (2006), 21-40. Also, B. Nardi, 'Il concetto dell'impero nello svolgimento del pensiero dantesco', in *Saggi di filosofia dantesca* (note 3 above), pp. 215-75 (especially pp. 215-28). More generally, H. Rondet, *Original Sin: the Patristic and Theological Background*, trans. C. Finegan (Shannon, Eire: Ecclesia Press, 1972; originally *Le Péché originel dans la tradition patristique et théologique* (Paris: Fayard, 1967)); H. M. Köster, *Urstand, Fall und Erbsünde in der Scholastik* (Freiburg: Herder, 1979); and, with reference to particular representatives of the tradition, J. B. Kors, O.P. *La Justice primitive et le peché originel d'après S. Thomas*, Bibliothèque Thomiste (Paris: Vrin, 1930); R. Martorelli Vico, 'La dottrina della giustizia originale e del peccato originale nel trattato *De peccato originali* di Egidio Romano', *Documenti e studi sulla tradizione filosofica medievale* 1 (1990), 1, 227-46; P. J. Weithman, 'Augustine and Aquinas on Original Sin and the Function of Political Authority', *Journal of the History of Philosophy* 30 (1992), 3, 353-76. Otherwise, N. P. Williams, *The Idea of the Fall and Original Sin* (London: Longmans, 1927); E. Yarnold, *The Theology of Original Sin* (Notre Dame, Ind.: Fides Publishers, 1971); M. Flick, *Il peccato originale* (Brescia: Queriniana, 1972).

> di proceder per tutte le sue vie,
> a rilevarvi suso, fu contenta.
>   Né tra l'ultima notte e 'l primo die
> sì alto o sì magnifico processo,
> o per l'una o per l'altra, fu o fie:
>   ché più largo fu Dio a dar sé stesso
> per far l'uom sufficiente a rilevarsi,
> che s'elli avesse sol da sé dimesso;
>   e tutti li altri modi erano scarsi
> a la giustizia, se 'l Figliuol di Dio
> non fosse umilïato ad incarnarsi.[60]

On the other hand we have the predicament of the one who, knowing himself as called to be in, through and for God as the beginning and end of all being, knows himself also by way of the alternative project and of the drastic phenomenology of this, of the disorientation, the directionlessness, the fear, the self-inexplicability, and, as the boundary and underlying condition of these and of every other symptom of being in its far-wandering, the despair contingent on radical lostness and fashioning from it a scourge of the spirit. This, then, is where Dante begins. Setting aside every preoccupation with the propaedeutics of faith and the methodology of sacred science, he begins with the substance and psychology of being in its proximity to non-being, with self itself under the aspect of imminent dissolution:

>   Nel mezzo del cammin di nostra vita
> mi ritrovai per una selva oscura,
> ché la diritta via era smarrita.
>   Ahi quanto a dir qual era è cosa dura
> esta selva selvaggia e aspra e forte
> che nel pensier rinova la paura!
>   Tant' è amara che poco è più morte;
> ma per trattar del ben ch'i' vi trovai,
> dirò de l'altre cose ch'i' v'ho scorte.
>   Io non so ben ridir com' i' v'intrai,
> tant' era pien di sonno a quel punto

---

[60] But because the deed is so much the more prized by the doer, the more it displays of the goodness of the heart whence it issued, the divine goodness which puts its imprint on the world, was pleased to proceed by all its ways to raise you up again; nor between the last night and the first day has there been or will there be so exalted and so magnificent a procedure, either by the one or by the other; for God was more bounteous in giving himself to make man sufficient to uplift himself again, than if he solely of himself had remitted; and all other modes were scanty in respect to justice, if the Son of God had not humbled himself to become incarnate.

che la verace via abbandonai ...
   Questi parea che contra me venisse
con la test'alta e con rabbiosa fame,
sì che parea che l'aere ne tremesse.
   Ed una lupa, che di tutte brame
sembiava carca ne la sua magrezza,
e molte genti fé già viver grame,
   questa mi porse tanto di gravezza
con la paura ch'uscia di sua vista,
ch'io perdei la speranza de l'altezza.

(*Inf.* I.1-12 and 46-54)[61]

With this, then, the way is open for a discourse turning, certainly, upon an act of intellection, of theological right understanding but, more fundamentally still, on intellection as a means of actualization *ex parte subiecti*, as that whereby self emerges into the fullness of its now transfigured humanity. First, then, comes the moment of *self-encounter*, the moment in which, quickened by grace as a principle of encouragement, the soul more than ever anxious in respect of the integrity and of the intelligibility of its presence in the world looks into the face, not of love, but of lovelessness as the truth of its own being and of being generally in the world, a process issuing, in the recesses of the pit, in a sense of the nothingless of it all, of being under the aspect of non-being. But in so far as lovelessness presupposes love as the ground of its intelligibility, the way is open to renewal, the moment of *self-encounter* thus giving way to that of *self-reconfiguration*, to the moment in which, with the taking of the guilt of estrangement into itself as the condition of its liquidation, the soul sets about bringing home every otherwise random love-impulse of the spirit to the kind of love given with the act itself of existence – a process culminating, Dante thinks, in a state of perfect spiritual self-possession, of governance as a matter of *self*-governance (the 'per ch'io te sovra te corono e mitrio' of *Purg.* XXVII.142).[62] But that, resplendent as it is, is not all, for the kind of *self-encounter* and *self-reconfiguration* whereby

---

[61] Midway in the journey of our life I found myself in a dark wood, for the straight way was lost. Ah, how hard it is to tell what that wood was, wild, rugged, harsh; the very thought of it renews my fear! It is so bitter that death is hardly more so. But, to treat of the good that I found in it, I will tell of the other things I saw there. I cannot rightly say how I entered it, I was so full of sleep at the moment I left the true way ... [the lion] seemed to be coming at me, head high and raging with hunger, so that the air seemed to tremble at it; and a she-wolf, that in her leanness seemed laden with every craving and had already caused many to live in sorrow; she put such heaviness on me with the fear that came from the sight of her that I lost hope of the height.

[62] wherefore I crown and mitre you over yourself.

the soul knows itself in the possibility of new life is in turn taken up in the kind of *self-transcendence* whereby it knows itself in the now ecstatic substance of self, in the opening out of self upon the kind of deiformity to which it is called from beforehand as to its proper destiny.[63] Having, in other words, known and struggled with self in its endless capacity for self-destruction, the soul at last rejoices in the kind of transhumanity (the 'trasumanar' of *Par.* I.70-72) proper to it as the most immanent of its immanent possibilities. Such at any rate is the Christian hope as Dante sees and understands it, at which point we return at last to Dante and Aquinas; for if on the one hand Thomas remains the undisputed master of Christian-theological discourse on the plane of the horizontal, of the forward thrust of the mind as it attends to the business of precise intellection, then Dante remains the undisputed master of Christian-theological discourse on the plane of the vertical, of the downward thrust of the mind – which is also its upward thrust – as it attends to the business of disclosure, of laying open the deep substance of self as embarked on the way of death and resurrection.

5. Where, then, does this leave us with respect to the massive and at times militant intervention of Nardi, Gilson and Foster with which we began? It leaves us first with an enhanced appreciation of what between them they accomplished in this area of Dante scholarship, for it is thanks to their combination of courage and clearsightedness that, not so much Dante, as we ourselves are set free for a new order of enquiry, for an account of the precise nature (*a*) of Dante's reading and reception of the Thomist text, and (*b*) of the theological issue as he himself sees and understands it. Of the second of these things, we have said sufficient, Dante's being a proposal of the theological project by way, not so much of the content in and for itself of dogmatic consciousness, as of the situation into which that content enters as a co-efficient of new life, as that whereby, in and through an ever more refined sense of its own

---

[63] For the terminology ('trasumanar'), S. Botterill, *Dante and the Mystical Tradition: Bernard of Clairvaux in the Commedia* (Cambridge: Cambridge University Press, 1994), Chapter 6 ('From deificari to transumanar? Dante's *Paradiso* and Bernard's *De diligendo Deo*'), pp. 194-241; V. Capelli, 'Lettura del canto I del *Paradiso*. L'esperienza del "trasumanar"', in *Letture dantesche tenute nella pieve di Polenta e nella basilica di S. Mercuriale in Forlì (1996-2005)* (Genoa and Milan: Marietti, 2006), pp. 215-29; G. Jori, 'Per un commento di "trasumanar e organizzar" (appunti di lettura)', in *E 'n guisa d'eco i detti e le parole. Studi in onore di Giorgio Barberi Squarotti*, 3 vols (Alessandria: Edizioni dell'Orso, 2006), vol. 2, pp. 959-81; B. Guthmüller, '"Trasumanar significar per verba / non si poria". Sul I canto del *Paradiso*', *L'Alighieri. Rassegna dantesca*, n.s. 29 (2007), 48, 107-20 (from the German original in the *Deutsches Dante-Jahrbuch* 82 (2007), 67-85, and updated in *Mito e metamorfosi. Da Dante al Rinascimento* (Rome: Carocci, 2009), pp. 75-90).

innermost reasons, the soul at last comes home to itself in the fullness of its proper humanity, its proper humanity being nothing other than its proper transhumanity. As far, however, as the first of them is concerned, namely the kind of relationship subsisting between the reader and the text he cherishes and by which he is in turn cherished, it is a question of the way in which otherness in respect of the idea pure and simple points on beyond itself to the kind of sameness whereby it is authorized from out of the depths. Something of the kind, at any rate, is the object of Dante's meditation in the exquisite tenth canto of the *Paradiso*, where, given the power of the idea, not so much to unite, as to divide one man from another, each alike remains indispensable to the collective proclamation:

> Tu vuo' saper di quai piante s'infiora
> questa ghirlanda che 'ntorno vagheggia
> la bella donna ch'al ciel t'avvalora.
>   Io fui de li agni de la santa greggia
> che Domenico mena per cammino
> u' ben s'impingua se non si vaneggia.
>   Questi che m'è a destra più vicino,
> frate e maestro fummi, ed esso Alberto
> è di Cologna, e io Thomas d'Aquino.
>   Se sì di tutti li altri esser vuo' certo,
> di retro al mio parlar ten vien col viso
> girando su per lo beato serto.
>   Quell' altro fiammeggiare esce del riso
> di Grazïan, che l'uno e l'altro foro
> aiutò sì che piace in paradiso.
>   L'altro ch'appresso addorna il nostro coro,
> quel Pietro fu che con la poverella
> offerse a Santa Chiesa suo tesoro.
>   La quinta luce, ch'è tra noi più bella,
> spira di tale amor, che tutto 'l mondo
> là giù ne gola di saper novella:
>   entro v'è l'alta mente u' sì profondo
> saver fu messo, che, se 'l vero è vero,
> a veder tanto non surse il secondo.
>   Appresso vedi il lume di quel cero
> che giù in carne più a dentro vide
> l'angelica natura e 'l ministero.
>   Ne l'altra piccioletta luce ride
> quello avvocato de' tempi cristiani
> del cui latino Augustin si provide.

> Or se tu l'occhio de la mente trani
> di luce in luce dietro a le mie lode,
> già de l'ottava con sete rimani.
>   Per vedere ogne ben dentro vi gode
> l'anima santa che 'l mondo fallace
> fa manifesto a chi di lei ben ode.
>   Lo corpo ond' ella fu cacciata giace
> giuso in Cieldauro; ed essa da martiro
> e da essilio venne a questa pace.
>   Vedi oltre fiammeggiar l'ardente spiro
> d'Isidoro, di Beda e di Riccardo,
> che a considerar fu più che viro.
>   Questi onde a me ritorna il tuo riguardo,
> è 'l lume d'uno spirto che 'n pensieri
> gravi a morir li parve venir tardo:
>   essa è la luce etterna di Sigieri,
> che, leggendo nel Vico de li Strami,
> silogizzò invidïosi veri.
>
>   (*Par.* X.91-138)[64]

    In a passage decisive for the now sublime sociology of it all, *over-againstness* gives way to *alongsidedness* as a paradigm of consciousness, to a species of circuminsession or 'inseatedness' as a means of seeing and

---

[64] You wish to know what plants these are that enflower this garland, which amorously circles round the fair lady who strengthens you for heaven. I was of the lambs of the holy flock which Dominic leads on the path where there is good fattening if they do not stray. He that is next beside me on the right was my brother and my master, and he is Albert of Cologne, and I Thomas of Aquino. If thus of all the rest you would be informed, come, following my speech with your sight, going round the blessed wreath. The next flaming comes from the smile of Gratian who served the one and the other court so well that it pleases in paradise. The other who next adorns our choir was that Peter who, like the poor widow, offered his treasure to holy Church. The fifth light, which is the most beautiful among us, breathes with such love that all the world there below thirsts to know tidings of it. Within it is the lofty mind to which was given wisdom so deep that, if the truth be true, there never rose a second of such full vision. At its side behold the light of that candle which, below in the flesh, saw deepest into the angelic nature and its ministry. In the next little light shines that defender of the Christian times, of whose discourse Augustine made use. If now you are bringing your mind's eye from light to light after my praises, you are already thirsting for the eighth. Therewithin, through seeing every good, the sainted soul rejoices who makes the fallacious world manifest to any who listen well to him. The body from which it was driven lies down below in Cieldauro, and he came from martyrdom and exile to this peace. See, flaming beyond, the glowing breath of Isidore, of Bede, and of Richard who in contemplation was more than man. This one from whom your look returns to me is the light of a spirit to whom, in his grave thoughts, it seemed that death came slow. It is the eternal light of Siger who, lecturing in Straw Street, demonstrated invidious truths.

celebrating the relationship between one man and another in the moment of emergence, this in turn pointing on to the nature of Dante's relationship with those of his *auctores* he most cherished – to a relationship lit up and sustained by its own perichoretic intensity.[65]

---

[65] O light eternal, who alone abidest in thyself, [and, known to thyself and knowing, lovest and smilest on thyself!]. A. Deneffe, 'Perichoresis, circumincessio, circuminsessio,' in *Zeitschrift für katholische Theologie* 47 (1923), 497-532; D. F. Stramara Jr, 'Gregory of Nyssa's Terminology for Trinitarian Perichoresis', *Vigiliae Christianae* 52 (1998), 3, 257-63; R. Cross, 'Perichoresis, Deification, and Christological Predication in John of Damascus', *Medieval Studies* 62 (2000), 69-124, after Gregory Nazianzen, *Epistula* ci.6; xxii.4; John of Damascus *De fide ortho*. i.14, etc.

The Twin Peaks of Dante's Theology in the *Paradiso*

> Né tra l'ultima notte e 'l primo die
> sì alto o sì magnifico processo,
> o per l'una o per l'altra, fu o fie:
>   ché più largo fu Dio a dar sé stesso
> per far l'uom sufficiente a rilevarsi,
> che s'elli avesse sol da sé dimesso;
>   e tutti li altri modi erano scarsi
> a la giustizia, se 'l Figliuol di Dio
> non fosse umilïato ad incarnarsi.
>
> ...
>
> *Regnum celorum* vïolenza pate
> da caldo amore e da viva speranza,
> che vince la divina volontate:
>   non a guisa che l'omo a l'om sobranza,
> ma vince lei perché vuole esser vinta,
> e, vinta, vince con sua beninanza.
>
> (*Par.* VII.112-20 and XX.94-99)[1]

1. Introduction: preliminary emphases – being, affectivity and a reconfiguration of the theological issue. 2. Atonement theology I: Anselm and the Christ event as a matter of reparation. 3. Atonement theology II: Dante and the Christ event as a matter of re-potentiation. 4. Election theology I: Thomas, implicit faith and salvation *in casu*. 5. Election theology II: Dante, explicit faith and the love-susceptibility of the Godhead.

Dante's is a love-interpretation of existence under the conditions of time and eternity. Everything that *is* in the world as an object of perception

---

[1] Nor between the last night and the first day has there been or will there be so exalted and so magnificent a procedure, either by one or the other; for God was more bounteous in giving himself to make man sufficient to uplift himself again, than if he solely of himself had remitted; and all other modes were scanty in respect to justice, if the Son of God had not humbled himself to become incarnate ... *Regnum celorum* suffers violence from fervent love and from living hope which vanquishes the divine will; not as man overcomes man, but vanquishes it because it wills to be vanquished, and, vanquished, vanquishes with its own benignity.

and delight stands to be understood in terms (*a*) of its proceeding from the Godhead as original and abiding love, and (*b*) of its tending from deep within itself – from out of the love given with the act itself of existence – towards its proper perfection in the world. Eloquent in respect of the first of these things, of the notion of God as original and abiding love and as forever opening out in fresh channels of creative and recreative concern, is the 'Non per aver a sé di bene acquisto' passage of *Par.* XXIX.13-18, an essay in the twofold love-immanence and love-extrinsication of the One who *is* as of the essence:

> Non per aver a sé di bene acquisto,
> ch'esser non può, ma perché suo splendore
> potesse, risplendendo, dir "*Subsisto*",
>   in sua etternità di tempo fore,
> fuor d'ogne altro comprender, come i piacque,
> s'aperse in nuovi amor l'etterno amore.[2]

while no less committed in respect of the second of them, of the notion of everything as tending from out of its connatural affectivity towards a consummate act of existence, is this passage from the *Convivio* (III.iii.2-5), an essay in being in general as but the sum total of its love-impulses:

> Onde è da sapere che ciascuna cosa, come detto è di sopra, per la ragione di sopra mostrata ha 'l suo speziale amore. Come le corpora simplici hanno amore naturato in sé a lo luogo proprio, e però la terra sempre discende al centro; lo fuoco ha [amore a] la circunferenza di sopra, lungo lo cielo de la luna, e però sempre sale a quello. Le corpora composte prima, sì come sono le minere, hanno amore a lo luogo dove la loro generazione è ordinata, e in quello crescono e acquistano vigore e potenza; onde vedemo la calamita sempre da la parte de la sua generazione ricevere vertù. Le piante, che sono prima animate, hanno amore a certo luogo più manifestamente, secondo che la complessione richiede; e però vedemo certe piante lungo l'acque quasi c[ontent]arsi, e certe sopra li gioghi de le montagne, e certe ne le piagge e dappiè monti: le quali se si transmutano, o muoiono del tutto o vivono quasi triste, sì come cose disgiunte dal loro amico. Li animali bruti hanno più manifesto amore non solamente a li luoghi, ma l'uno l'altro vedemo amare. Li uomini hanno loro proprio amore a le perfette e oneste cose. E però che l'uomo, avvegna che una sola sustanza sia, tuttavia [la] forma, per la sua nobilitade, ha in sé e la

---

[2] Not for gain of good unto himself, which cannot be, but that his splendour might, in resplendence, say "*Subsisto*" – in his eternity beyond time, beyond every other bound, as it pleased him, the eternal love opened into new loves.

natura [d'ognuna di] queste cose, tutti questi amori puote avere e tutti li ha.³

Thus everything that *is* in the world, be it animate or inanimate, is open to contemplation in terms of the affective economy of the whole, of being as, again, no more than the aggregate of its love-instances. And it is this sense of existence both severally and in the round as open to interpretation in terms of the love by which it is moved from deep within itself that determines the form and content of two of the great doctrinal emphases of the *Commedia*: in the area of atonement theology, its commitment to the notion of God's initiative in Christ as a matter of moral and ontological empowerment, as that whereby man as man is once again made sufficient on the planes of being and doing (the 'per far l'uom sufficiente a rilevarsi' moment of *Par.* VII.116);⁴ and, in the area of election theology, its sense of the love-susceptibility of it all, of God's willingness to be overcome, not only by the justified in Christ, but by all those living out the synderectic substance of their humanity (the 'ma vince lei perché vuole esser vinta' moment of *Par.* XX.98).⁵ Now neither of these things need scandalize the pious spirit, those sensitive (*a*) to the nature of grace as, always and everywhere, the condition of human being and becoming, and (*b*) to God's immunity to anything but the substance of his own intentionality, for each of them survives intact within the soteriological economy of the whole. But in surviving intact they are relieved of any sense (*a*) of the continuing poverty of the human situation in respect of its

---

³ It is important to know, therefore, that, as was said above and for the reason adduced there, everything has its own special kind of love. Just as simple bodies have an inborn love for the place proper to them – so that earth always descends to the centre, while fire has an inborn love for the circumference above us bordering the heaven of the Moon, and therefore always rises upwards towards that – so primary compound bodies, such as minerals, have a love for the place suited to their generation; in that place they grow, and from it they derive their vigour and power. That is why, as we observe, the magnet always receives power from the quarter in which it was generated. Plants, which are the primary form of animate life, even more clearly have a love for certain places, in accordance with what their constitution requires; and so we see that some plants rejoice, as it were, when alongside water, others when on the ridges of mountains, others when on slopes and on foothills; if they are transplanted, they either die completely or live a sad life, like beings so to speak separated from their friends. Brute animals not only more clearly still have a love for particular places, but, as we observe, they also love one another. Human beings have their specific love, for what is perfect and just. And since the human being, despite the fact that his whole form constitutes a single substance in virtue of its nobility, has a nature that embraces all these features, he can have all these loves, and indeed does have them.

⁴ [for God was more bounteous in giving himself] to make man sufficient to uplift himself again [than if he solely of himself had remitted].

⁵ but vanquishes it because it wills to be vanquished ...

power to significant determination, and (*b*) of the inevitable reprobation of those through no fault of their own a stranger to Christ. On the contrary, they testify between them to something more magnanimous and more magnificent than this, to a sense on Dante's part of the kind of love-encompassing whereby the human project may be said both to subsist in its intrinsic viability, and to commend itself in the sight of God as its author and architect.

2. Quite apart from the solutions it advances in the area of salvation theology, the *Cur Deus homo* of Anselm commended itself in Dante's time as the classic case of theology under the aspect of faith seeking understanding (*fides quaerens intellectum*), for what is going on here is a proposal of the faith component of the religious life in terms of its reasonableness, of its making good sense.[6] Without prejudice to the mystery of it all, the theologian seeks to throw light on the contents of faith as belief, to gloss the *how* and *why* of God's purposes under the aspect of their intelligibility. Anselm, availing himself of the obvious text here (I Peter 3:15), puts it thus:

> Saepe et studiosissime a multis rogatus sum et verbis et litteris, quatenus cuiusdam de fide nostra quaestionis rationes, quas soleo respondere quaerentibus, memoriae scribendo commendem. Dicunt enim eas sibi placere et arbitrantur satisfacere. Quod petunt, non ut per rationem ad fidem accedant, sed ut eorum quae credunt intellectu et contemplatione delectentur, et ut sint, quantum possunt, 'parati semper ad safisfactionem omni poscenti se rationem de ea quae in nobis est spe'.
>
> (*Cur Deus homo* I.i prin.)[7]

---

[6] K. Barth, *Fides quaerens intellectum. Anselm's Proof of the Existence of God in the Context of his Theological Scheme* (Pittsburg, Pickwick Press, 1985; originally 1960). More generally on the soteriological issue in Christian theology, R. S. Franks, *The Work of Christ. A Historical Study of Christian Doctrine* (London and New York: Nelson, 1962); F. W. Dillistone, *The Christian Understanding of Atonement* (Philadelphia: Westminster Press, 1968); A. McGrath, *Iustitia Dei. A History of the Christian Doctrine of Justification. The Beginnings to the Reformation* (Cambridge: Cambridge University Press, 1986); R. Cessario, *The Godly Image: Christ and Salvation in Catholic Thought from Anselm to Aquinas* (Petersham, MA: St Bede's Publications, 1990); J. McIntyre, *The Shape of Soteriology* (Edinburgh: T. & T. Clark, 1992). Older but still serviceable, H. Rashdall, *The Idea of Atonement in Christian Theology* (London: MacMillan, 1925; originally 1919); G. Aulén, *Christus Victor. An Historical Study of the Three Main Types of the Idea of Atonement*, trans. A. G. Hebert (New York: Macmillan, 1951).

[7] I have often been asked most earnestly, both by word of mouth and in writing, by many people, to set down a written record of the reasoned explanations with which I am in the habit of answering people who put enquiries to me about a certain position in our faith. For they say that these explanations please them, and they think them satisfactory. They make this request, not with a view to arriving at faith through reason, but in order

His, therefore, in the *Cur Deus homo*, is an *epoche* or parenthesizing of every given in respect of the Christ and of the Christ event in favour of its logicality, of its acceptibility even to the most sceptical of spirits:

> Quod secundum materiam de qua editum est, *Cur deus homo* nominavi et in duos libellos distinxi. Quorum prior quidem infidelium Christianam fidem, quia rationi putant illam repugnare, respuentium continet obiectiones et fidelium responsiones. Ac tandem remoto Christo, quasi numquam aliquid fuerit de illo, probat rationibus necessariis esse impossibile ullum hominem salvari sine

that they may take delight in the understanding and contemplation of the things which they believe, and may be, as far as they are able, "ready to give satisfaction to all who ask the reason for the hope that is in us [1 Peter 3:15]". The Latin text is F. S. Schmitt (ed.), *Anselmi Opera Omnia*, 6 vols (Edinburgh: Nelson, 1946-61), in facsimile in *S. Anselmi Cantuariensis archiepiscopi opera omnia ad fidem codicum recensuit Franciscus Salesius Schmitt*, 6 vols in 2 (Stuttgart: F. Frommann, 1968-84). It may also be consulted in Migne, *PL* CLVIII, 360C-432B. There are several translations, this one (from Schmitt, 1946) by J. Fairweather in *Anselm of Canterbury. The Major Works*, ed. B. Davies and G. R. Evans (Oxford: Oxford University Press, 1998), pp. 260-356 (slightly amended). On the *Cur Deus homo* (but the list is selective), J. McIntyre, *St Anselm and his Critics: A Re-Interpretation of the Cur Deus Homo* (Edinburgh and London: Oliver and Boyd, 1954); G. H. Williams, *Anselm: Communion and Atonement* (Saint Louis: Concordia, 1960); C. B. Gray, 'Freedom and Necessity in St Anselm's *Cur Deus homo*', *Franciscan Studies* 14 (1976-77), 177-91; G. R. Evans, '*Cur deus homo*: the Nature of St Anselm's Appeal to Reason', *Studia Theologica* 31 (1977), 33-50; B. Leftow, 'Anselm on the Beauty of the Incarnation', *The Modern Schoolman* 72 (1995), 109-24; idem, 'Anselm on the Necessity of the Incarnation', *Religious Studies* 31 (1995), 167-85; R. Campbell, 'The Conceptual Roots of Anselm's Soteriology', in D. E. Luscombe and G. R. Evans (eds), *Anselm: Aosta, Bec and Canterbury. Papers in Commemoration of the Nine-hundreth Anniversary of Anselm's Enthronement as Archbishop, 25 September 1093* (Sheffield: Sheffield Academic Press, 1996), pp. 256-63. More generally on Anselm, R. W. Southern, *St Anselm and His Biographer: a Study of Monastic Life and Thought, 1059-c.1130* (Cambridge: Cambridge University Press, 1963); idem, *St Anselm: A Portrait in a Landscape* (Cambridge: Cambridge University Press, 1990); J. R. Fortin (ed.), *Saint Anselm: His Origins and Influence* (Lewiston, N.Y.: E. Mellen Press, 2001); G. R. Evans, *Anselm* (London: Continuum, 2002; originally 1989); B. Davies and B. Leftow (eds), *The Cambridge Companion to Anselm* (Cambridge: Cambridge University Press, 2004). On Dante and Anselm, in addition to C. Ryan, 'Marking the Difference between Dante and Anselm', in *Dante and the Middle Ages*, ed. J. Barnes and C. Ó Cuilleanáin (Dublin: Irish Academic Press, 1995), pp. 117-37 (a piece to which I am much indebted in the first part of this essay), and to commentaries and *lecturae* on *Paradiso* VII generally (see especially G. Fallani, 'Il Canto VII del *Paradiso*', in *Paradiso: Letture degli anni 1979-81*, ed. S. Zennaro (Rome: Bonacci, 1989), pp. 233-39), A. Agresti, *Dante e S. Anselmo* (Naples: de Bonis, 1887); F. S. Schmitt, ad voc. 'Anselmo' in the *Enciclopedia dantesca*, 6 vols (Rome: Istituto dell'Enciclopedia Italiana, 1970-78), vol. 1, pp. 293-94; G. Muresu, 'Le "vie" della redenzione (*Paradiso* VII)', *Rassegna della letteratura italiana*, eighth series, 98 (1994), 1-2, 5-19 (subsequently in *Il richiamo dell'antica strega* (Rome: Bulzoni, 1997), pp. 203-24); R. McMahon, *Understanding the Medieval Meditative Ascent. Augustine, Anselm, Boethius, and Dante* (Washington, D.C., The Catholic University of America Press, 2006).

illo. In secundo autem libro similiter quasi nihil sciatur de Christo, monstratur non minus aperta ratione et veritate naturam humanam ad hoc institutam esse, ut aliquando immortalitate beata totus homo, id est in corpore et anima, fruereter; ac necesse esse ut hoc fiat de homine propter quod factus est, sed non nisi per hominem-deum; atque ex necessitate omnia quae de Christo credimus fieri oportere.

(*Cur Deus homo, praefatio*)[8]

Setting aside, then, all we have come to believe about the Christ as made known to us by revelation, we may begin by saying that man as man was created to live in a state of covenantal bliss, in the kind of happiness contingent upon his acknowledging himself as a child of the Most High. But in the moment of his disobedience, of his grasping at equality with God, reparation fell due, reparation not only *equal* to that disobedience but, in defiance of mere proportionality, *exceeding* it:

Hoc est debitum quod debet angelus et homo deo, quod solvendo nullus peccat, et quod omnis qui non solvit peccat. Haec est iustitia sive rectitudo voluntatis, quae iustos facit sive rectos corde id est voluntate. Hic est solus et totus honor, quem debemus deo et a nobis exigit deus. Sola namque talis voluntas opera facit placita deo, cum potest operari; et cum non potest, ipsa sola per se placet, quia nullum opus sine illa placet. Hunc honorem debitum qui deo non reddit, aufert deo quod suum est, et deum exhonorat; et hoc est peccare. Quamdiu autem non solvit quod rapuit, manet in culpa. Nec sufficit solummodo reddere quod ablatum est, sed pro contumelia illata plus debet reddere quam abstulit. Sicut enim qui laedit salutem alterius, non sufficit si salutem restituit, nisi pro illata doloris iniuria recompenset aliquid: ita qui honorem alicuius violat non sufficit honorem reddere, si non secundum exhonorationis factam molestiam aliquid, quod placeat illi quem exhonoravit, restituit. Hoc quoque

---

[8] I have named it, in consideration of its subject-matter, *Why God became man*, and have divided it into two books. The first book contains the objections of unbelievers who reject the Christian faith because they think it militates against reason, and the answers given by the faithful. And eventually it proves, by unavoidable logical steps, that, supposing Christ were left out of the case, as if there had never existed anything to do with him, it is impossible that, without him, any member of the human race could be saved. In the second book, similarly, the supposition is made that, even knowing nothing of Christ, it is open to demonstration with no less clear logic and truth: that human nature was instituted with the specific aim that at some stage the whole human should enjoy blessed immortality, 'whole' meaning 'with both body and soul'; that it was inevitable that the outcome concerning mankind which was the reason behind man's creation should become a reality, but that this could only happen through the agency of a Man-God; and that it is from necessity that all the things which we believe about Christ have come to pass.

attendendum quia, cum aliquis quod iniuste abstulit solvit, hoc debet dare, quod ab illo non posset exigi, si alienum non rapuisset. Sic ergo debet omnis qui peccat, honorem deo quem rapuit solvere; et haec est 'satisfactió, quam omnis peccator deo debet facere.

(ibid. i.xi)[9]

– at which point, given the depth of man's destitution and his manifest inequality to the task in hand, the inevitability of God's work in Christ, of his stepping in to do what man could not do for himself, moves clearly into view. Now here we need to be careful, for in speaking of the necessity – by which we mean the logical necessity – of Christ's coming amongst us, we have to acknowledge its love-dimensionality, the referability of everything God set out to do in Christ to his mercy in man's regard; so, for example, as transparent to the substance of Anselmian piety, these lines from ii.20 on the compassion which is God, on the generosity which is Christ, and on these between them as the ground of hope in the midst of hopelessness:

Misericordiam vero Dei quae tibi perire videbatur, cum iustitiam dei et peccatum hominis considerabamus, tam magnam tamque concordem iustitiae invenimus, ut nec maior nec iustior cogitari possit. Nempe quid misericordius intelligi valet, quam cum peccatori tormentis aeternis damnato et unde se redimat non habenti deus pater dicit: accipe unigenitum meum et da pro te; et ipse filius: tolle me et redime te? Quasi enim hoc dicunt, quando nos ad Christianam fidem vocant et trahunt.[10]

---

[9] This is the debt which man and angel owe to God, and no one who pays this debt commits sin; but every one who does not pay it sins. This is justice, or uprightness of will, which makes a being just or upright in heart, that is, in will; and this is the sole and complete debt of honour which we owe to God, and which God requires of us. For it is such a will only, when it can be exercised, that does works pleasing to God; and when this will cannot be exercised, it is pleasing of itself alone, since without it no work is acceptable. He who does not render this honour which is due to God, robs God of his own and dishonours him; and this is sin. Moreover, so long as he does not restore what he has taken away, he remains in fault; and it will not suffice merely to restore what has been taken away, but, considering the contempt offered, he ought to restore more than he took away. For as one who imperils another's safety does not enough by merely restoring his safety, without making some compensation for the anguish incurred, so he who violates another's honour does not enough by merely rendering honour again, but must, according to the extent of the injury done, make restoration in some way satisfactory to the person whom he has dishonoured. We must also observe that when any one pays what he has unjustly taken away, he ought to give something which could not have been demanded of him, had he not stolen what belonged to another. So then, every one who sins ought to pay back the honour of which he has robbed God; and this is the satisfaction which every sinner owes to God.

[10] Now, the mercy of God which, when we were considering the justice of God and the sin of mankind, seemed to you to be dead, we have found to be so great, and so consonant

Implicit, therefore, in the *Cur Deus homo*, and here explicit, is Anselm's referral of the calculative aspect of the atonement to its compassionate aspect, to the movement of love by which it is inaugurated and maintained. But this, for the moment, is not what interests him, for what interests him is, again, the logic of the case, thoughts of compassion not only not entering into it, but tending to compromise the nature of the Godhead as original and abiding justice; so, for example, as a caveat to the ii.20 passage noted above, the following lines from i.24, with their sense of God's brooking no excuse when it comes to exacting his due:

> Quod si vis dicere: misericors Deus dimittit supplicanti quod debet, idcirco quia reddere nequit: non potest dici dimittere, nisi aut hoc quod homo sponte reddere debet nec potest, id est quod recompensari possit peccato, quod fieri non deberet pro conservatione omnis rei quae Deus non est; aut hoc quod puniendo ablaturus erat invito, sicut supra dixi, id est beatitudinem. Sed si dimittit quod sponte reddere debet homo, ideo quia reddere non potest, quid est aliud quam: dimittit Deus quod habere non potest? Sed derisio est, ut talis misericordia Deo attribuatur. At si dimittit quod invito erat ablaturus, propter impotentiam reddendi quod sponte reddere debet: relaxat Deus poenam et facit beatum hominem propter peccatum, quia habet quod debet non habere. Nam ipsam impotentiam debet non habere, et idcirco, quamdiu illam habet sine satisfactione, peccatum est illi. Verum huiusmodi misericordia Dei nimis est contraria iustitiae illius, quae non nisi poenam permittit reddi propter peccatum. Quapropter quemadmodum Deum sibi esse contrarium, ita hoc modo illum esse misericordem impossibile est.[11]

with justice, that a greater and juster mercy cannot be imagined. What, indeed, can be conceived of more merciful than that God the Father should say to a sinner condemned to eternal torments and lacking any means of redeeming himself, "Take my only-begotten Son and give him on your behalf", and that the Son himself should say, "Take me and redeem yourself"? For it is something of this sort that they say when they call us and draw us towards the Christian faith.

[11] But if you want to say, "A merciful God remits the debt of anyone who begs forgiveness on the ground that he is incapable of making repayment", God cannot be said to be remitting anything except either that which the person ought to repay and cannot, that is, recompense which he might hypothetically be able to give for his sin – sin which ought not to be committed even for the sake of preserving everything that exists which is not God – or, alternatively, that which, by way of punishment, he was about to take away from a person against that person's will, that is, the state of blessed happiness. But if God remits what a person cannot give back of his own volition, for the reason that he is incapable of giving it back, how is this different from saying: "God remits what he is not able to have"? But it is mockery for mercy of this kind to be attributed to God. If, however, God remits what he was about to take away from a person against his will, because of that person's incapacity to make payment, in that case he is making his

There can be no question then, Anselm insists, of God's giving up or going back here, for giving up and going back when it comes to good order makes a mockery of the whole thing, and God will suffer no mockery. And this, as an aspect of his setting aside every kind of faith-awareness in the *Cur Deus homo* in favour of argumentation pure and simple, is a point he will not let go of; so, for example, in the same chapter, his statement to the effect that God is indeed a merciful God, but that, rather than the other way round, mercy follows upon justice as the dominant mode of God's dealings with man – at which point the good Boso, impressed (or maybe just oppressed) by the non-negotiability of it all, gives way:

> *B.* Si rationem sequitur Deus iustitiae, non est qua evadat miser homuncio, et misericordia Dei perire videtur.
> *A.* Rationem postulasti, rationem accipe. Misericordem Deum esse non nego, qui "homines et iumenta" salvat, "quemadmodum multiplicavit misericordiam suam" – Nos autem loquimur de illa ultima misericordia, qua post hanc vitam beatum facit hominem. Hanc beatitudinem nulli dari debere nisi illi, cui penitus dimissa sunt peccata, nec hanc dimissionem fieri nisi debito reddito, quod debetur pro peccato secundum magnitudinem peccati, supra positis rationibus puto me sufficienter ostendisse. Quibus si quid tibi videtur posse rationibus obici, dicere debes.
> *B.* Ego utique nullam tuarum rationum aliquatenus infirmari posse video.[12]

Now this again, as an account of what is going on in the *Cur Deus homo*, needs careful statement, since for Anselm as for every seasoned Christian spirit what God does he does in and through the love co-terminous

---

punishment lax and making a person happy on account of his sin, in that the person has what he ought not to have. For his very incapacity is something he ought not to have, and therefore, so long as he has it without paying recompense, it is sin on his part. But mercy of this kind is absolutely contrary to God's justice, which does not allow anything to be given in repayment for sin except punishment. Hence, given that it is impossible for God to be self-contradictory, it is impossible for him to be merciful in this way.

[12] *B.* If the God of justice acts according to logic, there is no route whereby man in his meanness may escape, and it seems that the mercy of God is dead.
A. You asked for logic, and so here it is. I do not deny that God is merciful, he who saves "men and beasts in accordance with how he has multiplied his mercy" [Ps. 36: 7-8; 35 *iuxta* LXX]. Moreover, we are talking about that final mercy, whereby, after this life, he makes a human being blessedly happy. That this state of bliss ought not to be given to anyone whose sins have not been utterly forgiven, and that this forgiveness ought not to happen except on repayment of a debt which is owed because of his sin and which is proportioned to the magnitude of his sin, I think I have demonstrated by the logical reasonings set out earlier. If it seems to you that any objection can be made to these logical reasonings, you ought to say so.
B. I see no way of showing your logical reasonings to be in the slightest invalid.

and thus consubstantial with his being. To look elsewhere in his work, therefore, particularly among his prayers and meditations, is to register his sense both of the incarnation and of the crucifixion as a matter of boundless self-giving, at which point legality is taken up in love as the currency of all God's dealings with man in his far-offness. But – and this now is the point – love, by reason of Anselm's chosen methodology in the *Cur Deus homo*, is contemplated across its judicial aspect, the judicial aspect, he thinks, being both excisable from the salvific scheme generally and furnishing an object of contemplation in its own right.[13]

3. It is by way, then, of Anselm's sense of the cross as God's way of seeing that justice was done and his honour preserved intact that we come to Dante's sense of Christ's work on Calvary as a matter of moral and ontological re-potentiation, as that whereby, in and through the Word made flesh, man was re-empowered in respect of what he already was, and now is once more, as a creature of reasonable self-determination. The key canto is Canto VII of the *Paradiso*, Dante's being a step-by-step reconstruction of the argument until at last he settles on the notion of moral and ontological co-adequation as his point of arrival, of God's once again making man equal to the business in hand. First, then, comes the offence itself, his sense of Eden as a matter of wilfulness, of the unwillingness of our first parents to suffer the yoke of their creatureliness.[14] In fact, the

---

[13] For a gentler view of the *Cur Deus homo*, a sense of the text as belonging to the mainstream of Anselmian piety, D. Brown in his 'Anselm on Atonement' in *The Cambridge Companion to Anselm* (note 7 above), pp. 279-302, at p. 290: 'He was no cold rationalist imposing purely external criteria on God but a devout monk concerned to explore his faith in a God, the internal logic of whose nature, he believed, entailed His never failing to act beautifully and well.' For a critique of the position in Anselm, ranging over both the strengths and the weaknesses of that position, A. Harnack, *History of Dogma*, seven volumes bound as four (unabridged republication of the English translation of the third German edn), trans. N. Buchanan (New York: Dover Publications, 1961), vol.6, p. 54 ff. More recently, J. McIntyre, *Saint Anselm and His Critics: A Re-interpretation of the Cur Deus homo* (note 7 above).

[14] B. Nardi, 'Il concetto dell'impero nello svolgimento del pensiero dantesco', in *Saggi di filosofia dantesca*, 2nd edn (Florence: La Nuova Italia, 1967), pp. 215-75 (especially pp. 215-28); N. Borsellino, 'Notizie sull'Eden (*Paradiso* XXVI)', *Lettere Italiane* 41 (1989), 3, 321-33 (and in *Sipario dantesco. Sei scenari della Commedia* (Rome: Salerno, 1991), pp. 88-101); L. Cardellino, 'Struttura del poema e senso del viaggio. Eden: peccato originale e umiltà', in *Autocritica infernale* (Milan: Jaca Book, 1992), pp. 25-51; C. A. Mangieri, 'L'Eden dantesco: allegorismo e significazione', in *Italian Quarterly* 41, 161-62 (2004), 5-53; W. W. Marshall, 'Dante and the Doctrine of Original sin. A Theological Gloss on *Purgatorio* XVI, 80-105 and *Paradiso* XXVII, 121-41', *Dante. Rivista internazionale di studi su Dante Alighieri* 3 (2006), 21-40. More generally, J. B. Kors, O.P., *La Justice primitive et le peché originel d'après S. Thomas: les sources, la doctrine*, (Paris: Vrin, 1930; originally 1922); H. Rondet, *Original Sin: the Patristic and Theological Background*, trans. C. Finegan

idea is already there in the twilight pages of the *Purgatorio*, where it is a question pre-eminently of melancholy and misgiving:

> E una melodia dolce correva
> per l'aere luminoso; onde buon zelo
> mi fé riprender l'ardimento d'Eva,
>   che là dove ubidia la terra e 'l cielo,
> femmina, sola e pur testé formata,
> non sofferse di star sotto alcun velo;
>   sotto 'l qual se divota fosse stata,
> avrei quelle ineffabili delizie
> sentite prima e più lunga fiata.
>
> (*Purg.* XXIX.22-30)[15]

But in the *Paradiso* melancholy and misgiving give way to something more drastic, to a sense of the co-implication of all men in the self-undoing of Adam:

> Per non soffrire a la virtù che vole
> freno a suo prode, quell' uom che non nacque,
> dannando sé, dannò tutta sua prole.
>
> (*Par.* VII.25-27)[16]

It was in response to this situation, then, to Adam's guilt as visited upon the generations and as borne by them in an attitude of patient expectation (the 'molt' anni lacrimata pace' of *Purg.* X.35),[17] that God looked to its resolution in Christ, to a descent into the flesh as the way of reconciliation:

> onde l'umana specie inferma giacque
> giù per secoli molti in grande errore,

(Shannon, Eire: Ecclesia Press, 1972; originally *Le Péché originel dans la tradition patristique et théologique* (Paris: Fayard, 1967)); H. Köster, *Urstand, Fall und Erbsünde in der Scholastik* (Freiburg: Herder, 1979); R. Martorelli Vico,'La dottrina della giustizia originale e del peccato originale nel trattato *De peccato originali* di Egidio Romano', *Documenti e Studi sulla Tradizione Filosofica Medievale* 1 (1990), 1, 227-46; P. J. Weithman, 'Augustine and Aquinas on Original Sin and the Function of Political Authority', *Journal of the History and Philosophy* 30 (1992), 3, 353-76.

[15] And a sweet melody ran through the luminous air; wherefore good zeal made me reprove Eve's daring, that, there where earth and heaven were obedient, a woman alone and but then formed, did not bear to remain under any veil, under which, if she had been devout, I should have tasted those ineffable delights before, and for a longer time.

[16] By not enduring for his own good a curb upon the power that wills, that man who was never born, in damning himself damned all his progeny.

[17] the peace wept for since many a year ...

> fin ch'al Verbo di Dio discender piacque
> u' la natura, che dal suo fattore
> s'era allungata, unì a sé in persona
> con l'atto sol del suo etterno amore.
>
> *(Par.* VII.28-33)[18]

But – and this now is the question – why? Why this complicated way of going about it? Would not a suitable reprimand, perhaps with a penalty proportionate to what man as man could afford to pay, have been enough? To this, Dante is ready with a reply, but not before establishing the ground of that reply, namely its rootedness in love as nothing other than the endless working out of the Pentateuchal *let it be*, as that whereby whatever *is* in the world as an object of perception and delight is confirmed from deep within itself in its equality to a consummate act of existence. The Christ event, in other words, necessary as it was and still is to man's homecoming as man, was necessary by virtue, not of the law, but of love, of the kind of love, which, in any adult understanding of what love is, functions as a principle of emancipation and, by way of emancipation, of actualization – the substance of the exquisite 'mature in the flame of love' tercet beginning at line 58:

> Questo decreto, frate, sta sepulto
> a li occhi di ciascuno il cui ingegno
> ne la fiamma d'amor non è adulto.[19]

Only now, on the basis of a developed sense of love as a matter of letting a thing be in the totality of that being, is it possible to see into the mystery of it all and to fashion from that mystery a moment of intelligibility. Dante, therefore, secure in the strength of his leading intuition, proceeds to its definitive statement, each successive emphasis serving to draw out and to develop the content of its predecessor. First, then, comes his sense of the Fall as forfeiture, as a foregoing of God's original gift to mankind: of the *immortality* whereby he himself would share in the sempiternity of the Godhead,[20] of the *freedom* whereby he would be unconstrained by

---

[18] wherefore the human race lay sick down there for many centuries in great error, until it pleased the word of God to descend where he, by the sole act of his eternal love, united with himself in person the nature which had estranged itself from its maker.

[19] This decree, brother, is buried from the eyes of everyone whose understanding is not mature in the flame of love. L. M. La Favia, *Soteriologia e poesia (Par. VII). Giustizia e amore* (Ravenna: Centro Dantesco dei Frati Minori Conventuali, 2011).

[20] Anselm, *Cur Deus homo* ii.2: 'Quod autem talis factus sit, ut necessitate non moreretur, hinc facile probatur, quia, ut iam diximus, sapientiae et iustitiae Dei repugnat, ut cogeret hominem mortem pati sine culpa, quem iustum fecit ad aeternam beatitudinem. Sequitur

anything other than his own righteousness,[21] and of these things between them as the substance and meaning of his God-likeness, of his subsisting in the image of his maker.[22] To forfeit any one of them, Dante thinks, is to know self in the disenfranchisement and thus in the dysfunctionality of self, in the falling away of self from its own high calling:

> La divina bontà, che da sé sperne
> ogne livore, ardendo in sé, sfavilla
> sì che dispiega le bellezze etterne.
>   Ciò che da lei sanza mezzo distilla
> non ha poi fine, perché non si move
> la sua imprenta quand' ella sigilla.
>   Ciò che da essa sanza mezzo piove
> libero è tutto, perché non soggiace
> a la virtute de le cose nove.

ergo, quia si nunquam peccasset nunquam moreretur'; ibid. ii.11: 'Non puto mortalitatem ad puram sed ad corruptam hominis naturam pertinere', etc. Thomas, *ST* Ia.97.1 resp.: 'Tertio modo dicitur aliquid incorruptibile ex parte causae efficientis. Et hoc modo homo in statu innocentiae fuisset incorruptibilis et immortalis. Quia, ut Augustinus dicit in libro de quaest. Vet. et Nov. Test., "Deus hominem fecit, qui quandiu non peccaret, immortalitate vigeret, ut ipse sibi auctor esset aut ad vitam aut ad mortem". Non enim corpus eius erat indissolubile per aliquem immortalitatis vigorem in eo existentem; sed inerat animae vis quaedam supernaturaliter divinitus data, per quam poterat corpus ab omni corruptione praeservare, quandiu ipsa Deo subiecta mansisset', etc. In Scripture, Ecclesiastes 3:14: 'Didici quod omnia opera, quae fecit Deus, perseverent in perpetuum', etc.

[21] *Purg.* XVI.79-81, but also, by way of the Dante-character's reply to Brunetto Latini's particular brand of astral determinism (*Inf.* XV.46-47; 55-57; 70-72), *Inf.* XV.88-96. Exact, in this sense, the commentary of Benvenuto da Imola *ad loc.*: 'Et addit aliam praerogativam, scilicet libertatis, dicens, repetendo eadem verba, *ciò che piove da essa*, idest, procedit ab eadem bonitate, *senza mezzo*, idest, organo coeli, *è tutto libero*, ab omni corruptione, ab omni coactione; et ecce rationem: *perchè non soggiace alla virtude*, scilicet informativae, *delle cose nuove*, scilicet planetarum et stellarum, quae de novo creatae sunt et non sunt ab aeterno. Et hic nota quod corpora coelestia influunt in terrestria et elementaria quantum ad distinctionem temporum et productionem generabilium et corruptibilium; non tamen influunt super liberum arbitrium per vim constellationum, quam quidam philosophi dixerunt factum, nec sunt certa signa futurorum contingentium, contra quae homo potest per liberum arbitrium ...'

[22] *Mon.* I.viii.2 (on the in-breathing of Godlikeness), *Par.* V.19-24 (with *Mon.* I.xii.6, on free will as the principle in man of Godlikeness). Thomas on the threefold modality of man's assimilation to God, *ST* Ia.93.4 resp.: 'imago Dei tripliciter potest considerari in homine. Uno quidem modo, secundum quod homo habet aptitudinem naturalem ad intelligendum et amandum Deum; et haec aptitudo consistit in ipsa natura mentis, quae est communis omnibus hominibus. Alio modo, secundum quod homo actu vel habitu Deum cognoscit et amat, sed tamen imperfecte; et haec est imago per conformitatem gratiae. Tertio modo, secundum quod homo Deum actu cognoscit et amat perfecte; et sic attenditur imago secundum similitudinem gloriae.'

> Più l'è conforme, e però più le piace;
> ché l'ardor santo ch'ogne cosa raggia,
> ne la più somigliante è più vivace.
> Di tutte queste dote s'avvantaggia
> l'umana creatura, e s'una manca,
> di sua nobilità convien che caggia.
>
> (ibid., 64-78)[23]

The situation, then, is bleak, man as man, in the wake of Eden, knowing himself only in the powerlessness of sin (the 'solo il peccato è quel che la disfranca' of line 79),[24] in the dissimilitude or God-*un*likeness of the guilty spirit (the 'falla dissimìle al sommo bene' of line 80),[25] in the darkling spirituality of the offender (the 'per che del lume suo poco s'imbianca' of line 81),[26] in the indignity of being in its remotion (the 'in sua dignità mai non rivene' of line 82),[27] and in the moral emptiness of it all (the 'se non r'iempie, dove colpa vòta' of line 83)[28] – bleakness shading off in these circumstances into impossibility, into a delivery of self to the near-nothingness of self. This at any rate is the meaning of the 'Ficca mo l'occhio per entro l'abisso' sequence beginning at line 94, where the notion of impasse ushers in that of a fresh initiative from on high, of an *auxilium Dei* designed to do for man what he cannot do for himself:

> Ficca mo l'occhio per entro l'abisso
> de l'etterno consiglio, quanto puoi
> al mio parlar distrettamente fisso.
> Non potea l'uomo ne' termini suoi
> mai sodisfar, per non potere ir giuso
> con umiltate obedïendo poi,
> quanto disobediendo intese ir suso;
> e questa è la cagion per che l'uom fue

---

[23] The divine goodness, which spurns all envy from itself, burning within itself so sparkles that it displays the eternal beauties. That which immediately derives from it thereafter has no end, because when it seals, its imprint may never be removed. That which rains down from it immediately is wholly free, because it is not subject to the power of new things. It is the most conformed to it and therefore pleases it the most; for the holy ardour, which irradiates everything, is most living in what is most like itself. With all these gifts the human creature is advantaged, and if one fails, it needs must fall from its nobility.

[24] Sin alone is that which disfranchises it ...

[25] and makes it unlike the supreme good ...

[26] so that it is little illumined by its light.

[27] and to its dignity it never returns ...

[28] unless, where fault has emptied, it is filled afresh [with just penalties against evil delight].

> da poter sodisfar per sé dischiuso.
> Dunque a Dio convenia con le vie sue
> riparar l'omo a sua intera vita,
> dico con l'una, o ver con amendue.[29]

God, then, alone equal to the task in hand, had just two options: either to wipe the slate clean and start all over again, or to leave man to sort it out for himself (the 'o che Dio solo per sua cortesia / dimesso avesse, o che l'uom per sé isso / avesse sodisfatto a sua follia' of lines 91-93)?[30] In the event he chose neither. Or, rather, he chose both, both to forgive with a suitable penalty (the penalty paid by Christ in his suffering as man for

---

[29] Fix your eyes now within the abyss of the eternal counsel, as closely focused on my words as you are able. Man, within his own limits, could never make satisfaction, for not being able to descend in humility, by subsequent obedience, so far as in his disobedience he had intended to ascend; and this is the reason why man was shut off from power to make satisfaction by himself. Therefore it was needful for God, with his own ways, to restore man to his full life – I mean with one way, or else with both.

[30] either that God alone, solely by his clemency, had pardoned; or that man should of himself have given satisfaction for his folly. Thomas on the impossibility of God's having forgiven man without satisfaction, *ST* IIIa.46.2 ad 3: 'Alioquin, si voluisset absque omni satisfactione hominem a peccato liberare, contra iustitiam non fecisset. Ille enim iudex non potest, salva iustitia, culpam sive poenam dimittere, qui habet punire culpam in alium commissam, puta vel in alium hominem, vel in totam rempublicam, sive in superiorem principem. Sed Deus non habet aliquem superiorem, sed ipse est supremum et commune bonum totius universi. Et ideo, si dimittat peccatum, quod habet rationem culpae ex eo quod contra ipsum committitur, nulli facit iniuriam, sicut quicumque homo remittit offensam in se commissam absque satisfactione, misericorditer, et non iniuste agit.' It was for various reasons more fitting that God should have proceeded in quite the way he did in Christ, for (*a*) Christ's passion shows forth God's love for man, (*b*) it provides a model of submission and humility, (*c*) it merits for man justifying grace and ultimate glory, (*d*) it binds him more strongly to obedience, and (*e*) it confirms him in his moral dignity (ibid. IIIa.46.3 resp.). On the depth, and thus the impossibility, of man's depravity in consequence of Eden (for the 'Non potea l'uomo ne' termini suoi' passage beginning at VII.97), Hugh of St Victor, *De verbi incarn.* viii: 'Ad hanc plenitudinem oportuit, ut tanta esset humiliatio in expiatione, quanta fuerit praesumptio in praevaricatione. Rationalis autem substantiae Deus tenet summum, homo vero imum gradum. Quando ergo homo praesumpsit contra Deum, facta est elatio de imo ad summum. Oportuit ergo, ut ad expiationis remedium fieret humiliatio de summo ad imum'; Thomas, *ST* IIIa.1.2 ad 2: 'Hominis puri satisfactio sufficiens esse non potuit pro peccato, tum quia tota humana natura erat per peccatum corrupta; nec bonum alicujus personae, vel etiam plurium, poterat per aequiparantiam totius naturae detrimentum recompensare; tum etiam qui peccatum contra Deum commissum quamdam infinitatem habet ex infinitate divinae majestatis; tanto enim offensa est gravior, quanto major est ille in quem delinquitur. Unde oportuit ad condignam satisfactionem ut actus satisfacientis haberet efficaciam infinitam, utpote Dei et hominis existens', etc. For the 'per sé isso' component of the formula, Thomas, *ST* Ia IIae.109.7 resp.: 'homo nullo modo potest resurgere a peccato *per seipsum* sine auxilio gratiae'; IIa IIae.164.2 resp.: 'Et quia ad illum statum primae innocentiae *per seipsum* redire non poterat', etc.

man) *and*, by identifying with him in the midst of his desolation, to make it possible for him to participate in his own renewal. This, then, is the substance of the 'Ma perché l'ovra tanto è più gradita' moment of Canto VII beginning at line 106, a passage tending in its sense of God's work in Christ as a matter of love-empowerment to fashion from atonement theology an essay, not so much in sacrifice, as in sufficiency, in the newly won adequacy of man to his proper destiny:

> Ma perché l'ovra tanto è più gradita
> da l'operante, quanto più appresenta
> de la bontà del core ond' ell' è uscita,
>   la divina bontà che 'l mondo imprenta,
> di proceder per tutte le sue vie,
> a rilevarvi suso, fu contenta.
>   Né tra l'ultima notte e 'l primo die
> sì alto o sì magnifico processo,
> o per l'una o per l'altra, fu o fie:
>   ché più largo fu Dio a dar sé stesso
> per far l'uom sufficiente a rilevarsi,
> che s'elli avesse sol da sé dimesso;
>   e tutti li altri modi erano scarsi
> a la giustizia, se 'l Figliuol di Dio
> non fosse umilïato ad incarnarsi.[31]

Now here too we must be careful, for just as Anselm's account in the *Cur Deus homo* of God's work in Christ as a matter of his exacting his due is enfolded at last by a sense of the love-dimensionality of it all, so Dante takes seriously its judicial component, the notion of a debt to be redeemed and of an account to be settled. Twice, then, in the course of *Paradiso* VII he lights on the retributive or legalistic aspect of the argument, its *quid pro quo* aspect (the 'nulla già mai sì giustamente morse' moment of line 42 and the 'tutti li altri modi erano scarsi / a la giustizia, se 'l Figliuol di Dio / non fosse umilïato ad incarnarsi' moment of lines 118-20),[32] Anselm, in this sense, never being far away. But for all that, the differences are greater

---

[31] But because the deed is so much the more prized by the doer, the more it displays of the goodness of the heart whence it issued, the divine goodness which puts its imprint on the world, was pleased to proceed by all its ways to raise you up again; nor between the last night and the first day has there been or will there be so exalted and so magnificent a procedure, either by the one or by the other; for God was more bounteous in giving himself to make man sufficient to uplift himself again, than if he solely of himself had remitted; and all other modes were scanty in respect to justice, if the Son of God had not humbled himself to become incarnate.

[32] none ever so justly stung ... and all other modes were scanty in respect to justice, if the Son of God had not humbled himself to become incarnate.

than the similarities; for this is a thinking through of the Christ event in terms, not of logic, but of love, not of the apologetic, but of the agapeic. It is a meditation turning upon the notion, not so much of debt and the paying off of debt, as upon the endless love-outpouring of the Godhead as that whereby man knows himself in the fullness of his humanity, at which point atonement theology, like every other species of theology in Dante, is drawn at last into the ambit of creation theology, of a theology both moved by and transparent to God's original and abiding concern for the human project in the viability of that project.

4. But that is not all, for this sense of love as a matter of *letting it be* and of this as a key to understanding in the area of salvation theology, extends also into the area of election theology, where as our control text we may take, not Anselm, but Aquinas, the Aquinas of the *De veritate* and of the *Summa theologiae*. Aquinas's, then, though not without qualification, is a proposal of this issue in terms of explicit faith, of a positive profession of the Christ as the condition in man of ultimate homecoming. In the *Summa theologiae* the matter arises in the course of the faith articles of the *Secunda secundae*, where in reply to the question as to whether a man is bound to believe anything explicitly ('utrum homo teneatur ad credendum aliquid explicite'), Thomas affirms that whereas the contingencies of the scriptural narrative need not compel in conscience, the leading propositions of the faith are binding for the purposes of salvation:

> Determinatio igitur virtuosi actus ad proprium et per se obiectum virtutis est sub necessitate praecepti, sicut et ipse virtutis actus. Sed determinatio actus virtuosi ad ea quae accidentaliter vel secundario se habent ad proprium et per se virtutis obiectum non cadit sub necessitate praecepti nisi pro loco et tempore. Dicendum est ergo quod fidei obiectum per se est id per quod homo beatus efficitur, ut supra dictum est. Per accidens autem vel secundario se habent ad obiectum fidei omnia quae in Scriptura divinitus tradita continentur, sicut quod Abraham habuit duos filios, quod David fuit filius Isai, et alia huiusmodi. Quantum ergo ad prima credibilia, quae sunt articuli fidei, tenetur homo explicite credere, sicut et tenetur habere fidem.
>
> (*ST* IIa IIae.2.5 resp.)[33]

[33] Accordingly, just as a virtuous act is required for the fulfilment of a precept, so is it necessary that the virtuous act should terminate in its proper and direct object: but, on the other hand, the fulfilment of the precept does not require that a virtuous act should terminate in those things which have an accidental or secondary relation to the proper and direct object of that virtue, except in certain places and at certain times. We must, therefore, say that the direct object of faith is that whereby man is made one of the blessed, as stated above [qu. 1, art. 8]; while the indirect and secondary object comprises

Attentive, therefore, to the distinction between what does and does not matter, or, more exactly, between what matters primarily and what matters secondarily, the text settles on a sense of explicit faith in the primary articles of religion as the ground of man's ultimate well-being. And what applies in the *Secunda secundae* at 2.5 applies in Articles 7 and 8 of the same question in relation to the mysteries of the incarnation and of the Trinity, where it is a question of faith as consent to the hypostatic union of the human and the divine in Christ and to the triune substance of the Godhead as the ground of salvation:

> illud proprie et per se pertinet ad obiectum fidei per quod homo beatitudinem consequitur. Via autem hominibus veniendi ad beatitudinem est mysterium incarnationis et passionis Christi, dicitur enim Act. IV, 'non est aliud nomen datum hominibus in quo oporteat nos salvos fieri'. Et ideo mysterium incarnationis Christi aliqualiter oportuit omni tempore esse creditum apud omnes ... mysterium Christi explicite credi non potest sine fide Trinitatis, quia in mysterio Christi hoc continetur quod filius Dei carnem assumpserit, quod per gratiam spiritus sancti mundum renovaverit, et iterum quod de spiritu sancto conceptus fuerit.
>
> (*ST* IIa IIae.2.7 resp. and 8 resp.)[34]

Thomas's, then, is a commitment to the notion of explicit faith as a principle of homecoming, formal profession of the Christian mysteries entering as of the essence into the salvific economy of the whole. But for all their consistency at this point, these articles of the *Secunda secundae* register a caveat, for in well-nigh the same breath Thomas acknowledges the notion of *implicit* faith as a means of salvation among two groups of people: (*a*) the Jewish *inferiores* or those living within the Old Law but

---

all things delivered by God to us in Holy Writ, for instance that Abraham had two sons, that David was the son of Jesse, and so forth. Therefore, as regards the primary points or articles of faith, man is bound to believe them, just as he is bound to have faith. Here, as elsewhere, in this essay, I am much indebted to the work of the late professor Christopher Ryan in his *Dante and Aquinas. A Study of Nature and Grace in the Comedy*, a text revised and edited by me on the basis of papers kindly made available by his widow and soon to be published.

[34] the object of faith includes, properly and directly, that thing through which man obtains beatitude. Now the mystery of Christ's incarnation and passion is the way by which men obtain beatitude; for it is written in Acts 4 [v. 12] that "there is no name under heaven given to men, whereby we must be saved". Therefore belief of some kind in the mystery of Christ's incarnation was necessary at all times and for all persons ... it is impossible to believe explicitly in the mystery of Christ, without faith in the Trinity, since the mystery of Christ includes that the Son of God took flesh, that he renewed the world through the grace of the Holy Ghost, and again that he was conceived by the Holy Ghost.

not learned in it, and (*b*) those who, knowing neither the Old nor the New Law, may nonetheless be said to have an inkling of the providentiality of it all and maybe even of their ultimate deliverance. Notable as far as the first of these groups is concerned, the Jewish *inferiores*, are the following lines from the *Secunda secundae* at 2.7 resp. and 2.8 resp. with their sense that, while in respect of the Christ now among us, an act of explicit faith is required both of the *inferiores* and of the *superiores*, in respect of the Christ as yet to come, implicit faith sufficed for the greater part of the people:

> Post peccatum autem fuit explicite creditum mysterium Christi non solum quantum ad incarnationem, sed etiam quantum ad passionem et resurrectionem, quibus humanum genus a peccato et morte liberatur. Aliter enim non praefigurassent Christi passionem quibusdam sacrificiis et ante legem et sub lege. Quorum quidem sacrificiorum significatum explicite maiores cognoscebant, minores autem sub velamine illorum sacrificiorum, credentes ea divinitus esse disposita de Christo venturo, quodammodo habebant velatam cognitionem ... Et ideo eo modo quo mysterium Christi ante Christum fuit quidem explicite creditum a maioribus, implicite autem et quasi obumbrate a minoribus, ita etiam et mysterium Trinitatis. Et ideo etiam post tempus gratiae divulgatae tenentur omnes ad explicite credendum mysterium Trinitatis. Et omnes qui renascuntur in Christo hoc adipiscuntur per invocationem Trinitatis, secundum illud Matth. ult., 'euntes, docete omnes gentes, baptizantes eos in nomine patris et filii et spiritus sancti.[35]

---

[35] But after sin, man believed explicitly in Christ, not only as to the incarnation, but also as to the passion and resurrection, whereby the human race is delivered from sin and death; for they would not, else, have foreshadowed Christ's passion by certain sacrifices both before and after the Law, the meaning of which sacrifices was known by the learned explicitly, while the simple folk, under the veil of those sacrifices, believed them to be ordained by God in reference to Christ's coming, and thus their knowledge was covered with a veil, so to speak ... wherefore just as, before Christ, the mystery of Christ was believed explicitly by the learned, but implicitly and under a veil, so to speak, by the simple, so too was it with the mystery of the Trinity. And consequently, when once grace had been revealed, all were bound to explicit faith in the mystery of the Trinity; and all who are born again in Christ, have this bestowed on them by the invocation of the Trinity, according to Matthew 28:19: "Going therefore teach ye all nations, baptizing them in the name of the Father, and of the Son and of the Holy Ghost." *De ver.* 14.11 resp.: 'Sed ante peccatum et post, omni tempore necessarium fuit a maioribus explicitam fidem de Trinitate habere; non autem a minoribus post peccatum usque ad tempus gratiae; ante peccatum enim forte talis distinctio non fuisset, ut quidam per alios erudirentur de fide. Et similiter etiam post peccatum usque ad tempus gratiae maiores tenebantur habere fidem de redemptore explicite; minores vero implicite, vel in fide patriarcharum et prophetarum, vel in divina providentia.'

Significant as far as the second of them is concerned – those, that is to say, without the Law but sensitive to the providentiality of things – is this passage, again from the *Secunda secundae* at 2.7, where in reply to the objection that some of the gentiles appear on the testimony of the Areopagite to have been brought home irrespective of their ignorance of Christ and of the Christian mysteries,[36] Thomas insists (*a*) that they were not, in fact, without oracular and other utterances testifying to the truth about to be revealed, and (*b*) that, though not party to Christian revelation precisely as such, they knew themselves in something approaching a sense of God's will to salvation:

> Si qui tamen salvati fuerunt quibus revelatio non fuit facta, non fuerunt salvati absque fide mediatoris. Quia etsi non habuerunt fidem explicitam, habuerunt tamen fidem implicitam in divina providentia, credentes Deum esse liberatorem hominum secundum modos sibi placitos et secundum quod aliquibus veritatem cognoscentibus ipse revelasset ...
>
> (*ST* IIa IIae.2.7 ad 3)[37]

to which, for the sake of confirming his consistency hereabouts, we should add these lines from the *De veritate* on the comparability of the old Jews living as *inferiores* under the Law and of the gentiles living beyond the Law but possessed even so of an inkling of it:

> gentiles non ponebantur ut instructores divinae fidei. Unde, quantumcumque essent sapientes sapientia saeculari, inter minores computandi sunt; et ideo sufficiebat eis habere fidem de redemptore implicite, vel in fide legis et prophetarum, vel etiam in ipsa divina providentia.
>
> (*De ver.* 14.11 ad 5)[38]

---

[36] *ST* IIa IIae.2.7 obj. 3: 'multi gentilium salutem adepti sunt per ministerium Angelorum, ut Dionysius dicit, IX cap. Cael. Hier. Sed gentiles non habuerunt fidem de Christo nec explicitam nec implicitam, ut videtur, quia nulla eis revelatio facta est. Ergo videtur quod credere explicite Christi mysterium non fuerit omnibus necessarium ad salutem.'

[37] If, however, some were saved without receiving any revelation, they were not saved without faith in a mediator, for, though they did not believe in him explicitly, they did, nevertheless, have implicit faith through believing in divine providence, since they believed that God would deliver mankind in whatever way was pleasing to him, and according to the revelation of the Spirit to those who knew the truth ...

[38] the gentiles were never deemed to be teachers in faith and divinity, whence, although they were wise in the secular way of being wise, they are to be counted as *minores*. It was therefore enough for them to have implicit faith in the redeemer or in the law or the prophets, or even in that same divine providence.

True, as Thomas himself suggests, it is all somewhat hypothetical (the 'Si qui tamen salvati fuerunt quibus revelatio non fuit facta' of the *Secunda secundae* passage), but, given his commitment to belief in the Christ either as to come or else as already with us as the only sure way of salvation, the door is left ajar, Thomas's, as far as the pagans are concerned, being to this extent a generous sense of the matter. Persuaded as he is of the centrality of the Christ to every definitive account of God's dealings with man and thus of man's with God under the conditions of time and eternity, and thus, all other things being equal, of the indispensability of explicit faith as a condition of man's ultimate happiness, his, nonetheless, is a sense of the efficacy of implicit faith as a principle *in casu* of homecoming.

5. Now Dante, when it comes to those living outside the Christian dispensation but under the Old Law, is not too far removed, either in substance or in spirit, from Thomas, for though doing without the distinction between explicit and implicit faith decisive for the precise complexion of Thomas's position, he too is eager to bring home the Jewish patriarchs on the basis of their living in anticipation of the Christ to come; so, for example, on the threshold of the poem, the harrowing of hell passage of *Inferno* IV, at once inclusive and exclusive in spirit, inclusive as regards those living within the Old Law and exclusive as regards those living beyond it:

> "Dimmi, maestro mio, dimmi, segnore",
> comincia' io per voler esser certo
> di quella fede che vince ogne errore:
> "uscicci mai alcuno, o per suo merto
> o per altrui, che poi fosse beato?".
> E quei che 'ntese il mio parlar coverto,
> rispuose: "Io era nuovo in questo stato,
> quando ci vidi venire un possente,
> con segno di vittoria coronato.
> Trasseci l'ombra del primo parente,
> d'Abèl suo figlio e quella di Noè,
> di Moïsè legista e ubidente;
> Abraàm patrïarca e Davìd re,
> Israèl con lo padre e co' suoi nati
> e con Rachele, per cui tanto fé,
> e altri molti, e feceli beati.
> E vo' che sappi che, dinanzi ad essi,
> spiriti umani non eran salvati".

(*Inf.* IV.46-63)[39]

---

[39] "Tell me, master, tell me, sir", I began, wishing to be assured of the faith that conquers

while further on in the poem, the Hebrew women passage of *Paradiso* XXXII, where, as Dante himself puts it (the 'secondo lo sguardo che fée / la fede in Cristo' of lines 19-20), it is a question of directionality, of those looking forward rather than backward upon the Christ event as the pivotal point of world-historical understanding:

> E dal settimo grado in giù, sì come
> infino ad esso, succedono Ebree,
> dirimendo del fior tutte le chiome;
>   perché, secondo lo sguardo che fée
> la fede in Cristo, queste sono il muro
> a che si parton le sacre scalee.
>   Da questa parte onde 'l fiore è maturo
> di tutte le sue foglie, sono assisi
> quei che credettero in Cristo venturo;
>   da l'altra parte onde sono intercisi
> di vòti i semicirculi, si stanno
> quei ch'a Cristo venuto ebber li visi.
>
> (*Par.* XXXII.16-27)[40]

But when it comes to those living before and beyond the Old and New Law he is not so sure, for these, though sensitive to the providentiality of it all, were nonetheless bereft of the word which, quickened as it is by the Spirit, alone brings a man to the fullness of faith and the blessedness thereof. And this, for Dante, makes all the difference, for while for Thomas faith and the blessedness thereof are the product of a movement of grace notionally and substantially independent of their external occasions,[41] for

---

every error, did ever anyone go forth from here, either by his own or by another's merit, who afterwards was blessed?" And he, who understood my covert speech, replied, "I was new in this condition when I saw a mighty one come here, crowned with sign of victory. He took hence the shade of our first parent, Abel his son, and Noah, and Moses, obedient giver of laws, Abraham the patriarch and David the king, Israel with his father and his children and with Rachel, for whom he did so much, and many others; and he made them blessed. And I would have you know that before these no human souls were saved."

[40] And from the seventh row downwards, even as down to it, Hebrew women follow in succession, dividing all the trees of the flower; because, according to the look which their faith turned to Christ, these are the wall by which the sacred stairway is divided. On this side, wherein the flower is mature in all its petals, are seated those who believed in Christ yet to come. On the other side, where the half-circles are broken by vacant places, sit those who turned their faces towards Christ already come.

[41] *ST* IIa IIae 6.1 resp.: 'Quantum vero ... ad assensum hominis in ea quae sunt fidei, potest considerari duplex causa. Una quidem exterius inducens, sicut miraculum visum, vel persuasio hominis inducentis ad fidem. Quorum neutrum est sufficiens causa, videntium enim unum et idem miraculum, et audientium eandem praedicationem, quidam credunt

Dante the external occasions of faith, including above all Scripture as the living word of God, constitute *in themselves* a channel of grace, herein lying their indispensability to a coming home of the individual to his proper happiness; so, for example, on the power of Scripture *in and through itself* – irrespective, that is to say of any movement of the Spirit other than that by which it is itself irradiated – to persuasion, the 'silogismo che la m'ha conchiusa' sequence of *Paradiso* XXIV.91-96:

> E io: "La larga ploia
> de lo Spirito Santo, ch'è diffusa
> in su le vecchie e 'n su le nuove cuoia,
>   è silogismo che la m'ha conchiusa
> acutamente sì, che 'nverso d'ella
> ogne dimostrazion mi pare ottusa."[42]

the 'e a tal creder non ho io pur prove / fisice e metafisice' sequence of the same canto at lines 130-38:

> E io rispondo: Io credo in uno Dio
> solo ed etterno, che tutto 'l ciel move,
> non moto, con amore e con disio;
>   e a tal creder non ho io pur prove
> fisice e metafisice, ma dalmi
> anche la verità che quinci piove
>   per Moïsè, per profeti e per salmi,
> per l'Evangelio e per voi che scriveste
> poi che l'ardente Spirto vi fé almi.[43]

and the 'Avete il novo e 'l vecchio Testamento' passage of *Paradiso* V.73-78:

et quidam non credunt. Et ideo oportet ponere aliam causam interiorem, quae movet hominem interius ad assentiendum his quae sunt fidei. Hanc autem causam Pelagiani ponebant solum liberum arbitrium hominis, et propter hoc dicebant quod initium fidei est ex nobis, inquantum scilicet ex nobis est quod parati sumus ad assentiendum his quae sunt fidei; sed consummatio fidei est a Deo, per quem nobis proponuntur ea quae credere debemus. Sed hoc est falsum. Quia cum homo, assentiendo his quae sunt fidei, elevetur supra naturam suam, oportet quod hoc insit ei ex supernaturali principio interius movente, quod est Deus. Et ideo fides quantum ad assensum, qui est principalis actus fidei, est a Deo interius movente per gratiam.'

[42] And I: "The plenteous rain of the Holy Spirit which is poured over the old and new parchments is a syllogism that has proved it to me so acutely that, in comparison with this, every demonstration seems obtuse to me."

[43] And I reply: I believe in one God, sole and eternal, who, unmoved, moves all the heavens with love and with desire; and for this belief I have not only proofs physical and metaphysical, but it is given to me also in the truth that rains down hence through Moses and the prophets and the psalms, through the gospel, and through you who wrote when the fiery Spirit made you holy.

> Siate, Cristiani, a muovervi più gravi:
> non siate come penna ad ogne vento,
> e non crediate ch'ogne acqua vi lavi.
>   Avete il novo e 'l vecchio Testamento,
> e 'l pastor de la Chiesa che vi guida;
> questo vi basti a vostro salvamento.[44]

each alike secure in its sense of Scripture, along with the inspired teaching of the Church (the 'e 'l pastor de la Chiesa che vi guida' of the *Paradiso* V passage), as salvifically sufficient. Throughout, then, the pattern is the same. Dispensing with the notion of grace as dispositive in respect of faith as a property of the spirit (a notion which, especially when taken in conjunction with that of implicit faith, leaves considerable room for manoeuver), Dante opts instead for the encounter pure and simple as a means of grace and principle of salvation, an option, however, at once making for the exclusion of whole tracts of humanity from the feast of the Lamb. And it is precisely this – the melancholy of a position not entirely innocent of effrontery in respect of the wideness of God's mercy – that urged him to rethink the issue here with a view to resolving it at the highest conceivable level, in terms, that is to say, less of the revelatory instant in all its historical contingency, than of the love and thus of the love-susceptibility of One whose being *is* his loving. It is, in other words, the sadness of a soteriology making only for repudiation as its point of arrival, that, in a moment of exhilaration, encouraged him, indeed compelled him, to revise the whole question of ultimate being and becoming in turns of the willingness of God (*a*) to accommodate all those who in good faith plead the cause of the righteous spirits of antiquity (the case of Trajan), and (*b*) to grace those who, though unChristed and unchurched, nevertheless lived or live still according to their lights (the case of Rhipeus). First, then, in the order of exposition comes the predicament of the good man and true, who, though bereft of Christ through no fault of his own, lives even so a just and honourable life. Where, the pilgrim protagonist wonders, is the justice which condemns him?:

> Assai t'è mo aperta la latebra
> che t'ascondeva la giustizia viva,
> di che facei question cotanto crebra;
>   ché tu dicevi: "Un uom nasce a la riva
> de l'Indo, e quivi non è chi ragioni
> di Cristo né chi legga né chi scriva;
>   e tutti suoi voleri e atti buoni

---

[44] Be graver, you Christians, in moving. Be not like a feather to every wind, and think not that every water may cleanse you. You have the New Testament and the Old, and the Shepherd of the Church to guide you. Let this suffice for your salvation.

> sono, quanto ragione umana vede,
> sanza peccato in vita o in sermoni.
>   Muore non battezzato e sanza fede:
> ov' è questa giustizia che 'l condanna?
> ov' è la colpa sua, se ei non crede?".
>
> <div align="right">(<i>Par.</i> XIX.67-78)[45]</div>

The answer, delivered by the celestial eagle, comes in two parts, the first of which, taken alone, is no answer at all, merely a preliminary admonition: let no one, the eagle says, jump to conclusions, for all justice is grounded in the righteousness of God, which, forever consistent with the goodness of which it is but the outshining, informs steadily – if, as far as man is concerned, inscrutably – his every decree:

> Or tu chi se', che vuo' sedere a scranna,
> per giudicar di lungi mille miglia
> con la veduta corta d'una spanna?
>   Certo a colui che meco s'assottiglia,
> se la Scrittura sovra voi non fosse,
> da dubitar sarebbe a maraviglia.
>   Oh terreni animali! oh menti grosse!
> La prima volontà, ch'è da sé buona,
> da sé, ch'è sommo ben, mai non si mosse.
>   Cotanto è giusto quanto a lei consuona:
> nullo creato bene a sé la tira,
> ma essa, radïando, lui cagiona.
>
> <div align="right">(<i>Par.</i> XIX.79-90)[46]</div>

---

[45] Now is laid well open to you the hiding place which concealed from you the living justice concerning which you have made question so incessantly. For you said, "A man is born on the banks of the Indus, and none is there to speak, or read, or write of Christ, and all his wishes and acts are good, so far as human reason sees, without sin in life or in speech. He dies unbaptized, and without faith. Where is this justice which condemns him? Where is his sin if he does not believe?"

[46] Now who are you who would sit upon the seat to judge at a thousand miles away with the short sight that carries but a span? Assuredly, for him who subtilizes with me, if the Scriptures were not set over you, there would be marvelous occasion for questioning. O earthly animals! O gross minds! The primal will, which of itself is good, has never moved from itself, which is the supreme good. All is just that accords with it; no created good draws it to itself, but it, raying forth, is the cause of it. *Mon.* II.ii.4-5: 'Ex hiis iam liquet quod ius, cum sit bonum, per prius in mente Dei est; et, cum omne quod in mente Dei est sit Deus, iuxta illud "Quod factum est in ipso vita erat", et Deus maxime se ipsum velit, sequitur quod ius a Deo, prout in eo est, sit volitum. Et cum voluntas et volitum in Deo sit idem, sequitur ulterius quod divina voluntas sit ipsum ius. Et iterum ex hoc sequitur quod ius in rebus nichil est aliud quam similitudo divine voluntatis; unde fit quod quicquid divine voluntati non consonat, ipsum ius esse non possit, et quicquid divine voluntati est consonum, ius ipsum sit.'

– an emphasis straightaway confirmed in the 'Roteando cantava' tercet beginning at line 97 of the same canto:

> Roteando cantava, e dicea: "Quali
> son le mie note a te, che non le 'ntendi,
> tal è il giudicio etterno a voi mortali".[47]

But, then, from out of the stillness (the 'Poi si quetaro quei lucenti incendi / de lo Spirito Santo ...' of XIX.100-101)[48] comes the reply proper to Dante's question, a reply nicely attentive once again to its periodization, its step-by-step unfolding. First, then, comes the Johannine moment of the argument to the effect that no one comes to the Father other than by way of the Son as crucified (the 'A questo regno / non salì mai chi non credette 'n Cristo, / né pria né poi ch'el si chiavasse al legno' of lines 103-105),[49] and then the Matthean moment to the effect that many of those crying 'Christ! Christ!' will be turned away as strangers to him (the 'Ma vedi: molti gridan "Cristo, Cristo!", / che saranno in giudicio assai men *prope* / a lui, che tal che non conosce Cristo' of lines 106-108),[50] the latter, however, serving merely to reinforce the pathos everywhere generated by the spectacle of those living out the synderectic substance of their being but even so far off. And with this – this recognizably Pauline sense of the claim set up by those not so much proclaiming the law as bearing it inscribed on their hearts[51] – we come to the nub of the matter, to Dante's

---

[47] Wheeling it sang and said, "As are my notes to you who understand them not, such is the eternal judgement to you mortals".

[48] After those glowing flames of the Holy Spirit became quiet ...

[49] To this realm none ever rose who believed not in Christ, either before or after he was nailed to the tree. John 14:6: 'Dicit ei Jesus: ego sum via et veritas et vita; nemo venit ad Patrem nisi per me.'

[50] But behold, many cry Christ, Christ, who, at the judgement, shall be far less near to him than he who knows not Christ. Matt. 7:21-23: 'Non omnis qui dicit mihi Domine, Domine intrabit in regnum cœlorum, sed qui facit voluntatem Patris mei, qui in cœlis est, ipse intrabit in regnum cœlorum. Multi dicent mihi in illa die: Domine, Domine, nonne in nomine tuo prophetavimus, et in nomine tuo dæmonia ejecimus, et in nomine tuo virtutes multas fecimus? Et tunc confitebor illis, quia nunquam novi vos, discedite a me, qui operamini iniquitatem.'

[51] Romans 2:14-15: 'Cum enim Gentes, quae legem non habent, naturaliter ea quae legis sunt, faciunt, ejusmodi legem non habentes, ipsi sibi sunt lex. Qui ostendunt opus legis scriptum in cordibus suis, testimonium reddente illis conscientia ipsorum et inter se invicem cogitationum accusantium, aut etiam defendentium, in die, cum judicabit Deus occulta hominum, secundum evangelium meum per Jesum Christum.' P. S. Hawkins, 'Dante, St Paul, and the Letter to the Romans', in *Medieval Readings in Romans*, ed. W. S. Campbell, P. S. Hawkins and B. D. Schildgen (Edinburgh and New York: Continuum and T. & T. Clark, 2007), pp. 115-31. More generally, J. A. Mazzeo, 'Dante and the Pauline Modes of Vision', in *Structure and Thought in the 'Paradiso'* (Ithaca, N.Y.: Cornell University

account, not simply of the susceptibility, but of the vulnerability of God as seeing and delighting in the good works of the pagan spirit. Startled, then, by the presence in paradise of Trajan and Rhipeus as innocent of Christ and clergy, but invited by the eagle of righteousness to think through the deep reasons of it all, the pilgrim poet is at last initiated in an act of understanding, in a sense of God's readiness, not only to love, but to be won over by love, herein lying the triumph of love over lovelessness:

> *Regnum celorum* vïolenza pate
> da caldo amore e da viva speranza,
> che vince la divina volontate:
>   non a guisa che l'omo a l'om sobranza,
> ma vince lei perché vuole esser vinta,
> e, vinta, vince con sua beninanza.
>
> (*Par.* XX.94-99)[52]

Press, 1958; reprint New York: Greenwood, 1968), pp. 84-110; G. Petrocchi, 'San Paolo in Dante', in G. Barblan (ed.), *Dante e la Bibbia. Atti del Convegno internazionale promosso da Biblia, Florence, 26-28 settembre 1986* (Florence: Olschki, 1988), pp. 235-48 (subsequently in *La selva del protonotario. Nuovi studi danteschi* (Naples: Morano, 1988), pp. 65-82); R. Hollander, *Dante and Paul's 'Five Words with Understanding'* (Binghampton, N.Y.: Center for Medieval and Early Renaissance Studies, 1992); G. Di Scipio, *The Presence of Pauline Thought in the Works of Dante* (Lewiston, Queenston and Lampeter: Edwin Mellen, 1995).

[52] *Regnum celorum* suffers violence from fervent love and from living hope which vanquishes the divine will; not as man overcomes man, but vanquishes it because it wills to be vanquished, and, vanquished, vanquishes with its own benignity. G. Cannavò, *Regnum celorum vïolenza pate. Dante e la salvezza dell'umanità. Letture Dantesche Giubilari, Vicenza, ottobre 1999 - giugno 2000* (Montella (Avellino): Accademia Vivarium Novum, 2002), with, at pp. 193-203, A. M. Chiavacci Leonardi, 'La salvezza degli infedeli: il canto XX del *Paradiso*' (subsequently in *Le bianche stole. Saggi sul Paradiso di Dante* (Florence: Sismel, 2009), pp. 97-112). Also, F. Ruffini, 'Dante e il problema della salvezza degli infedeli', *Studi danteschi* 14 (1930), 79-92; B. Quilici, *Il destino dell'infidele virtuoso nel pensiero di Dante* (Florence: Ariani, 1936); T. O'H. Hahn, 'I "gentili" e "un uom nasce a la riva / de l'Indo" (*Par.* XIX, vv.70 sqq.)', *L'Alighieri. Rassegna bibliografica dantesca* 18 (1977), 2, 3-8; R. Morghen, 'Dante tra l'"umano" e la storia della salvezza', in *L'Alighieri. Rassegna bibliografica dantesca* 21 (1980), 1, 18-30; N. Iliescu, 'Will Virgil be saved?', *Mediaevalia* 12 (1986), 93-114 and as 'Sarà salvo Virgilio?' in *Dante. Summa medievalis. Proceedings of the Symposium of the Center for Italian Studies, SUNY Stony Brook*, ed. C. Franco and L. Morgan (Stony Brook, N.Y.: Forum Italicum, 1995), pp. 112-33; M. Allan, 'Does Dante hope for Vergil's Salvation?', *Modern Language Notes* 104 (1989), 193-205; M. Picone, 'La "viva speranza" di Dante e il problema della salvezza dei pagani virtuosi. Una lettura di *Paradiso* 20', *Quaderni di Italianistica* 10 (1989), 1-2, 251-68 ; idem, '*Auctoritas* classica e salvezza cristiana: una lettura tipologica di *Purgatorio* XXII', in *Studi in memoria di Giorgio Varanini* (Pisa: Giardini, 1992), vol. I (*Dal Duecento al Quattrocento*), pp. 379-95; T. Barolini, 'Q: Does Dante hope for Vergil's Salvation?', *Modern Language Notes* 105 (1990), 1, 138-44 and 147-49 (and in *Dante and the Origins of Italian Literary Culture* (New York: Fordham University Press, 2006), pp. 151-57); B. D. Schildgen, 'Dante and the Indus', *Dante*

Taking as his core text the difficult saying of Christ in Matthew 11:12 to the effect that 'ever since the coming of John the Baptist the kingdom of heaven has been subject to violence and violent men are seizing it',[53] Dante fashions from it a notion reaching as far into the essential nature of the Godhead as it is possible for man to go, a notion which, transcending as it does the customary τοποι of God-discourse relative to his impassivity and unmoveability, settles on his love-responsiveness, on his willingness, where love is concerned, to reply in kind. Now here, clearly, we have to be careful, for tempting as it is to see in this a breaking of the mould in the area of election theology, we need to note that neither the 'viva speranza' nor the 'caldo amore' of which the eagle speaks originates with the beneficiary of that love, the former, the lively hope, proceeding from the prayers of the supplicant spirit, and the latter from the storehouse of God's own graciousness:

> D'i corpi suoi non uscir, come credi,
> Gentili, ma Cristiani, in ferma fede

Studies 111 (1993), 177-93; eadem, 'Dante's Utopian Political Vision, the Roman Empire, and the Salvation of Pagans', *Annali d'Italianistica* 19 (2001), 51-69; G. Muresu, 'Le "vie" della redenzione (*Paradiso* VII)', *Rassegna della letteratura italiana*, ser. 8, 98 (1994), 1-2, 5-19; N. Cacciaglia, '"Per fede e per opere" (una lettura del tema della salvezza nella *Divina Commedia*)', in *Critica Letteraria* 30 (2002), 2-3, 265-74 (also in *Annali dell'Università per Stranieri di Perugia* 29 (2002), 123-131); B. Martinelli, 'Canto XIX', in *Lectura Dantis Turicensis. Paradiso*, ed. G. Güntert and M. Picone (Florence: Cesati, 2002), pp. 281-305 (revised with the title 'La fede in Cristo. Dante e il problema della salvezza (*Paradiso* XIX)', *Rivista di Letteratura Italiana* 20 (2002), 2, 11-39, and in *Dante. L'"altro viaggio"* (Pisa: Giardini, 2007), pp. 289-319); G. Inglese, 'Il destino dei non credenti. Lettura di *Paradiso* XIX', *La Cultura. Rivista trimestrale di filosofia letteratura e storia* 42 (2004), 2, 315-29; A. Lanza, 'Giustizia divina e salvezza dei "senza fede", in *Dante eterodosso* (Bergamo: Moretti Honegger, 2004), pp. 113-24; C. O'Connell Baur, *Dante's Hermeneutics of Salvation. Passages to Freedom in the Divine Comedy* (Toronto, Buffalo and London: University of Toronto Press, 2007). More generally, S. Harent, 'Infidèles, Salut des', *Dictionnaire de Théologie Catholique*, 15 vols, ed. P. Moraux et al. (Paris: Letouzey et Ané, 1909-46), vol. 7, ii, cols 1276-1930; L. Capéran, *Le Problème du salut des infidèles*, 2 vols, revised edn (Toulouse: Grand Séminaire, 1934); T. P. Dunning, 'Langland and the Salvation of the Heathen', *Medium Aevum* 12 (1943), 45-54; M. Frezza, *Il problema della salvezza dei pagani (da Abelardo al Seicento)* (Naples: Fiorentino, 1962); R. V. Turner, '"Descendit ad Inferos". Medieval Views on Christ's descent into Hell and the Salvation of the Ancient Just', *Journal of the History of Ideas* 27 (1966), 173-94; C. L. Vitto, *The Virtuous Pagan in Middle English Literature. Transactions of The American Philosophical Society* 79, part 5 (Philadelphia: The American Philosophical Society, 1989), pp. 36-49; N. Watson, 'Visions of Inclusion. Universal Salvation and Vernacular Theology in Pre-Reformation England', *Journal of Medieval and Early Modern Studies* 27 (1997), 145-88. On the cases of Trajan and Rhipeus, G. Whatley, 'The Uses of Hagiography: the Legend of Pope Gregory and the Emperor Trajan in the Middle Ages', *Viator* 15 (1984), 25-63.

[53] 'a diebus autem Joannis Baptistae usque nunc, regnum cælorum vim patitur, et violenti rapiunt illud'; Luke 16:16: 'Lex et prophetae, usque ad Joannem; ex eo regnum Dei evangelizatur, et omnis in illud vim facit.' Translation *NEB*.

> quel d'i passuri e quel d'i passi piedi.
> Ché l'una de lo 'nferno, u' non si riede
> già mai a buon voler, tornò a l'ossa;
> e ciò di viva spene fu mercede:
> di viva spene, che mise la possa
> ne' prieghi fatti a Dio per suscitarla,
> sì che potesse sua voglia esser mossa.
> L'anima glorïosa onde si parla,
> tornata ne la carne, in che fu poco,
> credette in lui che potëa aiutarla;
> e credendo s'accese in tanto foco
> di vero amor, ch'a la morte seconda
> fu degna di venire a questo gioco.
> L'altra, per grazia che da sì profonda
> fontana stilla, che mai creatura
> non pinse l'occhio infino a la prima onda,
> tutto suo amor là giù pose a drittura:
> per che, di grazia in grazia, Dio li aperse
> l'occhio a la nostra redenzion futura;
> ond' ei credette in quella, e non sofferse
> da indi il puzzo più del paganesmo;
> e riprendiene le genti perverse.
>
> (*Par.* XX.103-26)[54]

---

[54] They came forth from their bodies not as you think, gentiles, but Christians, with firm faith, the one in the feet that were to suffer, the other in the feet that had suffered. For the one came back to his bones from hell, where none ever returns to right will; and this was the reward of living hope, of living hope that gave power to the prayers made to God to raise him up, that it might be possible for his will to be moved. The glorious soul I tell of, having returned to the flesh for a short time, believed in him that was able to help him; and, believing, was kindled to such a fire of true love that on his second death he was worthy to come to this rejoicing. The other, through grace that wells from a fountain so deep that never did creature thrust eye down to its first wave, set all his love below on righteousness; wherefore, from grace to grace, God opened his eye to our future redemption, so that he believed in it, and therefore endured not the stench of paganism, and reproved the perverse peoples for it. On Dante and the virtuous pagans (in addition to commentaries and *lecturae* on *Inferno* IV), G. Rizzo, 'Dante and the Virtuous Pagans', in *Dante Symposium in Commemoration of the 700th Anniversary of the Poet's Birth (1265-1965)*, ed. W. De Sua and G. Rizzo (Chapel Hill: University of North Carolina Press, 1965), pp. 115-40; K. Foster, O.P., 'The Two Dantes (III). The Pagans and Grace', in *The Two Dantes and Other Studies* (London: Darton, Longman and Todd, 1977), pp. 220-53 (also, in the same volume, pp. 137-55, 'The Son's Eagle: *Paradiso* XIX'); D. Thompson, 'Dante's Virtuous Romans', *Dante Studies* 96 (1978), 145-62; H.A. Mason, 'A Journey through Hell: Dante's *Inferno* Revisited. Virtuous pagans – "gente di molto valore". Canto IV', *The Cambridge Quarterly* 16 (1987), 3, 187-211; M. Picone, 'La "viva speranza" di Dante e il problema della salvezza dei pagani virtuosi. Una lettura di *Paradiso* 20' (note 52

There can, then, be no inferring from this passage a theology of election unconstrained by the customary contents of Christian consciousness, a theology of election, that is to say, countenancing the dispensability of grace, and above all of the grace made available to us in Christ, to any ultimate homecoming of the soul. At the same time something stirs in the depths, a sense of God's concern, not simply for those seated at his table, but for the stranger at the gate, and for his status too as a guest. Something of the kind, at any rate, would seem to be the substance of Dante's final reflection in this canto, of his sense of the wind as blowing where it listeth and of this as its sweetness:

> O predestinazion, quanto remota
> è la radice tua da quelli aspetti
> che la prima cagion non veggion tota!
>   E voi, mortali, tenetevi stretti
> a giudicar: ché noi, che Dio vedemo,
> non conosciamo ancor tutti li eletti;
>   ed ènne dolce così fatto scemo,
> perché il ben nostro in questo ben s'affina,
> che quel che vole Iddio, e noi volemo.
>
> (ibid. XX.130-38)[55]

---

above); C. L. Vitto, 'The Virtuous Pagan in Legend and in Dante', in *The Virtuous Pagan in Middle English Literature* (note 52 above); M. L. Colish, 'The Virtuous Pagan: Dante and the Christian Tradition', in *The Unbounded Community. Papers in Christian Ecumenism in Honor of Jaroslav Pelikan*, ed. W. Caferro and D. G. Fisher (New York: Garland, 1996), pp. 43-91; G. Inglese, 'Il destino dei non credenti. Lettura di *Paradiso* XIX', *La Cultura. Rivista trimestrale di filosofia letteratura e storia* (note 52 above). On Virgil (Dante's Virgil) in particular, and in addition to the *Enciclopedia dantesca* ad voc. (Rome: Istituto dell'Enciclopedia Italiana, 1970-78), vol. 5, pp. 1030-44; E. Auerbach, *Dante Poet of the Secular World*, trans. R. Manheim (Chicago and London: Chicago University Press, 1961 and reprints; originally 1929), with 'Dante und Virgil', *Das Humanistiches Gymnasium* 42 (1931), 136-44; D.Consoli, *Significato del Virgilio dantesco* (Florence: Le Monnier, 1967); R. Hollander, *Il Virgilio dantesco: tragedia nella 'Commedia'* (Florence: Olschki, 1983); T. Barolini, *Dante's Poets. Textuality and Truth in the 'Comedy'* (Princeton NJ: Princeton University Press, 1984). More generally, D. Comparetti, *Vergil in the Middle Ages*, trans. E. F. M. Benecke (Princeton, N.J.: Princeton University Press, 1997; original Italian 1872). On the Dantean limbo, G. Busnelli, 'La colpa del "non fare" degli infedeli negativi', *Studi danteschi* 23 (1938), 79-97; G. Padoan, 'Il limbo dantesco', *Lettere italiane* 21 (1969), 369-88 (and in *Il pio Enea, l'empio Ulisse* (Ravenna: Longo, 1977), pp. 103-24); K. Foster, O.P., 'The Two Dantes (I). Limbo and Implicit Faith', in *The Two Dantes* (above), pp. 156-89; A. A. Iannucci, 'Limbo: the Emptiness of Time', *Studi danteschi* 52 (1979-80), 69-128.

[55] O predestination, how remote is thy root from the vision of those who see not the first cause entire! And you mortals, keep yourselves restrained in judging; for we who see God, know not yet all the elect. And to us such defect is sweet, because our good in this good is refined, that what God wills we also will.

To rest in God, in other words, is to rest in the sweet understanding that, however he chooses to resolve it all, his will be a resolution in love, understanding to this effect serving but to refine still further the joy of the elect.

Love-magnanimity, therefore, and love-responsiveness, these are the twin emphases of Dante's mature meditation in the areas of atonement and of election theology: the kind of love-magnanimity whereby, in the midst of his destitution, man is freshly empowered as man and the kind of love-responsiveness whereby, consubstantial and co-extensive with his own loving, God cannot but reply in kind to a movement of love wherever he sees it. Good theology? Most certainly. For this is theology which, jealous of its credentials and communicability, is forever on the point of being undone by its own agapeic substance, its fundamental inequality to the business in hand.

Dante and the Modalities of Grace

> Né tra l'ultima notte e 'l primo die
> sì alto o sì magnifico processo,
> o per l'una o per l'altra, fu o fie:
> ché più largo fu Dio a dar sé stesso
> per far l'uom sufficiente a rilevarsi,
> che s'elli avesse sol da sé dimesso ...
>
> (*Par.* VII.112-17)[1]

1. Preliminary considerations: Singleton, Singletonians and patterns of grace-theological consciousness. 2. Dante and the revised geometry of grace awareness. 3. Dante and the modalities of grace: grace as a principle of encouragement (being under the aspect of fortitude) – grace as a principle of emancipation (being under the aspect of freedom) – grace as a principle of ecstasy (being under the aspect of rejoicing). 4. Conclusion: grace as but love by another name.

In 1990 a book appeared which, by way of its knack both of uplifting and of upsetting the reader at the same time, called into question an interpretation of the *Commedia* in its theological aspect going back through Giuseppe Mazzotta and John Freccero to Charles Singleton in his seminal *Journey to Beatrice*. The book was Antonio Mastrobuono's *Dante's Journey of Sanctification*,[2] which, in the course of

---

[1] Nor between the last night and the first day has there been or will there be so exalted and so magnificent a procedure, either by one or by the other; for God was more bounteous in giving himself to make man sufficient to raise himself again, than if he solely of himself had remitted ...

[2] A. C. Mastrobuono, *Dante's Journey of Sanctification* (Washington, D.C.: Gateway, 1990), especially Chapter 1 ('Justification and Merit'). C. S. Singleton, *Journey to Beatrice* (Cambridge, Mass.: Harvard University Press, 1958), cited by Mastrobuono in the 1967 edition from the same press. G. Mazzotta, *Dante: Poet of the Desert. History and Allegory in the Divine Comedy* (Princeton, N.J.: Princeton University Press, 1979); J. Freccero (relative to whom Mastrobuono's lengthy appendix 'A Book Twenty-Five Years in the Making', pp. 212-79), *Dante. The Poetics of Conversion* (Cambridge, Mass.: Harvard University Press, 1986). Peter Armour on the merits of Mastrobuono's book as a timely critique of 'the most influential American Dante scholar of recent years' but as 'intemperate' and apt to 'alienate the reader, *Modern Language Review* 88 (1993) 1, 219-20; similarly Christopher Ryan, *Italian Studies* 46 (1991), 110-14.

its preface (page x), reproduces the following passage from Singleton to the effect that

> what we are finally privileged to see is clear: Dante has continued to work with the metaphor 'return to Eden' even in this respect. At the summit and end of the climb up the mountain, when Eden is reached, we may see history somehow repeating itself; as it was with Adam in his formation, so now with this man, so now with 'man', in his reformation. Only now do we glimpse an aspect of the metaphor we might otherwise have missed. There had been a moment in Adam's formation when Adam was not yet in Eden, when Adam was formed outside of Eden in a first condition 'secundum naturam'. What corresponds to this, in a 'return' to Eden, is the moment when Virgil proclaims that Dante the Wayfarer is now reformed in justice, a justice discernible by the natural light. This then is the moment 'secundum naturam' in the reformation.
>
> The pattern of the original formation of man is thus seen to repeat itself in the reformation of a man named Dante, who attains first to a condition of justice with Virgil, within the proportion of his nature and under the natural light, and then, in a second moment attains to Eden proper, crossing the river to a kind of justice with Beatrice that is truly beyond all human measure.

In fact, Mastrobuono would have done better to quote in full at this point, for occupying the space between what here look like consecutive paragraphs there is, in the original, additional material summing up Singleton's main thesis in the book – namely, his sense of how it is that, having been confirmed under the auspices of Virgil in a state of natural justice, Dante aspires in the earthly paradise, and in the presence of Beatrice, to one of supernatural justice, to a species of righteousness ushered in by grace:

> Dante advances to a stream which cuts across his path and blocks his way. He may go no further for the moment, nor may Virgil ever go further than this. Beatrice is expected and when she comes Virgil has disappeared. The light of grace flashes through the forest, from beyond the stream. And when after contrition and confession, Dante may cross through the water to the far shore, to attain to Beatrice and the infused virtues, we know that he crosses to a condition of grace and justice beyond Virgil and beyond nature. And we come to understand better why that further bank of the stream where Beatrice comes is called a 'blessed' shore.
>
> The stream of Lethe in Eden is as a boundary, marking the confines of the Paradise proper. Return to Eden is thus not complete until the wayfarer has crossed over. Only when he stands on the far

shore, where Beatrice and Matelda are, does he stand in that place where God has placed him *after* He had formed him outside the Garden, according to nature.

Fully restored, then, the passage offers a faithful account of what, theologically, Singleton thinks is going on in the *Commedia*. Everything leading up to the gracing of the pilgrim's soul in the Earthly Paradise is, he believes, a preparation for that gracing, a *praeparatio ad gratiam* accomplished by way of an as yet ungraced movement of the spirit, of the kind of natural reasonableness proper to one such as Virgil. This situation is open to exploration, he thinks, on the basis of the analogy to be drawn between justification and generation, for just as God is said to breathe the rational soul into the sensitive soul generated *ex materia*,[3] so also might he be said to grace the natural activity of man as a creature of reasonable moral determination with a view to its ulterior perfection, to its resolution on a higher plane of knowing and loving; so, for example, these lines from page 46 of the *Journey to Beatrice*, secure in their sense of grace and gracing as a matter of something like formal specification:

> This clearly becomes a point of very particular interest to our consideration of the substance and basic structural progression of Dante's poem, when we realize that the whole area of Virgil's guidance in

---

[3] *Purg.* XXV.67-75: 'Apri a la verità che viene il petto; / e sappi che, sì tosto come al feto / l'articular del cerebro è perfetto, / lo motor primo a lui si volge lieto / sovra tant'arte di natura, e spira / spirito novo, di vertù repleto, / che ciò che trova attivo quivi, tira / in sua sustanzia, e fassi un'alma sola, / che vive e sente e sé in sé rigira', with a parallel passage in the *Convivio* at IV.xxi.4: 'E però dico che quando l'umano seme cade nel suo recettaculo, cioè ne la matrice, esso porta seco la vertù de l'anima generativa e la vertù del cielo e la vertù de li elementi legati, cioè la complessione; e matura e dispone la materia a la vertù formativa, la quale diede l'anima del generante; e la vertù formativa prepara li organi a la vertù celestiale, che produce de la potenza del seme l'anima in vita'. G. Di Giannatale, 'Considerazioni sull'origine dell'anima in Dante', *Sapienza* 30 (1977), 4, 450-54; B. Nardi, 'L'origine dell'anima umana secondo Dante', in *Studi di filosofia medievale* (Rome: Edizioni di storia e letteratura, 1979; originally 1960), pp. 9-68; idem, 'Sull'origine dell'anima umana', in *Dante e la cultura medievale*, ed. P. Mazzantini (Bari: Laterza, 1983; originally 1942), pp. 207-24, with 'L'immortalità dell'anima' at pp. 225-43; idem, 'Il canto XXV del *Purgatorio*', in *Lecturae ed altri studi danteschi*, ed. R. Abardo with an introduction by F. Mazzoni and A. Vallone (Florence: Le Lettere, 1990), pp. 139-50; S. Bemrose, '"Come d'animal divenga fante". The Animation of the Human Embryo in Dante', in *The Human Embryo. Aristotle and the Arabic and European Traditions*, ed. G. R. Dunstan (Exeter: University of Exeter Press, 1990), pp. 123-35; idem, 'God so Loves the Soul. Intellections of Immortality in Dante', in *Medium Aevum* 74 (2005), 1, 86-108; M. Gragnolati, *Experiencing the Afterlife. Soul and Body in Dante and Medieval Culture* (Notre Dame, Ind.: University of Notre Dame Press, 2005), especially Chapter 2 ('Embryology and Aerial Bodies in Dante's *Comedy*'), pp. 53-87 – much of this discussion turning on the evolutionary character of Dantean psychogenesis over against Thomist substitutionalism.

the *Comedy* is that of *praeparatio ad gratiam*, and that had the Aristotelian notion of *generatio* not prevailed so generally in the thought of the poet's time, the event of the journey would not have been at all as it is.

If, then, sanctifying grace is 'form' and if the process of conversion is construed on such a pattern of *generatio*, what exactly are we to understand the 'matter' to be which is made ready to receive that form? The matter is, in the broadest sense, some human creature ...

More exactly, Singleton thinks, it is a question here of grace as that whereby reason and will are 'elevated above the limits of what is natural to man', of what he is able to do from out of his ordinary power to moral self-determination. It is by way of grace and its power to 'transhumanization' that he is raised above himself in point of understanding and confirmed in his status as an adopted son of God:

> But the advent of Beatrice is not merely the advent of light. By such grace as she (in allegory) is, man's whole nature is transformed, elevated above the limits of what is natural to man. A *trasumanar* takes place, not in the intellect alone but also in the will. A new orientation of the inner man prevails, *itinerarium mentis* 'turns' and moves in a new way. Through sanctifying grace the soul is uplifted and turned toward God as to its special object of beatitude. By such grace alone do we become the 'adopted sons of God'. (ibid., p. 42)

But on both accounts, Mastrobuono maintains, Singleton is mistaken. He is mistaken as regards the analogy to be drawn between justification and generation in that, while the latter is accomplished in the order of time, the former is accomplished in the order of being. Grace as a principle of justification, in other words, functions on the plane, not of the horizontal or of the before and after of the moment, but on that of the vertical or of the height and depth of the instant, successionality thus giving way to simultaneity or all-at-onceness as a means of understanding here; so, for example, this from the *Prima secundae* at 113.7 resp.:

> tota justificatio impii originaliter consistit in gratiae infusione. Per eam enim et liberum arbitrium movetur, et culpa remittitur. Gratiae autem infusio fit in instanti absque successione ... Cum igitur virtus divina sit infinita, potest quamcumque materiam creatam subito disponere ad formam, et multo magis liberum arbitrium hominis, cujus motus potest esse instantaneus secundum naturam. Sic igitur justificatio impii fit a Deo in instanti.[4]

---

[4] The entire justification of the ungodly consists as to its origin in the infusion of grace. For it is by grace that free will is moved and sin is remitted. Now the infusion of grace

But that is not all, for we do not speak of the powers of the soul, but rather of the soul itself, as graced. True, it is by faith as an infused virtue of the intellect and by charity as an infused virtue of the will that man is said to participate in the life of the Godhead, but preceding these things and subsisting as their indispensable condition is the recreative work of grace in the recesses of the soul itself. Thomas again:

> ... ista quaestio ex praecedenti dependet. Si enim gratia sit idem quod virtus, necesse est quod sit in potentia animae sicut in subiecto; nam potentia animae est proprium subiectum virtutis, ut supra dictum est. Si autem gratia differt a virtute, non potest dici quod potentia animae sit gratiae subiectum; quia omnis perfectio potentiae animae habet rationem virtutis, ut supra dictum est. Unde relinquitur quod gratia, sicut est prius virtute, ita habeat subiectum prius potentiis animae, ita scilicet quod sit in essentia animae. Sicut enim per potentiam intellectivam homo participat cognitionem divinam per virtutem fidei, et secundum potentiam voluntatis amorem divinum per virtutem caritatis; ita etiam per naturam animae participat secundum quamdam similitudinem naturam divinam per quamdam regenerationem, sive recreationem.
>
> (*ST* Ia IIae.110.4 resp.)[5]

takes place in an instant and without succession ... Therefore, since the divine power is infinite, it can suddenly dispose any matter whatsoever to its form; and much more man's free will, whose movement is by nature instantaneous. Therefore the justification of the ungodly by God takes place in an instant. *De verit.* 28.9 resp. ult.: 'Dico igitur, quod extrema iustificationis sunt gratia et privatio gratiae, inter quae non cadit medium circa proprium susceptibile: unde oportet quod transitus de uno in alterum sit in instanti, quamvis causa huius privationis successive tollatur; vel secundum quod homo cogitando disponit se ad gratiam, vel saltem secundum quod tempus praeterit postquam Deus se gratiam daturum praeordinavit; et sic gratiae infusio fit in instanti. Et quia expulsio culpae est formalis effectus gratiae infusae, inde est quod tota iustificatio impii in instanti est. Nam forma et dispositio ad formam completam et abiectio alterius formae, totum est in instanti', etc. Mastrobuono, p. 49.

[5] this question depends on the preceding. For if grace is the same as virtue, it must necessarily be in the powers of the soul as in a subject; since the soul's powers are the proper subject of the virtue, as stated above [qu. 56, art. 1]. But if grace differs from virtue, it cannot be said that a power of the soul is the subject of grace, since every perfection of the soul's powers has the nature of virtue, as stated above [qu. 55, art. 1; qu. 56, art. 1]. Hence it remains that grace, as it is prior to virtue, has a subject prior to the powers of the soul, so that it is in the essence of the soul. For as man in his intellective power participates in the divine knowledge through the virtue of faith, and in his power of the will participates in the divine love through the virtue of charity, so also in the nature of the soul does he participate in the divine nature, after the manner of a likeness, through a certain regeneration or re-creation. Mastrobuono, pp. 17-18.

Grace, then, is present to the individual, not *operationally* or as empowering reason and will as faculties of the rational soul, but *entitatively* or as a principle of transformation in respect of the soul in its totality (which is why we speak of it as a matter of accidental or superadditional formality).[6] And it is this sense in Aquinas of the ontological as distinct from the merely operational character of grace in its positive working out that enables Mastrobuono to reconstruct over against the Singletonians the position in Dante. Grace, he believes, is understood in the *Commedia* to function both operatively and co-operatively.[7] It functions co-

---

[6] Thomas, *ST* Ia IIae.110.2 ad 1 and ad 2: 'gratia, secundum quod est qualitas, dicitur agere in animam non per modum causae efficientis, sed per modum causae formalis, sicut albedo facit album, et iustitia iustum ... Et quia gratia est supra naturam humanam, non potest esse quod sit substantia aut forma substantialis; sed est forma accidentalis ipsius animae'; *ScG* III.cl.6: 'Oportet quod homo ad ultimum finem per proprias operationes perveniat. Unumquodque autem operatur secundum propriam formam. Oportet igitur, ad hoc quod homo perducatur in ultimum finem per proprias operationes, quod superaddatur ei aliqua forma, ex qua eius operationes efficaciam aliquam accipiant promerendi ultimum finem', etc.

[7] Cf. Thomas, *ST* Ia IIae.111.2, resp.: 'Est autem in nobis duplex actus: primus quidem interior voluntatis; et quantum ad istum actum voluntas se habet ut mota, Deus autem ut movens; et praesertim cum voluntas incipit bonum velle, quae prius malum volebat; ei ideo, secundum quod Deus movet humanam mentem ad hunc actum, dicitur *gratia operans*. Alius autem actus est exterior, qui cum a voluntate imperetur, ut supra habitum est [qu. 17, art. 9], consequens est quod ad hunc actum operatio attribuatur voluntati. Et quia etiam ad hunc actum Deus nos adjuvat, et interius confirmando voluntatem, ut ad actum perveniat, et exterius facultatem operandi praebendo; respectu huiusmodi actus dicitur *gratia cooperans*. Unde post praemissa verba subdit Augustinus [*De gratia et lib. arb.* xvii, in the *sed contra*]: "Ut autem velimus, operatur; cum autem volumus, ut perficiamus, nobis cooperatur"' (Augustine, in the *De gratia et lib. arb.* xvii.33, has the following: 'Et quis istam etsi parvam dare coeperat caritatem, nisi ille qui praeparat voluntatem, et cooperando perficit, quod operando incipit? Quoniam ipse ut velimus operatur incipiens, qui volentibus cooperatur perficiens. Propter quod ait Apostolus: "Certus sum quoniam qui operatur in vobis opus bonum, perficiet usque in diem Christi Iesu" [Philip. 1:6]. Ut ergo velimus, sine nobis operatur; cum autem volumus, et sic volumus ut faciamus, nobiscum cooperatur; tamen sine illo vel operante ut velimus, vel cooperante cum volumus, ad bona pietatis opeera nihil valemus. De operante illo ut velimus, dictum est: "Deus est enim qui operatur in vobis et velle" [Philip. 2:13]. De cooperante autem cum iam volumus et volendo facimus: "Scimus", inquit, "quoniam diligentibus Deum omnia cooperatur in bonum" [Rom. 8:28]'); Bonaventure, II *Sent.* d. 5, c. 4: '*Operans* quidem gratia dicitur, qua iustificatur impius, id est de impio fuit pius, de malo bonus. *Cooperans* vero, qua iuvatur ad bene volendum efficaciter et Deum prae omnibus diligendum et ad operandum bonum et ad perseverandum in bono et huiusmodi', etc. R. Garrigou-Lagrange, O.P., *La Prédestination des saints et la grâce: doctrine de Saint Thomas comparée aux autres systèmes théologiques* (Paris: Desclée de Brouwer, 1936); idem, *Grace: Commentary on the* Summa Theologica *of St Thomas, Ia IIae, 109-14*, trans. from the *Commentarius* of 1947 (Rome: Pontificium Institutum Internationale 'Angelicum') by the Dominican Nuns of the Corpus Christi Monastery, Menlo Park, California (St. Louis: B. Herder, 1952); B.

Dante and the Modalities of Grace 87

operatively in that it is everywhere on hand, in circumstances at any rate of justification, to assist and strengthen the individual in his commitment to right being and right doing, to living out the substance of his nature as a creature of moral and ontological accountability. But first comes the moment of justification, the moment in which, quickened by grace under the aspect of operation, the soul is (*a*) turned away from self towards God, (*b*) deflected from its old habits, and (*c*) absolved from its sin, these between them constituting the basis of everything coming next by way either of infused or of acquired virtue.[8] This, then, Mastrobuono maintains, is where Dante begins. Having reconstructed in the person of his protagonist the substance and psychology of estrangement from self and from the innermost reasons of self, he begins with the grace proclaimed by Virgil in the second canto of the *Inferno* whereby the soul is duly disposed towards God (the 'Tu m'hai con desiderio il cor disposto' of II.136) and quickened afresh in point of willing (the 'Or va, ch'un sol volere

---

J. F. Lonergan, S.J., 'St Thomas's Thought on *Gratia Operans*', *Theological Studies* 2 (1941), 3, 289-324; 3 (1942), 1, 69-88; 3, 375-402 and 4. 533-78; idem, *Grace and Freedom: Operative Grace in the Thought of St Thomas Aquinas*, ed. F. E. Crowe and R. M. Doran (Toronto: University of Toronto Press, 2000; originally 1971); H. Bouillard, *Conversion et grâce chez s. Thomas d'Aquin: étude historique* (Paris: Aubier, 1944); M. Flick, *L'attimo della giustificazione secondo S. Tommaso* (Rome: Apud aedes Universitatis Gregorianiae, 1947); P. Wehbrink (trans), *Thomas von Aquin. Die menschliche Willensfreiheit* (Düsseldorf: L. Schwann, 1954; selections from the *Quaestiones disputatae de malo* and *de veritate* with an introduction by G. Siewerth); C. Ernst, O.P. (ed. and comm.), *St Thomas Aquinas. Summa theologiae*, vol. 30 (*The Gospel of Grace. 1a 2a. 106-114*) (London: Eyre and Spottiswoode, 1972); J. P. Wawrykow, *God's Grace and Human Action. 'Merit' in the Theology of Thomas Aquinas* (Notre Dame: University of Notre Dame Press, 1995); idem, 'Grace', in *The Theology of Thomas Aquinas*, ed. R. Van Nieuwenhove and J. Wawrykow (Notre Dame: University of Notre Dame Press, 2005), pp. 192-221; J. F. Wippel, 'Natur und Gnade (*S.th.* I-II, qq. 109-114)', in *Thomas von Aquin: Die Summa theologiae. Werkinterpretationen*, ed. A. Speer (Berlin: de Gruyter, 2005), pp. 246-70. More generally on grace theology (but with reference still to Thomas), J. Auer, *Die Entwicklung der Gnadenlehre in der Hochscholastik*, 2 vols (Freiburg: Herder, 1951); R. W. Gleason, S.J., *Grace* (London and New York: Sheed and Ward, 1962); N. P. Williams, *The Grace of God* (London: Hodder and Stoughton, 1966, originally 1930).

[8] Thomas, *ST* Ia IIae.113.6 resp.: 'quatuor enumerantur quae requiruntur ad iustificationem impii, scilicet gratiae infusio; motus liberi arbitrii in Deum per fidem; et motus liberi arbitrii in peccatum; et remissio culpae. Cuius ratio est quia, sicut dictum est, iustificatio est quidam motus quo anima movetur a Deo a statu culpae in statum iustitiae. In quolibet autem motu quo aliquid ab altero movetur, tria requiruntur, primo quidem, motio ipsius moventis; secundo, motus mobilis; et tertio, consummatio motus, sive perventio ad finem. Ex parte igitur motionis divinae, accipitur gratiae infusio; ex parte vero liberi arbitrii moti, accipiuntur duo motus ipsius, secundum recessum a termino a quo, et accessum ad terminum ad quem; consummatio autem, sive perventio ad terminum huius motus, importatur per remissionem culpae, in hoc enim iustificatio consummatur.'

è d'ambedue' of II.139).⁹ Grace, then, far from intervening subsequently to perfect the hitherto ungraced work of nature, is there from the outset as both the antecedent and the subsistent principle of man's proper striving as man, of every creative inflexion of the spirit on the plane of properly human being and becoming:

> All of this, according to Singleton, is within the proportion of Dante's nature to accomplish, aided, of course, by Virgil's natural light of reason ... Singleton does not seem to understand that the natural reason symbolized by Virgil is an immanent power, and as such is absolutely impotent to erase the effects of sin from Dante's soul. For this, Dante needs the transcendent power of grace. Since it does in fact happen that on the mountain of Purgatory the effects of sin (the stains) are erased from Dante's soul, as the 'P's are erased from his forehead, that in itself is proof, as we have noted, that Dante has already received an infusion of sanctifying grace before he entered the world beyond. The erasing of the effects of sin from Dante's soul is an effect of sanctifying grace, not a preparation for it, which also means that the whole area of Virgil's guidance through the world beyond is an effect of sanctifying grace, not a preparation for it as Singleton also believes.¹⁰

Dante's, in other words, though at every point a sense both of the power in man to moral self-determination and of this as the ground of his eschatological triumph and tragedy, is at the same time a commitment to the priority of grace as the condition of his righteousness, of the individual's knowing himself in the fullness and functionality of his proper humanity. To suppose otherwise – to imagine that, for the Dante of the *Commedia*, it is a question of the periodization of these things, of what comes next in the order of time – is to implicate him in a species of theological absurdity.

2. Dante's, for all his commitment to the notion of grace as *incomingness*, is a tendency to see and to celebrate it under the aspect of *alongsidedness*, and indeed of a species of alongsidedness amounting in its intimacy to something closer to co-immanence, to a commingling of human and divine intentionality at the still centre of existence;¹¹ so, for example, as

---

⁹ By your words you have made me so eager [to come with you that I have returned to my first resolve] ... Now on, for a single will is in us both ...

¹⁰ Mastrobuono, p. 59.

¹¹ Recently on Dante and grace: S. Rossi, 'Il trionfo della grazia nell'episodio di Bonconte da Montefeltro', *L'Alighieri. Rassegna bibliografica dantesca* 35, n.s. 3/4 (1994), 83-93; C. Ryan, '"Natura dividitur contra gratiam": concetti diversi della natura in Dante e nella cultura filosofico-teologica medievale', in *Dante e la scienza. Atti del Convegno*

eloquent in respect of the first of these things, of incomingness under the aspect of alongsidedness, these passages from Cantos XXV, XXVIII and XXIX of the *Paradiso*, each of them turning on the parallelization as distinct from the prioritization of grace with respect to nature in the moment of its verification:

> "Spene", diss' io, "è uno attender certo
> de la gloria futura, il qual produce
> grazia divina e precedente merto".
>
> ...
>
> Quinci si può veder come si fonda
> l'esser beato ne l'atto che vede,
> non in quel ch'ama, che poscia seconda;
> e del vedere è misura mercede,
> che grazia partorisce e buona voglia
>
> ...
>
> per che le viste lor furo essaltate
> con grazia illuminante e con lor merto,
> si c'hanno ferma e piena volontate.
>
> (*Par.* XXV.67-69, XXVIII.109-13 and XXIX.61-63)[12]

Internazionale di Studi, Ravenna 28-30 maggio 1993, ed. P. Boyde and V. Russo (Ravenna: Longo, 1995), pp. 363-73; L. Scorrano, 'Paradiso XXXII. La legge, la grazia', *L'Alighieri. Rassegna bibliografica dantesca* 37, n.s. 7 (1996), 19-36, subsequently in *Tra il 'banco' e 'l'alte rote'. Letture e note dantesche* (Ravenna: Longo, 1996), pp. 103-22; I. Biffi, *La poesia e la grazia nella Commedia di Dante* (Milan: Jaca Book, 1999), especially pp. 29-35 ('Un viaggio che parte dalla grazia'); J. T. Chiampi, 'The role of freely bestowed grace in Dante's journey of legitimation', in *Rivista di Studi Italiani* 17 (1999), 1, 89-111; J. Trabant, '"Gloria" oder "grazia". Oder: Wonach die "questione della lingua" eigentlich fragt', *Romanistisches Jahrbuch* 51 (2000), 29-52; P. Cherchi, 'Da me stesso non vegno (*Inf.* X, 61)', *Rassegna europea di letteratura italiana* 18 (2001), 103-106. Notable prior to Mastrobuono are G. Getto, 'L'"epos" della grazia in *Paradiso*', in *Scrittori e idee in Italia: Antologia della critica. (Dalle Origini al Trecento)*, ed. P. Pullega (Bologna: Zanichelli, 1982), pp. 209-14; G. Godenzi, 'Il viaggio spirituale di Dante dal peccato alla grazia', in *Quaderni Grigionitaliani. Rivista trimestrale delle valli Grigionitaliane* 56 (1987), 3-4, 234-39; B. Panvini, 'La concezione tomistica della grazia nella *Divina Commedia*', in *Letture classensi* 17 (Ravenna: Longo, 1988), pp. 69-85.

[12] "Hope", I said, "is a sure expectation of future glory, which divine grace produces, and preceding merit" ... From this it may be seen that the state of blessedness is founded on the act of vision, not on that which loves, which follows after; and the merit, to which grace and good will give birth, is the measure of their vision ... wherefore their vision was exalted with illuminating grace and with their merit, so that they have their will full and established. Peter Lombard's text to the effect that 'est autem spes virtus qua spiritualia et aeterna bona sperantur, id est cum fiducia expectantur. Est enim certa expectatio futurae beatitudinis, veniens ex Dei gratia et ex meritis praecedentibus vel ipsam spem, quam natura praeit caritas; vel rem speratam, id est beatitudinem aeternam' (III *Sent.* xxvi), though variously cited by Thomas, is glossed, at any rate in the *Secunda secundae*

while exemplary in respect of the second of them, of the resolution of alongsidedness in co-immanence, in a 'commingling of human and divine intentionality at the still centre of existence', these lines from the Piccarda canto of the *Paradiso*, explicit in their sense of *willing* in man as a matter of *in-willing*, of a reconfiguration of human willing by way of an in-breathing of divine willing in the recesses of personality:

> Frate, la nostra volontà quïeta
> virtù di carità, che fa volerne
> sol quel ch'avemo, e d'altro non ci asseta.
>   Se disïassimo esser più superne,
> foran discordi li nostri disiri
> dal voler di colui che qui ne cerne;
>   che vedrai non capere in questi giri,
> s'essere in carità è qui necesse,
> e se la sua natura ben rimiri.
>   Anzi è formale ad esto beato esse
> tenersi dentro a la divina voglia,
> per ch'una fansi nostre voglie stesse;
>   sì che, come noi sem di soglia in soglia
> per questo regno, a tutto il regno piace
> com' a lo re che 'n suo voler ne 'nvoglia.
>   E 'n la sua volontade è nostra pace:
> ell' è quel mare al qual tutto si move
> ciò ch'ella crïa o che natura face.
>
> (*Par.* III.70-87)[13]

(17.1 ad 2), in such a way as to stress the notion of hope as an infused virtue of the spirit and thus as radically independent of merit: 'spes dicitur ex meritis provenire quantum ad ipsam rem expectatam, prout aliquis sperat se beatitudinem adepturum ex gratia et meritis. Vel quantum ad actum spei formatae. Ipse autem habitus spei, per quam aliquis expectat beatitudinem, non causatur ex meritis, sed pure ex gratia.' J.-G. Bougerol, *La Théologie de l'espérance aux XIIe et XIIIe siècles*, 2 vols (Paris: Etudes augustiniennes, 1985), vol. 1, pp. 97-99. Otherwise on Peter Lombard and the *Sentences* (in addition to the general histories of medieval thought), M. L. Colish, *Peter Lombard*, 2 vols (Leiden and New York: Brill, 1994); J.-G. Bougerol, 'The Church Fathers and the *Sentences* of Peter Lombard', in I. Backus (ed.), *The Reception of the Church Fathers in the West from the Carolingians to the Maurists*, 2 vols (Leiden and New York: Brill, 1997; also Boston: Brill Academic Publishers, 2001), vol. 1, pp. 113-64. On Dante and Peter Lombard, M. Papio, ad voc. 'Peter Lombard' in R. Lansing (ed.), *Dante Encyclopaedia* (London: Garland, 2000), pp. 682-83, with bibliography. Also, M. Da Carbonara, *Dante e Pier Lombardo ; Sent, lib. IV, distt. 43-49* (Città di Castello: Lapi, 1897).

[13] Brother, the power of love quiets our will and makes us wish only for that which we have and gives us no other thirst. Did we desire to be more aloft, our longings would be discordant with his will who assigns us here, which you will see is not possible in these circles if to exist in charity here is of necessity, and if you well consider what is love's

Now here, clearly, we have to be careful, for grace, for all its subsisting as a matter of alongsidedness and indeed of co-immanence in respect of the power in man to significant determination, subsists also both as an antecedent and as an extrinsic principle of new life, as a principle, that is to say, operative both from beforehand and from beyond. But for all that, Dante's, when it comes to a question famous for its distribution and redistribution of emphases, remains a tendency to proceed by way, less of antecedence and exteriority than of simultaneity and companionship, of what for the sake of capturing the intensity – not to mention the beauty – of it we may call a species of formed friendship. No longer, in other words, is it a question of grace as a stranger to nature, as visited upon it in all its otherwise unspeakable poverty, but of a welcoming home of the one by the other in the deepest and most sacred places of historical selfhood. And it is this resolution of the *antecedent* in the *alongsided* as a way of proposing the grace-theological issue in the moment of its positive living out that inclines Dante, less to a metaphysic, than to a phenomenology of grace, to an account of grace and of gracing in terms, less of its mechanism, than of its modality, of the *how* of its experiencing as a principle of self-actualization.

3. Grace, then, as a matter of its *how* or showing forth, not only abounds, but abounds in every sector of human experience in the living out of that experience. Thus it is by grace that the penitent soul knows itself in the free passage from seeing and understanding to being and doing (the 'se tosto grazia resolva le schiume / di vostra coscienza sì che chiaro / per essa scenda de la mente il fiume' of *Purg.* XIII.88-90),[14] and it is by

---

nature. Indeed, it is of the essence of this blessed existence to keep itself within the divine will, whereby our wills are made one; so that our being thus from threshold to threshold throughout this realm is a joy to all the realm as to the king, who inwills us with his will; and in his will is our peace. It is that sea to which all moves, both what it creates and what nature makes.

[14] so may grace soon clear the scum of your conscience that the stream of memory may flow down through it pure ... On synderesis and conscience, O. Lottin, '"Syndérèse" et conscience au XIIe et XIIIe siècles', in *Psychologie et morale aux XIIe et XIIIe siècles* (Louvain: Abbaye du Mont César, 1948), vol. 2, pp. 103-349; P. Siwek, *La conscience du libre arbitre* (Rome: Herder, 1976); M. G. Baylor, *Action and Person: Conscience in Late Scholasticism and the Young Luther* (Leiden: Brill, 1977); T. Potts, *Conscience in Medieval Philosophy* (Cambridge: Cambridge University Press, 1980); idem, 'Conscience', in *The Cambridge History of Later Medieval Philosophy* (Cambridge: Cambridge University Press, 1982), pp. 687-704. On Thomas, L. Elders, 'La doctrine de la conscience de saint Thomas d'Aquin', *Revue Thomiste* 83 (1983), 533-57; O. Benetollo, 'Il problema della formazione della coscienza retta', *Divus Thomas* 95 (1992), 113-28; G. Cavalcoli, 'Il concetto di coscienza in s. Tommaso', *Divus Thomas* 95 (1992), 53-77. More generally on the notion of synderesis, and in addition to Lottin above, J. de Blic, 'Syndérèse ou conscience?', *Revue d'ascétique et de mystique* 25 (1949), 146-57; M. B. Crowe, 'The Term Syneresis in

grace that it knows itself in its equality to every kind of intemperance and extravagance of the spirit (the 'Beati cui alluma / tanto di grazia, che l'amor del gusto / nel petto lor troppo disir non fuma' of *Purg.* XXIV.151-53).[15] It is by grace that it knows itself as encircled by the love of God (the 'se Dio m'ha in sua grazia rinchiuso' of *Purg.* XVI.40),[16] and it is by grace that it knows itself in the exhilaration of self-surpassing on the planes of knowing and of loving (the 'Ringrazia, / ringrazia il Sol de li angeli, ch'a questo / sensibil t'ha levato per sua grazia' of *Par.* X.52-54 and the 'Con tutto 'l core e con quella favella / ch'è una in tutti, a Dio feci olocausto, / qual conveniesi a la grazia novella' of *Par.* XIV.88-90).[17] It is by grace, moreover, that the mind is caressed by the truth to which it is now party (the 'Grazia, che donnea / con la tua mente' of *Par.* XXIV.118-19),[18] and it is by grace that the individual knows himself in the bliss of spiritual sonship (the 'Figliuol di grazia' of *Par.* XXXI.112). Grace, then, is everywhere present to the individual as the context and co-efficient of his every creative inflexion of the spirit, Dante's in this sense being a never less than fervent commitment to its status both as an immanent and as an overarching principle of human experience in its historical

---

the Scholastics', *The Irish Theological Quarterly* 23 (1956), 151-64 and 228-45; T. L. Miethe, 'Natural Law, the Synderesis Rule, and St Augustine', *Augustinian Studies* 11 (1980), 91-97; V. J. Bourke, 'The Background of Aquinas's Synderesis Principle', in *Graceful Reason. Essays in Ancient and Medieval Philosophy presented to James Owens*, ed. L. P. Gerson (Toronto: Pontifical Institute of Mediaeval Studies, 1983), pp. 345-60; R. A. Greene, 'Synderesis, the Spark of Conscience, in the English Renaissance', *Journal of the History of Ideas* 52 (1991), 2, 195-219; idem, 'Instinct of Nature. Natural Law, Synderesis and Moral Sense', *Journal of the History of Ideas* 58 (1997), 173-98; I. Sciuto, 'Sinderesi, desiderio naturale e fondamento dell'agire morale nel pensiero medievale. Da San Tommaso a Meister Eckhart', in *L'etica e il suo altro*, ed. C. Vigna (Milan: Vita e pensiero, 1994); idem, *La felicità e il male. Studi di etica medievale* (Milan: Franco Angeli, 1995). Dante on conscience as a principle of interrogation and affirmation, *Inf.* XV.91-93 and (especially) XXVIII.112-17, and as a principle of remorse or 'biting back', *Inf.* XIX.118-20, *Purg.* III.7-9, XIX.131-32 and XXXIII. 91-93 (cf. Augustine, *Serm. de script.* XLVII.xiv.23: 'Forte alius conscientia mordetur, alius in conscientiae, tanquam in eremo, requiescit'; *Serm. de temp.* ccxi.3: 'Si autem mordet conscientia fragilitatis ...', etc.).

[15] Blessed are they who are so illumined by grace that the love of taste kindles not too great a desire in their breasts, and who hunger always so far as is just.

[16] and since God has received me so far into his grace [that he wills that I see his court in a manner wholly outside modern usage, do not hide from me who you were before death ...]

[17] Give thanks, give thanks to the sun of the angels who of his grace has raised you to this visible one ... with all my heart, and with that speech which is one in all men, I made a holocaust to God such as befitted the new grace.

[18] the grace that holds amorous discourse with your mind [till now has opened your lips aright, so that I approve what has come from them].

unfolding. But it is under three aspects in particular that, for the Dante of the *Commedia*, grace is most powerfully present to the one graced, namely as a principle (*a*) of *encouragement* or as that whereby the soul knows itself in its power to moral and ontological self-confrontation (the infernal phase of its journey into God); (*b*) of *emancipation* or as that whereby it knows itself in its power to affective self-reconfiguration (the purgatorial phase of the journey); and (*c*) of *ecstasy* or as that whereby it knows itself in its power to self-transcendence (the paradisal phase of the journey). Now this, as we have said, is by no means to exclude the many other ways in which grace is experienced by the pilgrim spirit, for the ways and means of grace are as infinite and infinitely varied as the One from whom it proceeds. But it is under these three aspects especially – under the aspects of encouragement, emancipation and ecstasis as between them facilitating and confirming this or that instance of properly human being in the world – that grace as but the overflowing of the Godhead in ever fresh channels of creative and recreative concern commends itself to Dante as an object of contemplation.

Grace is present to those graced as a principle of encouragement in that, irrespective of everything within the economy of personality making for fear as the dominant mood of being under the conditions of time and space, the soul reaches out to affirm itself in the fullness of its proper humanity. Straightaway, then, it is a question in the *Inferno* of doubt and energization, of an empowerment of the crippled spirit in and through a movement of grace mediated by Virgil; on the one hand, these lines (37-42) from *Inferno* II on the demonic character not, certainly, of pure thought as such, but of pure thought in its endless capacity for reiteration, for staving off the moment of decision:

> E qual è quei che disvuol ciò che volle
> e per novi pensier cangia proposta,
> sì che dal cominciar tutto si tolle,
>   tal mi fec' ïo 'n quella oscura costa,
> perché, pensando, consumai la 'mpresa
> che fu nel cominciar cotanto tosta.[19]

---

[19] And like one who unwills what he has willed and with new thoughts changes his resolve, so that he quite gives up the thing he had begun, such did I become on that dark slope, for by thinking on it I rendered null the undertaking that had been so readily embarked on. Cf. *Purg.* V.13-18: 'Vien dietro a me, e lascia dir le genti: / sta come torre ferma, che non crolla / già mai la cima per soffiar di venti; / ché sempre l'omo in cui pensier rampolla / sovra pensier, da sé dilunga il segno, / perché la foga l'un de l'altro insolla.' On the gnawing of reflection and the issuelessness of pure thought, Søren Kierkegaard, *The Present Age*, trans. A Dru (London: Collins, 1962), p. 45: 'ambiguity enters into life when the qualitative distinctions are weakened by a gnawing reflection'; ibid., p. 52: 'With every means in its

while on the other these from the same canto (lines 121-42) on the revitalization of self by way of a movement of grace as solicitude from on high:

> "Dunque: che è? perché, perché restai?
> perché tanta viltà nel core allette?
> perché ardire e franchezza non hai?
>   poscia che tai tre donne benedette
> curan di te ne la corte del cielo,
> e 'l mio parlar tanto ben ti promette?".
>   Quali fioretti dal notturno gelo
> chinati e chiusi, poi che 'l sol li 'mbianca
> si drizzan tutti aperti in loro stelo,
>   tal mi fec' io di mia virtude stanca,
> e tanto buono ardire al cor mi corse,
> ch'i' cominciai come persona franca:
>   "Oh pietosa colei che mi soccorse!
> e te cortese ch'ubidisti tosto
> a le vere parole che ti porse!
>   Tu m'hai con disiderio il cor disposto
> sì al venir con le parole tue,
> ch'i' son tornato nel primo proposto.
>   Or va, ch'un sol volere è d'ambedue:
> tu duca, tu segnore, e tu maestro".
> Così li dissi; e poi che mosso fue,
>   intrai per lo cammino alto e silvestro.
>
> (*Inf.* II.121-42)[20]

power reflection prevents people from realizing that both the individual and the age are thus imprisoned, not imprisoned by tyrants or priests or nobles or the secret police, but by reflection itself, and it does so by maintaining the flattering and conceited notion that the *possibility* of reflection is far superior to a mere *decision*'; Karl Jaspers, *Philosophy*, trans. E. B. Ashton (Chicago: University of Chicago Press, 1970, originally 1932), vol. 2, p. 37, has the following: 'This is the way of succombing to self-reflection without coming to myself. My honesty does not go beyond a will to have clarity; a will which does not amount to self-being. This will as such does not affect my future, does not make me hazard any realization. Under its absolute sway I would avoid the risks involved in every manifestation of myself. I would like to know what is true, then, before trying it. I no sooner set out to be real than self-reflection will cast doubt upon my start and destroy it. I cannot take a step any more; I have been paralyzed by my will to be clear.'

[20] "Why, why do you hold back? Why do you harbour such cowardice in your heart? Why are you not bold and free, when in heaven's court three such blessed ladies are mindful of you, and my words pledge you so great a good?" As little flowers, bent down and closed by chill of night, straighten and all unfold on their stems when the sun brightens them, such in my faint strength did I become; and so much good courage rushed to my heart that I began, as one set free, "Oh, how compassionate was she who

Now for Mastrobuono these lines are in the highest degree significant, for it is here, he believes that, on the threshold of a discourse turning on death and resurrection as the way of emergence, Dante, taking his cue from Thomas, sets out his theology of justification, his sense of grace (*a*) as a matter of preliminary disposition, and (*b*) as that whereby, as part of its justification, the soul is renewed in point of willing; and the parallel is indeed tempting, the 'Tu m'hai con disiderio il cor disposto' of line 136 chiming well with the 'Primo igitur modo accipiendo gratiam, praeexigitur ad gratiam aliqua gratiae praeparatio; quia nulla forma potest esse nisi in materia disposita' of *ST* Ia IIae.112.2 resp.,[21] and the 'Or va, ch'un sol volere è d'ambedue' of line 139 with the 'non fit motio a Deo ad iustitiam absque motu liberi arbitrii; sed ita infundit donum gratiae iustificantis, quod etiam simul cum hoc movet liberum arbitrium ad donum gratiae acceptandum, in his qui sunt huius motionis capaces' of Ia IIae.113.3 resp.[22] But this, for all its suggestion of Dante's taking up and acquiescing in the Thomist text, is not what he has in mind here; for his is an essay, not so much in the theology of justification, in the complex process whereby the soul in receipt of grace eschews sin, espouses God, and is absolved from its guilt,[23] as in the kind of existential courage whereby the individual commits himself to the business of self-actualization by way of an encounter with self in the depths. Quickened, then, by the grace-proclamation of Virgil and by all this means by way of a movement of divine solicitude, the soul squares up to the necessities of its presence in the world as a creature of eschatological accountability, this,

---

helped me, and how courteous were you, so quick to obey the true words she spoke to you! By your words you have made me so eager to come with you, that I have returned to my first resolve. Now on, for a single will is in us both; you are my leader and my teacher". So I said to him, and when he moved on, I entered along the deep and savage way.

[21] Now taking grace in the first sense, a certain preparation of grace is required for it, since a form can only be in disposed matter.

[22] God's motion to justice does not take place without a movement of free will; but he so infuses the gift of justifying grace that at the same time he moves the free will to accept the gift of grace, in such as are capable of being moved thus.

[23] *ST* Ia IIae.113.6 resp.: 'quatuor enumerantur quae requiruntur ad iustificationem impii, scilicet gratiae infusio; motus liberi arbitrii in Deum per fidem; et motus liberi arbitrii in peccatum; et remissio culpae. Cuius ratio est quia, sicut dictum est, iustificatio est quidam motus quo anima movetur a Deo a statu culpae in statum iustitiae. In quolibet autem motu quo aliquid ab altero movetur, tria requiruntur, primo quidem, motio ipsius moventis; secundo, motus mobilis; et tertio, consummatio motus, sive perventio ad finem. Ex parte igitur motionis divinae, accipitur gratiae infusio; ex parte vero liberi arbitrii moti, accipiuntur duo motus ipsius, secundum recessum a termino a quo, et accessum ad terminum ad quem; consummatio autem, sive perventio ad terminum huius motus, importatur per remissionem culpae, in hoc enim iustificatio consummatur.'

therefore, being the first great work of grace in its positive verification. The first work of grace in its positive verification is the in-breathing of courage, the courage whereby the soul in the grip of ontological dread feels able to contemplate the risk of losing all for the sake of finding all, of essaying death in the interests of life.

But the grace whereby the individual squares up to the necessities of his presence in the world as a creature of eschatological accountability is at the same time the grace whereby he knows himself in the truth of his moral and ontological freedom, in the freedom to affirm self over against everything within the economy of personality making less for being than for non-being. Having, then, taken on board the possibility of losing all for the sake of finding all, the soul encouraged in respect of its proper destiny embarks on the search for freedom thus understood, trusting as it does so to the grace whereby that freedom becomes a possibility. This then, as far as the *Purgatorio* is concerned, is where Dante starts. Looking now to emancipation as the leading idea, he starts with a referral of the whole project to a movement of grace from above:

> Questi non vide mai l'ultima sera;
> ma per la sua follia le fu sì presso,
> che molto poco tempo a volger era.
> Sì com' io dissi, fui mandato ad esso
> per lui campare; e non lì era altra via
> che questa per la quale i' mi son messo.
> Mostrata ho lui tutta la gente ria;
> e ora intendo mostrar quelli spirti
> che purgan sé sotto la tua balìa.
> Com' io l'ho tratto, saria lungo a dirti;
> de l'alto scende virtù che m'aiuta
> conducerlo a vederti e a udirti.
> Or ti piaccia gradir la sua venuta:
> libertà va cercando, ch'è sì cara,
> come sa chi per lei vita rifiuta.
>
> (*Purg.* I.58-72)[24]

---

[24] This man has not seen his last evening, but by his folly was so near to it that very little time was left to run. Even as I said, I was sent to him to rescue him, and there was no other way than this along which I have set myself. I have shown him all the guilty people, and now I intend to show him those spirits that purge themselves under your charge. How I have brought him would be long to tell you; for on high descends the power that aids me to conduct him to see you and to hear you. Now may it please you to approve his coming. He goes seeking freedom , which is so precious, as he knows who renounces life for it.

And what, as far as the *Purgatorio* is concerned, is begun in grace is consummated in grace, this being the substance of Dante's final hymn to Beatrice as the means of his emergence as a free spirit:

> O donna in cui la mia speranza vige,
> e che soffristi per la mia salute
> in inferno lasciar le tue vestige,
>   di tante cose quant' i' ho vedute,
> dal tuo podere e da la tua bontate
> riconosco la grazia e la virtute.
>   Tu m'hai di servo tratto a libertate
> per tutte quelle vie, per tutt' i modi
> che di ciò fare avei la potestate.
>   La tua magnificenza in me custodi,
> sì che l'anima mia, che fatt' hai sana,
> piacente a te dal corpo si disnodi.
>
> (*Par.* XXXI.79-90)[25]

These certainly, are passages fraught with every kind of theological possibility, not least in respect of the basis they offer for what nowadays we would call a theology of culture, a theology turning on the function of the cultural encounter generally – of, in effect, the Virgilian and Beatrician presence in the life of every man – as a channel of grace in its own right. But that for the moment is neither here nor there, what matters at present being the notion of grace as a principle of emancipation, as that whereby self is freed for self in the untrammeled substance of self. This, then, is the second great work of grace in its positive verification. The second great work of grace in its positive verification is the freeing of the soul for communion with God as the end of all desiring, for the kind of service which is but perfect freedom.[26]

---

[25] O lady, in whom my hope is strong, and who for my salvation did endure to leave in hell your footprints, of all those things which I have seen I acknowledge the grace and the virtue to be from your power and your excellence. It is you who have drawn me from bondage into liberty by all those paths, by all those means by which you had the power so to do. Preserve me in your great munificence, so that my soul, which you have made whole, may be loosed from the body, pleasing unto you.

[26] *Purg.* XVI.73-81: 'Lo cielo i vostri movimenti inizia; / non dico tutti, ma, posto ch'i' 'l dica, / lume v'è dato a bene e a malizia, / e libero voler; che, se fatica / ne le prime battaglie col ciel dura, / poi vince tutto, se ben si notrica. / A maggior forza e a miglior natura / liberi soggiacete; e quella cria / la mente in voi, che 'l ciel non ha in sua cura.' E. Travi, '"Liberi soggiacete" (*Purg.* XVI. 80)', in *Dal cerchio al centro* (1990), pp. 25-33; M. Roddewig, '*Purgatoio* XVI – Zorn und Willensfreiheit', *Deutsches Dante-Jahrbuch* 74 (1999), 123-35; L. Pretto, 'La ricerca e il senso della libertà nella *Divina Commedia*', in *Con Dante e Cusano alla ricerca della verità* (Verona: Mazziana, 2005), pp. 111-39.

But there is more, for the grace whereby the soul is encouraged in respect of the journey ahead and the grace whereby it is sustained in its search for freedom, is also the grace whereby it projects itself upon its proper ecstasis or self-surpassing on the planes of knowing and loving, upon its proper transhumanization. Now here again we need to be careful, for inasmuch as he chooses to stress the atemporality of the ascent, its accomplishment in the order, less of time, than of being, Dante's looks after all to be a theology of created grace, a theology turning upon the notion of entitative renewal; so for example, these lines (22-26) from Canto II of the *Paradiso*:

> Beatrice in suso, e io in lei guardava;
> e forse in tanto in quanto un quadrel posa
> e vola e da la noce si dischiava,
>   giunto mi vidi ove mirabil cosa
> mi torse il viso a sé ...[27]

or these (lines 91-93) from Canto V:

> e sì come saetta che nel segno
> percuote pria che sia la corda queta,
> così corremmo nel secondo regno.[28]

or these (lines 34-39) from Canto X:

> e io era con lui; ma del salire
> non m'accors' io, se non com' uom s'accorge,
> anzi 'l primo pensier, del suo venire.
>   È Beatrice quella che sì scorge
> di bene in meglio, sì subitamente
> che l'atto suo per tempo non si sporge.[29]

or these (lines 97-105) from Canto XXII:

> Così mi disse, e indi si raccolse
> al suo collegio, e 'l collegio si strinse;
> poi, come turbo, in sù tutto s'avvolse.
>   La dolce donna dietro a lor mi pinse

---

[27] Beatrice was gazing upward, and I on her; and perhaps in that time that a bolt strikes, flies, and from the catch is released, I saw myself arrived where a wondrous thing drew my sight to it ...

[28] and as an arrow that strikes the target before the bowcord is quiet, so we sped into the second realm.

[29] and I was with him, but of my ascent I was no more aware than is a man, before his first thought, aware of its coming. It is Beatrice who thus conducts from good to better, and so swiftly that her act does not extend through time.

> con un sol cenno su per quella scala,
> sì sua virtù la mia natura vinse;
> né mai qua giù dove si monta e cala
> naturalmente, fu sì ratto moto
> ch'agguagliar si potesse a la mia ala.[30]

– passages nothing if not secure in their sense of the momentary character of the soul's movement into God, of the a-successionality of it all.[31] But the

---

[30] Thus he spoke to me, then drew back to his company, and the company closed together; then like a whirlwind all were gathered upward. My sweet lady, with only a sign, thrust me up after them by that ladder, so did her power overcome my nature; nor ever here below, where we mount and descend by nature's law, was motion so swift as might match my flight.

[31] So too VIII.13-15, XIV.79-84 and XXVII.88-99: 'Io non m'accorsi del salire in ella; / ma d'esservi entro mi fé assai fede / la donna mia ch'i' vidi far più bella ... Ma Bëatrice sì bella e ridente / mi si mostrò, che tra quelle vedute / si vuol lasciar che non seguir la mente / Quindi ripreser li occhi miei virtute / a rilevarsi; e vidimi translato / sol con mia donna in più alta salute ... E la virtù che lo sguardo m'indulse, / del bel nido di Leda mi divelse, / e nel ciel velocissimo m'impulse ... La mente innamorata, che donnea / con la mia donna sempre, di ridure / ad essa li occhi più che mai ardea; / e se natura o arte fé pasture / da pigliare occhi, per aver la mente, / in carne umana o ne le sue pitture, / tutte adunate, parrebber nïente / ver' lo piacer divin che mi refulse, / quando mi volsi al suo viso ridente. / E la virtù che lo sguardo m'indulse, / del bel nido di Leda mi divelse, / e nel ciel velocissimo m'impulse.' Thomas, *ST* Ia IIae.113.7 resp.: 'tota iustificatio impii originaliter consistit in gratiae infusione, per eam enim et liberum arbitrium movetur, et culpa remittitur. Gratiae autem infusio fit in instanti absque successione. Cuius ratio est quia quod aliqua forma non subito imprimatur subiecto, contingit ex hoc quod subiectum non est dispositum, et agens indiget tempore ad hoc quod subiectum disponat. Et ideo videmus quod statim cum materia est disposita per alterationem praecedentem, forma substantialis acquiritur materiae, et eadem ratione, quia diaphanum est secundum se dispositum ad lumen recipiendum, subito illuminatur a corpore lucido in actu. Dictum est autem supra quod Deus ad hoc quod gratiam infundat animae, non requirit aliquam dispositionem nisi quam ipse facit. Facit autem huiusmodi dispositionem sufficientem ad susceptionem gratiae, quandoque quidem subito, quandoque autem paulatim et successive, ut supra dictum est. Quod enim agens naturale non subito possit disponere materiam, contingit ex hoc quod est aliqua disproportio eius quod in materia resistit, ad virtutem agentis, et propter hoc videmus quod quanto virtus agentis fuerit fortior, tanto materia citius disponitur. Cum igitur virtus divina sit infinita, potest quamcumque materiam creatam subito disponere ad formam, et multo magis liberum arbitrium hominis, cuius motus potest esse instantaneus secundum naturam. Sic igitur iustificatio impii fit a Deo in instanti.' Already at 110.2 resp.: 'sicut iam dictum est, in eo qui dicitur gratiam Dei habere, significatur esse quidam effectus gratuitae Dei voluntatis. Dictum est autem supra quod dupliciter ex gratuita Dei voluntate homo adiuvatur. Uno modo, inquantum anima hominis movetur a Deo ad aliquid cognoscendum vel volendum vel agendum. Et hoc modo ipse gratuitus effectus in homine non est qualitas, sed motus quidam animae, actus enim moventis in moto est motus, ut dicitur in III Physic. Alio modo adiuvatur homo ex gratuita Dei voluntate, secundum quod aliquod habituale donum a Deo animae infunditur. Et hoc ideo, quia non est conveniens quod Deus minus

a-successionality of it all, suggesting once again a discourse attuned less to time than to being as a dominant parameter of consciousness, should not be allowed to waylay us here, for Dante's, in the *Commedia*, is not, in fact, an essay in the entitative and in the strangeness thereof, but rather in the opening out of self upon what it already has it in itself to be and to become, on the kind of greater humanity, or 'transhumanity', present to it from beforehand as at once the innermost and 'ownmost' ('eigenst') of its proper possibilities. His, in other words, is the logic and lexis, not of modification, but of emergence, of a progressive and progressively ecstatic process of self-implementation; so, for example, with their talk of dilation ('dilatarsi'), of 'magnification' ('farsi più grande') and of 'issuing forth' ('di sé uscire') as a way of seeing and celebrating the process of drawing nigh (the 'appropinquare' of *Par.* XXXIII.47), these lines (34-45) from *Paradiso* XXIII:

> Oh Bëatrice, dolce guida e cara!
> Ella mi disse: "Quel che ti sobranza
> è virtù da cui nulla si ripara.
>   Quivi è la sapïenza e la possanza
> ch'aprì le strade tra 'l cielo e la terra,
> onde fu già sì lunga disïanza".
>   Come foco di nube si diserra
> per dilatarsi sì che non vi cape,
> e fuor di sua natura in giù s'atterra,
>   la mente mia così, tra quelle dape
> fatta più grande, di sé stessa uscìo,
> e che si fesse rimembrar non sape.[32]

provideat his quos diligit ad supernaturale bonum habendum, quam creaturis quas diligit ad bonum naturale habendum. Creaturis autem naturalibus sic providet ut non solum moveat eas ad actus naturales, sed etiam largiatur eis formas et virtutes quasdam, quae sunt principia actuum, ut secundum seipsas inclinentur ad huiusmodi motus. Et sic motus quibus a Deo moventur, fiunt creaturis connaturales et faciles; secundum illud Sap. VIII, et disponit omnia suaviter. Multo igitur magis illis quos movet ad consequendum bonum supernaturale aeternum, infundit aliquas formas seu qualitates supernaturales, secundum quas suaviter et prompte ab ipso moveantur ad bonum aeternum consequendum. Et sic donum gratiae qualitas quaedam est.' Otherwise, *De verit.* 28. 9, *sed contra* 1 and resp. ult.: 'Iustificatio impii est quaedam spiritualis illuminatio. Sed illuminatio corporalis fit in instanti, non in tempore ... Nam forma et dispositio ad formam completam et abiectio alterius formae, totum est in instanti.'

[32] O Beatrice, sweet guide and dear! She said to me, "That which overcomes you is power against which naught defends itself. Therein are the wisdom and the power that opened the roads between heaven and earth, for which of old there was such long desire". Even as fire breaks from a cloud, and dilates so that it has not room there, and contrary to its own nature, falls down to earth, so my mind, becoming greater amid those feasts, issued from itself, and of what it became has no remembrance.

or, with their talk of soaring and strengthening ('sormontare' and 'avvalorarsi') as the way of ultimate affirmation, these (lines 52-63 and 106-14) from Cantos XXX and XXXIII:

> "Sempre l'amor che queta questo cielo
> accoglie in sé con sì fatta salute,
> per far disposto a sua fiamma il candelo".
> Non fur più tosto dentro a me venute
> queste parole brievi, ch'io compresi
> me sormontar di sopr' a mia virtute;
> e di novella vista mi raccesi
> tale, che nulla luce è tanto mera,
> che li occhi miei non si fosser difesi;
> e vidi lume in forma di rivera
> fulvido di fulgore, intra due rive
> dipinte di mirabil primavera.
> ...
> Omai sarà più corta mia favella,
> pur a quel ch'io ricordo, che d'un fante
> che bagni ancor la lingua a la mammella.
> Non perché più ch'un semplice sembiante
> fosse nel vivo lume ch'io mirava,
> che tal è sempre qual s'era davante;
> ma per la vista che s'avvalorava
> in me guardando, una sola parvenza,
> mutandom' io, a me si travagliava.[33]

Now the soul's movement into God is indeed a movement into the strangeness of God, into the a-referentiality — the timelessness, spacelessness, everywhereness and nowhereness — of what *is* as of the essence. But for all the strangeness of that movement into God, there can be no question here of a metaphysical or magical co-adaptation of the subject to the object of its desiring, grace, far from modifying the individual at the level of form (albeit of accidental form) and thus in some sense modifying

---

[33] "Ever does the love which quiets this heaven receive into itself with such like salutation, in order to prepare the candle for its flame." No sooner had these brief words come within me than I comprehended that I was surmounting beyond my own power, and such new vision was kindled in me that there is no light so bright that my eyes could not have withstood it. And I saw a light in the form of a river glowing tawny between two banks painted with marvelous spring ... Now will my speech fall more short, even in respect to what I remember, than that of an infant which still bathes his tongue at the breast. Not because more than one simple semblance was in the living light wherein I was gazing, which is ever such as it was before; but through my sight, which was growing strong in me as I looked, one sole appearance, even as I changed, was altering itself to me.

the original project, serving rather to confirm it in its natural capacity for self-transcendence as the most immanent of its immanent possibilities. This, then is the third great work of grace in its positive verification. The third great work of grace in its positive verification is the confirming of self in the power to transhumanity, transhumanity, for Dante, being but humanity under the aspect of ecstasy.

4. Adolph Harnack, the great German historian of Christian dogmatics, pauses in a moment of melancholy to consider the gap in medieval theology between God and grace, between on the one hand the superabundant love which *is* God, and, on the other, grace as that whereby that same love is known to man under the conditions of time and space. There was, he says, among the great theological spirits of the Middle Ages

> no recognition of *personality*, neither of the personality of God, nor of man as a *person*. If even in earthly relations man cannot be otherwise raised to a higher stage, than by passing into a person who is superior, more mature, and greater, that is, by entering into spiritual fellowship with such an one, and attaching one's self to him by reverence, love, and trust, then the same holds good, but in a way that transcends comparison, of the rising of man from the sphere of sin and guilt into the sphere of God. Here no communications of things avail, but only fellowship of person with person; the disclosure to the soul, that the holy God who rules heaven and earth is its Father, with whom it can, and may, live as a child in its father's house – that is grace, nay, that *alone* is grace, the trustful confidence in God, namely, which rests on the certainty that the separating guilt has been swept away. That was seen by Augustine as little as by Thomas, and it was not discerned even by the medieval Mystics, who aspired to having intercourse with Christ as with a friend ; for it was the *man* Jesus of whom they thought in seeking this. But all of them, when they think of God, look, not to the heart of God, but to an inscrutable Being, who, as He has created the world out of nothing, so is also the productive source of inexhaustible forces that yield *knowledge* and *transformation of essence*. And when they think of themselves, they think, not of the centre of the human ego, the spirit, which is so free and so lofty that it cannot be influenced by benefits that are objective, even though they be the greatest perceptions and the most glorious investiture, and at the same time is so feeble in itself that it can find support only in another *person*. Therefore they constructed the thesis: *God and gratia* (*i.e.*, knowledge and participation in the divine nature), in place of the personal fellowship with God, *which is the gratia*. That gratia, only a little separated from God in the thesis, became in course of time

always further removed from Him. It appears deposited in the merit of Christ, and then in the Sacraments. But in the measure in which it becomes more impersonal, more objective, and more external, confidence in it is also impaired, till at last it becomes a magical means, which stirs to activity the latent good agency of man, and sets in motion the standing machine, that it may then do *its* work, and that its work may be of account before God.[34]

Now this, in so far as it holds good in respect of a literature endlessly nuanced in respect of the substance and psychology of grace as the means of renewal and of resurrection, and indeed of the precise nature of man's relationship with God under the conditions of the time and space, is indeed melancholy. But in so far as it touches on Dante, it helps to account for his relative indifference, not, certainly, to grace precisely as such (on the contrary!), but to anything resembling a theology of grace. Faith, hope, love, atonement, election, yes, all these and much else besides are there as a matter of systematic concern, but not grace. How, then, are we to account

---

[34] A. Harnack, *History of Dogma*, trans. N. Buchanan (New York: Dover Publications, 1961), vol. 6, pp. 279-80. John Burnaby, however (*Amor Dei. A Study of the Religion of St Augustine* (The Hulsean Lectures for 1938) (London: Hodder and Stoughton, 1938), p. 313), commenting on Nygren's position in his *Agape and Eros*, Part II, *The History of the Christian Idea of Love* (London: SPCK, 1954) is gentler in Augustine's regard, seeing there a more intimate association between the notion of grace and the working of the Spirit: 'It is a conspicuous merit in Nygren's treatment of Augustine to have decisively rejected the superficial criticism which alleges that the Catholic doctrine of grace – as distinct from perversions of practice – is "magical" or "mechanical". What St Thomas calls the "infusion" of charity is that same working of the Holy Spirit for which Augustine found his *locus classicus* in the Epistle to the Romans. It is no 'thing-like' substance introduced from without, but the purely spiritual influence of the divine Person whose dwelling is within the believer's heart.' Nygren's text (pp. 522-23) runs as follows: 'This idea of the infusion of grace and love (*infusio caritatis*) has often been taken to prove that Augustine's conception of grace was magical and naturalistic. Thus Harnack says: "The love of God is infused into the soul in portions." The root error of Augustine's doctrine of grace is supposed to lie in its "objective character" (ihres *dinglichen* Charakters); indeed, he is accused of believing that "love can be poured in like a medicine". Similarly, W. Herrmann finds the weakness of Augustine's idea of grace in the fact that he failed to make it psychologically intelligible how man is converted by the grace of God which meets us in the historical Christ, and was content to think of grace as a mysterious power. But here the need for caution is indicated by the very fact that Augustine's idea of the "infusion" of Caritas is directly connected with Paul's saying in Rom. v.5 that "the love of God hath been shed abroad in our hearts through the Holy Ghost which was given unto us". Nothing was further from Augustine's intention than a magical or naturalistic idea of grace. If we are to apply the alternative "magical and naturalistic" or "personal and psychological", then it is the latter that describes Augustine's view. Caritas is infused into our hearts, not in a manner that is unconnected with our relation to God, but by the fact that the Holy Spirit is given to us.'

for this situation? By way of the status of grace in Dante as but love by another name, at which point motion, remotion, magic and metaphysics, indeed the entire apparatus of high-scholastic grace-consciousness, give way to something simpler and more sublime.

Events and Their Inner Life: an Essay in Actual Eschatology

> quel giorno più non vi leggemmo avante.
>
> *(Inf.* V.138)[1]

1. Preliminary considerations: patterns of eschatological awareness in Dante. 2. Axes of concern: the triumph of the *innermost* over the *aftermost* (the cases of Francesca da Rimini, Pier della Vigna and Guido da Montefeltro). 3. Conclusion: eschatology, immanence and the power to terrify.

Inasmuch as eschatology is ever ordinary, Dante's, in the *Commedia*, is an ordinary eschatology.[2] Like most eschatology, it is expectational in

---

[1] that day we read no farther in it.

[2] In general on Christian and Christian-medieval eschatology, R. Bultmann, *History and Eschatology* (Edinburgh: Edinburgh University Press, 1957); J. Moltmann, *Theology of Hope: On the Ground and the Implications of a Christian Eschatology* (London: SCM Press, 1968; also New York: Harper and Row, 1967); J. A. T. Robinson, *In the End God* (London and Glasgow: Fontana, 1968); J. Ratzinger, *Eschatology* (Washington DC: Catholic University of America Press, 1988; originally *Eschatologie. Tod und ewiges Leben* (Regensburg: Verlag, 1977)); W. Verbeke et al. (eds), *The Use and Abuse of Eschatology in the Middle Ages* (Leuven: Leuven University Press, 1988); Z. Hayes, *Vision of a Future: A Study of Christian Eschatology* (Wilmington DL: Michael Glazier, 1989); C. W. Bynum and P. Freedman (eds), *Last Things: Death and Apocalypse in the Middle Ages* (Philadelphia: University of Pennsylvania Press, 2000).

On Dante and eschatology, G. Barberi Squarotti, 'Artificio ed escatologia della *Vita Nuova*', in *L'artificio dell'eternit*à. *Studi danteschi* (Verona: Fiorini, 1972), pp. 35-106; idem, 'Retorica ed escatologia', in *Psicoanalisi e strutturalismo di fronte a Dante. Dalla letteratura profetica medievale agli odierni strumenti critici* (Florence: Olschki, 1972), vol. 2 (*Lettura della Commedia*), pp. 441-65; R. Palgen, *Mittelalterliche Eschatologie in Dantes 'Komödie'. Motive und motivketten aus der mittelalterlichen Sagen literatur. Die Timaiosmotive in der Göttlichen Komödie* (Graz: Hugo-Schuchardtsche Malwinenstiftung, 1975); A. K. Cassell, *Dante's Fearful Art of Justice* (Toronto: Toronto University Press, 1984); C. T. Davis, 'Poverty and Eschatology in the *Commedia*', in *Dante's Italy* (Philadelphia: University of Pennsylvania Press, 1984), pp. 42-70; M. P. Ciccarese, 'Le "Visiones" dell'aldilà nel cristianesimo occidentale. Genere letterario e tematiche predantesche', in *La fine dei tempi. Storia ed escatologia*, ed. M. Naldini (Florence: Nardini, 1994), pp. 101-15 (also, eadem (ed.), *Visioni dell'aldil*à *in occidente: fonti, modelli, testi* (Florence: Nardini, 1987) and 'L'anticipazione della

character, anticipatory in respect of the moment in which, summoned before Christ in judgement, the individual will at last be confirmed in the truth of what he has been, of what he is, and of what now he always will be. And this, as a way of seeing and understanding it, chimes with the typological idea similarly decisive for an overall interpretation of the poem, with the notion that events severally disposed on the plane of the horizontal may by dint of their shared significance be said to inhabit the same space, to relate one with another by way of a complex process of pre- and post-shadowing.[3] Eschatology and typology are in this sense all of a piece, each alike turning on a sense of the continuity of human experience in time and eternity, on a resolution of the *what is* under the aspect of the former in terms of the *what will be* under the aspect of the latter.[4] But to

fine: l'immaginario dell'aldilà nei primi secoli cristiani', in R. Uglione (ed.) *'Millennium': l'attesa della fine nei primi secoli cristiani. Atti delle III Giornate Patristiche Torinesi, Torini 23- 24 ottobre 2000* (Turin: CELID, 2002), pp. 183-208); M. A. Palacios, *Dante e l'islam. I. L'escatologia islamica nella 'Divina Commedia'. II. Storia e critica di una polemica*, trans. R. R. Testa and Y. Tawfik, with an introduction by C. Ossola (Parma: Nuova Pratiche Editrice, 1994 and 1997; based on 2nd edn, 1943); M. Gragnolati, *Experiencing the Afterlife. Soul and Body in Dante and Medieval Culture* (Notre Dame, Ind.: University of Notre Dame Press, 2005); F. Livi, 'La *Divina Commedia* e l'escatologia cristiana', in *Dante e la teologia* (Rome: Casa Editrice Leonardo da Vinci, 2008), pp. 29-69.

[3] E. Auerbach, 'Figurative Texts Illustrating Certain Passages of Dante's *Commedia'*, *Speculum* 21 (1946), 474-89 (also in *Studi su Dante*, ed. Dante Della Terza, 8th edn (Milan: Feltrinelli, 1991) pp. 239-63, with 'Figura' at pp. 176-226); idem, *Typologische Motive in der mittelalterlichen Literatur; Schriftere und Vorträge desPetrarca-Instituts, Koln* 2 (Krefeld: Scherpe, 1953); J. Chydenius, *The Typological Problem in Dante: A Study in the History of Medieval Ideas* (Helsinki: Societas scientiarum fennica, 1958); idem, *The Theory of Medieval Symbolism* (Helsinki: Societas scientiarum fennica, 1960); A. C. Charity, *Events and Their Afterlife: The Dialectics of Christian Typology in the Bible and Dante* (Cambridge: Cambridge University Press, 1966); G. Padoan, 'La "mirabile visione" di Dante e l'epistola a Cangrande', in *Il pio Enea, l'empio Ulisse. Tradizione classica e intendimento medievale in Dante* (Ravenna: Longo, 1977), pp. 30-63. Also, P. Armour, 'The Theme of Exodus in the First Two Cantos of the *Purgatorio*', in *Dante Soundings. Eight Literary and Historical Essays*, ed. D. Nolan (Dublin: Irish Academic Press, 1981), pp. 59-99. More generally on the typological issue, C. Spicq, *Esquisse d'une histoire de l'éxègese latine au moyen âge* (Paris: Vrin, 1944); J. Daniélou, *Sacramentum futuri. Etudes sur les origines de la typologie biblique* (Paris: Beauchesne, 1950); idem, 'The Conception of History in the Christian Tradition', *Journal of Religion* 30 (1950), 3, 171-79; idem, *Gospel Message and Hellenistic Culture* (London: Darton, Longman and Todd, 1973; originally 1961); B. Smalley, *The Study of the Bible in the Middle Ages*, 2nd edn (Oxford: Blackwell, 1952); G. W. H. Lampe and K. J. Woollcombe, *Essays on Typology* (London: SCM Press, 1957); H. de Lubac, *Exégèse médiévale. Les Quatre sens de l'écriture* (Paris: Aubier, 1959-1964); idem, 'A propos de l'allégorie chrétienne', *Recherches de science religieuse* 47 (1959), 5-43 (also 'Typologie et allégorisme' in vol. 34 (1947), 180-226); J. N. D. Kelly, 'The Bible and the Latin Fathers', in *The Church's Use of the Bible, Past and Present*, ed. D. E. Nineham (London: SPCK, 1963), pp. 41-56.

[4] On concepts of time and eternity in general and in Dante, P. Duhem, *Le Système du monde. Histoire des doctrines cosmologiques de Platon à Copernic* (Paris: Hermann, 1913-17 and

live for any length of time with the *Commedia* is sooner rather than later to sense something of its restiveness with this kind of expectationalism, with its all being a matter, as far as the ἔσχατος is concerned, of postponed intelligence. More exactly, it is to become aware of Dante's sense of the power of the historical instant to signify from out of the depths, the horizontal thus giving way to the vertical as a means of stating the eschatological issue. Now this needs careful statement, for to speak of the verticality of eschatological concern in the *Commedia*, of its sense of the ἔσχατος as dwelling in the depths of the historical instant, is by no means to sit lightly to what we have described as the expectational aspect of the argument, to the status of the ἔσχατος as *coming next* or as *following on*; for everywhere built into the consciousness both of Dante himself and of his clientèle in the poem is a sense of the truth of their existence as but a truth in waiting, as subsisting in anticipation of its definitive statement. In

reprints, with a selection in *Medieval Cosmology. Theories of Infinity, Place, Time, Void, and the Plurality of the Worlds*, ed. and trans. R. Ariew (Chicago: University of Chicago Press, 1985)); W. Kneale, 'Time and Eternity in Theology', *Proceedings of the Aristotelian Society* 61 (1960-61), 87-108; W. von Leyden, 'Time, Number and Eternity in Plato and Aristotle, *Philosophical Quarterly* 14 (1964), 35-52; M. Kneale, 'Eternity and Sempiternity', *Proceedings of the Aristotelian Society* 69 (1968-69), 223-38; E. Stump and N. Kretzmann, 'Eternity', *Journal of Philosophy* 78 (1981), 429-58; R. C. Dales, 'Time and Eternity in the Thirteenth Century', *Journal of the History of Ideas* 49 (1988), 27-45; A. G. Padgett (with reference to Boethius and Aquinas), 'God and Time. Towards a New Doctrine of Divine Timeless Eternity', *Religious Studies* 25 (1989), 209-15; B. Leftow, 'Eternity and Simultaneity', *Faith and Philosophy* 8 (1991), 148-79; K. A. Rogers, 'Eternity has no Duration', *Religious Studies* 30 (1994), 1, 1-16; R. Sorabji, *Time, Creation and the Continuum. Theories in Antiquity and the Early Middle Ages* (Chicago: Chicago University Press, 2006, originally 1983). In relation to Dante, F. Masciandaro, *La problematica del tempo nella "Commedia"* (Ravenna: Longo, 1976); M. M. Chiarenza, 'Time and Eternity in the Myths of *Paradiso* XVII', in *Dante, Petrarch, Boccaccio. Studies in the Italian Trecento in Honor of C. S. Singleton*, ed. A. S. Bernardo and A. L. Pellegrini (Binghampton, NY: Centre for Medieval and Early Renaissance Studies, 1983), pp. 133-50; G. Giacalone, 'Tempo ed eternità nella *Divina Commedia*', in *Dante Alighieri. La Divina Commedia* (Roma: Signorelli, 1988), vol. 3, pp. 66-82 (subsequently in *Atti della Dante Alighieri a Treviso 1984-1989* (Treviso: Matteo, 1989), pp. 170-81 and *Da Malebolge alla Senna. Studi letterari in onore di Giorgio Santangelo* (Palermo: Palumbo, 1993), pp. 259-78); I. Sciuto, 'Eternità e tempo in Dante', in *Tempus, aevum, aeternitas. La concettualizzazione del tempo nel pensiero tardomedievale. Atti del Colloquio Internazionale, Trieste, 4-6 marzo 1999*, ed. G. Alliney and L. Cova (Florence: Olschki, 2000), pp. 1-20; R. Bodei, *Tempo ed eternità in Dante e in Petrarca*, in *Letture classensi* 32-34, ed. N. Ancarani (Ravenna: Longo, 2005), pp. 67-76. More generally, P. Salm, *Pinpoint of Eternity. European Literature in Search of the All-encompassing Moment*, (Lanham: University Press of America, 1986). For Dante on eternity as duration, the 'e io etterno duro' of *Inf.* III.8, while on eternity as all-at-onceness (*tota simul*), *Par.* XVII.13-18 (the 'il punto / a cui tutti li tempi son presenti' of lines 17-18) and XXIX.10-12 ('Poi cominciò: "Io dico, e non dimando, / quel che tu vuoli udir, perch' io l'ho visto / là 've s'appunta ogne *ubi* e ogne *quando*"'), where *extension* is present to the transfigured mind as a matter pre-eminently of *intension*, of the resolution of the quantitative in the qualitative as an inkling of the spirit.

this sense, the ἔσχατος is indeed the last thing horizontally, the *terminus ad quem* on the plane of temporality. But for all that, there can for Dante be no resolution of this matter in terms purely and simply of successionality, for his is a sense of ultimacy as a matter of intimacy, of what Kierkegaard used to call the 'infinite contentfulness' of the moment,[5] at which point eschatology as often enough an afterthought in the mind of the theologian, an item under any other business, moves up the agenda.

2. What amounts, then, to a privileging of the vertical over the horizontal as a parameter of eschatological awareness, of the height and depth of that awareness over its before and after, is throughout discernible in the *Commedia*, Dante's at every stage being a preoccupation with the kind of awareness whereby self stands in the truth of self as confirmed from deep within it, from out of the innermost recesses of personality. Turning, then, to the case of Francesca in *Inferno* V, we have first its symptomatology, its registration (*a*) of the surface sensation of being as adrift in respect of its own inner reasons, and (*b*) of the process of self-

---

[5] Søren Kierkegaard, *The Concept of Anxiety*, ed. and trans. R. Thomte in collaboration with A. B. Anderson (Princeton: Princeton University Press, 1980), p. 86: 'For representation, [the eternal] is a going forth that nevertheless does not get off the spot, because the eternal is for representation the infinitely contentful present.' Among the moderns, Paul Tillich, *The Religious Situation*, trans. R. Niebuhr (New York: Meridian Books, 1956), p. 35: 'it would not be worthwhile to speak at all of the fact that all sorts of things, ideas or feelings or deeds or works, move out of the past into the future across the mysterious boundary line of the present if all this were nothing but a moving, a flowing, a becoming and decaying without ultimate meaning or final importance. All of this is really important if it has unconditioned meaning, an unconditioned depth, an unconditioned reality. That it possesses this unconditioned meaning cannot be made a matter of proof or disproof but only of faith in the unconditioned meaning of life.' Karl Jaspers, *Philosophy*, trans. E. B. Ashton (Chicago: Chicago University Press, 1970; originally 1932), vol. 2, p. 17: 'Confronting necessity, the existence of an object *at all times*, we have, instead of endless time, the *fulfilled time of the moment*. As present eternity, this fulfilled time confronts Kant's time at large ... The latter is objective, measurable, and can be experienced as reality; the former is the depth of original, free Existenz. The latter is validly extant for everyone; the former turns a time that is tied to choice and decision into a phenomenon, as current time. Existenz has *its* time, not *time pure and simple*. Objective time exists for consciousness at large; existential time exists for the historical consciousness of Existenz alone' (emphases those of the translator). Among the depth-psychologists and psychoanalysts, Rollo May in *Man's Search For Himself* (New York: Norton, 1953, p. 269) speaks of eternity, not as a 'given quantity of time', but as its 'qualitative significance'. It is the form of man's relationship to life, 'not a succession of "tomorrows"'. Also, idem, *The Discovery of Being* (New York: Norton, 1983), p. 137: 'the *Eigenwelt*, the own world of self-relatedness, self-awareness, and insight into the meaning of an event for one's self, has practically nothing to do with Aristotle's clock time. The essence of self-awareness and insight are that they are "there" – instantaneous, immediate – and the moment of awareness has its significance for all time.'

exoneration whereby the soul in its contritionlessness seeks to sidestep the pain of moral and ontological disintegration; on the one hand, then, there is the 'bufera infernal' passage beginning at line 28, an essay, precisely, in freefloatingness, in the agony of self-separation:

> Io venni in loco d'ogne luce muto,
> che mugghia come fa mar per tempesta,
> se da contrari venti è combattuto.
>   La bufera infernal, che mai non resta,
> mena li spirti con la sua rapina;
> voltando e percotendo li molesta.
>   Quando giungon davanti a la ruina,
> quivi le strida, il compianto, il lamento;
> bestemmian quivi la virtù divina.
>   Intesi ch'a così fatto tormento
> enno dannati i peccator carnali,
> che la ragion sommettono al talento.
>   E come li stornei ne portan l'ali
> nel freddo tempo, a schiera larga e piena,
> così quel fiato li spiriti mali
>   di qua, di là, di giù, di sù li mena;
> nulla speranza li conforta mai,
> non che di posa, ma di minor pena.[6]

while on the other, there is the 'Amor ... Amor ... Amor' sequence beginning at line 100 and constituting an essay this time in the substance and psychology of self-evasion, in shifting the burden of guilt in the interests of a modicum of self-consistency:

> "Amor, ch'al cor gentil ratto s'apprende
> prese costui de la bella persona
> che mi fu tolta; e 'l modo ancor m'offende.
>   Amor, ch'a nullo amato amar perdona,
> mi prese del costui piacer sì forte,
> che, come vedi, ancor non m'abbandona.

---

[6] I came into a place mute of all light, which bellows like the sea in tempest when it is assailed by warring winds. The hellish hurricane, never resting, sweeps along the spirits with its rapine; whirling and smiting, it torments them. When they arrive before the ruin, there the shrieks, the moans, the lamentations; there they curse the divine power. I learned that to such torment are condemned the carnal sinners, who subject reason to desire. And as their wings bear the starlings along in the cold season, in wide, dense flocks, so does that blast the sinful spirits; hither, thither, downward, upward, it drives them. No hope of less pain, not to say of rest, ever comforts them.

Amor condusse noi ad una morte.
Caina attende chi a vita ci spense".
Queste parole da lor ci fuor porte.⁷

⁷ Love, which is quickly kindled in a noble heart, seized this one for the fair form that was taken from me – and the way of it afflicts me still. Love, which absolves no one from loving, seized me so strongly with delight in him, that, as you see, it does not leave me even now. Love brought us to one death. Caina awaits him who quenched our life. On contrition as the breaking down of hardheartedness and as the condition, therefore, of regeneration, [Aquinas], *ST* IIIa supp. 1.1 resp.: 'Respondeo dicendum quod, ut dicitur Eccli. 10:15, *initium omnis peccati est superbia*, per quam homo sensui suo inhaerens, a mandatis divinis recedit. Et ideo oportet quod illud quod destruit peccatum, hominem a proprio sensu discedere faciat. Ille autem qui in suo sensu perseverat, rigidus, et durus per similitudinem vocatur; sicut durum in materialibus dicitur quod non cedit tactui; unde et frangi dicitur aliquis quando a suo sensu divellitur. Sed inter fractionem, et comminutionem, sive contritionem in rebus materialibus, unde haec nomina ad spiritualia transferuntur, hoc interest, ut dicitur, quod frangi dicuntur aliqua quando in magnas partes dividuntur, sed comminui vel conteri, quando ad partes minimas reducitur hoc quod in se solidum erat. Et quia ad dimissionem peccati requiruntur quod affectum peccati homo totaliter dimittat, quem per quamdam continuitatem, et soliditatem in sensu suo habebat; ideo actus ille quo peccatum dimittitur, contritio dicitur per similitudinem.' Bernard, *In festo omnium sanct.* I.x (*PL* 183, 458A): 'Equum indomitum flagella domant; animam immitem contritio spiritus et assiduitas lacrymarum'; Aelred of Rievaulx, *Serm. de oner.* XX (*PL* 195, 441A): 'Scopa terens cordis contritio est, qua Babylon in anima nostra teritur et conteritur, et omnes spurcitiae ejus egeruntur', etc.

Augustine on the alienation of responsibility in circumstances of far-offness, *De civ. Dei* xiv.14: 'Sed est peior damnabilior superbia qua etiam in peccatis manifestis suffugium excusationis inquiritur, sicut illi primi homines, quorum et illa dixit: "Serpens seduxit me, et manducavi", et ille dixit: "Mulier, quam dedisti mecum, haec mihi dedit a ligno, et edi". Nusquam hic sonat petitio veniae, nusquam inploratio medicinae. Nam licet isti non, sicut Cain, quod commiserunt negent, adhuc tamen superbia in aliud quaerit referre quod perperam fecit, superbia mulieris in serpentem, superbia viri mulierem. Sed accusatio potius quam excusatio vera est ubi mandati divini est aperta transgressio'; *De lib. arb.* III.ii.5: 'Verumtamen maximam partem hominum ista quaestione torqueri non ob aliud crediderim, nisi quia non pie quaerunt, velocioresque sunt ad excusationem, quam ad confessionem peccatorum suorum'; *En. in psalm.* vii.19 (v. 18): 'Ista confessio ita Dominum laudat, ut nihil possint impiorum valere blasphemiae, qui volentes excusare facinora sua, nolunt suae culpae tribuere quod peccant, hoc est, nolunt suae culpae tribuere culpam suam. Itaque aut fortunam, aut fatum inveniunt quod accusent; aut diabolum, cui non consentire in potestate nostra esse voluit qui nos fecit; aut aliam naturam inducunt, quae non sit ex Deo, fluctuantes miseri et errantes, potius quam confitentes Deo, ut eis ignoscat', etc. Peter Lombard, *Comm. in ps. XL*, v. 4: 'Miserere ita: "Sana" per flagella "animam meam", quoniam nullo modo excuso peccatum, sed accuso dicens: "Quia peccavi tibi", non accuso fortunam, non dico: Hoc mihi facit fatum; non dico: Adulterum me fecit Venus, et latronem Mars, et avarum Saturnus'; Bernard, *Cant. cantic.* xvi.11: '[Confessio] oportet autem esse et simplicem. Non intentionem (forte quia latet homines) excusare delectet, si sit rea ... Primum illud non confessio est, sed defensio; nec placat, sed provocat ... Jam a postremo primi hominis dehortetur, exemplum, nec culpam siquidem diffitentis, nec tamen consequentis veniam non dubium quin ob reatus mulieris admissionem (Gen. 3:2). Genus excusationis est, cum argueris tu, alium incusare

But of the strategies of self-preservation in the context of catastrophe Dante will have nothing, his being straightaway a referral of the horizontal to the vertical as the dominant axis of awareness, of the strategic to the synderectic as a principle of self-interpretation. 'Tell me', then, he has the poet-pilgrim say, 'how was it with you in the moment of love's sweet sighs, in the moment of knowing and of being known by love in its power both to delight and to destroy?' ('Ma dimmi: al tempo d'i dolci sospiri, / a che e come concedette amore / che conosceste i dubbiosi disiri?'; lines 118-20),[8] a question which, for all its apparent innocence, leaves no room for manoeuvre, nowhere else for Francesca to look other than into the recesses of her soul there to contemplate yet again the enormity of it all, the awesome moment of moral and ontological self-delivery:

> E quella a me: "Nessun maggior dolore
> che ricordarsi del tempo felice
> ne la miseria; e ciò sa 'l tuo dottore.
>   Ma s'a conoscer la prima radice
> del nostro amor tu hai cotanto affetto,
> dirò come colui che piange e dice.
>   Noi leggiavamo un giorno per diletto
> di Lancialotto come amor lo strinse;
> soli eravamo e sanza alcun sospetto.
>   Per più fiate li occhi ci sospinse
> quella lettura, e scolorocci il viso;
> ma solo un punto fu quel che ci vinse.
>   Quando leggemmo il disïato riso
> esser basciato da cotanto amante,
> questi, che mai da me non fia diviso,
>   la bocca mi basciò tutto tremante.
> Galeotto fu 'l libro e chi lo scrisse:
> quel giorno più non vi leggemmo avante".
>
> (*Inf.* V.121-38)[9]

... In animam etenim suam peccat qui se excusat, repellens proinde a se indulgentiae medicinam, et sic vitam sibi proprio ore intercludens'; idem, *De grad. humil.* xvii.45: 'Si autem et de illa, sicut Adam vel Eva, convincitur, aliena suasione excusare se nititur', etc.

[8] But tell me, in the time of the sweet sighs, by what and how did Love grant you to know the dubious desires?

[9] And she to me, "There is no greater sorrow than to recall, in wretchedness, the happy time; and this your teacher knows. But if you have such great desire to know the first root of our love, I will tell as one who weeps and tells. One day, for pastime, we read of Lancelot, how love constrained him; we were alone, suspecting nothing. Several times that reading urged our eyes to meet and took the colour from our faces, but one moment alone it was that overcame us. When we read how the longed-for smile was kissed by so great a lover, this one, who never shall be parted from me, kissed my mouth all trembling.

Straightaway, then, the ἔσχατος, hitherto subsisting on the far limit of human experience in its moment-by-moment unfolding, is brought forward into the centre of that experience, at which point its power to terrify is intensified beyond words. Nothing, clearly, is lost here by way of horizontality, the terrified subject living on in a state of fear and trembling, of living dread in respect of the last judgement and of the second death. But everything is gained by way of immediacy, of a sense on the part of the subject of her standing even now in the truth of her existence under the conditions of time and eternity, at which point verticality – meaning by this the knowledge of self urged upon self from out of the depths – once again takes over as the dominant axis of concern.

As a further example of the ascendancy of the vertical over the horizontal as a plane of eschatological awareness in the *Commedia* we may take the case of Pier della Vigna in *Inferno* XIII, where again it is a question of self as summoned into its own presence from out of the recesses of self. Here too Dante starts out with the symptomatology of the case, with (*a*) the kind of paranoia characteristic of being in its remotion and referable to dividedness at the point of fundamental willing, and (*b*) the kind of self-exoneration functioning in circumstances of contritionlessness as the sole means of self-intelligibility in the individual, of his standing significantly in his own company. On the one hand, then, as an essay in the pathology of captivity and enslavement, in being under the aspect of intimidation, we have the 'Non fronda verde' passage beginning at line 1:

> Non era ancor di là Nesso arrivato,
> quando noi ci mettemmo per un bosco
> che da neun sentiero era segnato.
> Non fronda verde, ma di color fosco;
> non rami schietti, ma nodosi e 'nvolti;
> non pomi v'eran, ma stecchi con tòsco.[10]

A Gallehault was the book and he who wrote it; that day we read no farther in it."

[10] Nessus had not yet reached the other side when we moved forward through a wood which was not marked by any path. No green leaves, but of dusky hue; no smooth boughs, but gnarled and warped; no fruits were there, but thorns with poison. Thomas on despair as, under one at least of its aspects, the gravest of sins, *ST* IIa IIae.20.3 resp.: 'Et ideo illud quod primo et per se habet aversionem a Deo est gravissimum inter peccata mortalia. Virtutibus autem theologicis opponuntur infidelitas, desperatio et odium Dei. Inter quae odium et infidelitas, si desperationi comparentur, invenientur secundum se quidem, idest secundum rationem propriae speciei, graviora. Infidelitas enim provenit ex hoc quod homo ipsam Dei veritatem non credit; odium vero Dei provenit ex hoc quod voluntas hominis ipsi divinae bonitati contrariatur; desperatio autem ex hoc quod homo non sperat se bonitatem Dei participare. Ex quo patet quod infidelitas et odium Dei sunt contra Deum secundum quod in se est; desperatio autem secundum quod eius bonum participatur a nobis. Unde maius peccatum est, secundum se loquendo, non credere Dei

and, as similarly attuned to the notion of antagonism as a principle of cosmic interpretation, to the soul's inability to see in the world anything other than ill will, the 'Perché mi schiante' passage beginning at line 31:

> Allor porsi la mano un poco avante
> e colsi un ramicel da un gran pruno;
> e 'l tronco suo gridò: "Perché mi schiante?".
> Da che fatto fu poi di sangue bruno,
> ricominciò a dir: "Perché mi scerpi?
> non hai tu spirto di pietade alcuno?
> Uomini fummo, e or siam fatti sterpi:
> ben dovrebb' esser la tua man più pia,
> se state fossimo anime di serpi".[11]

while on the other hand, and as an essay this time in the kind of deflection whereby self is saved from the otherwise intolerable sensation of its inconsistency, of its delivery of self despite self to its own annihilation, there is the ''nfiammati infiammar sì Augusto' passage beginning at line 64:

> La meretrice che mai da l'ospizio
> di Cesare non torse li occhi putti,
> morte comune e de le corti vizio,
> infiammò contra me li animi tutti;
> e li 'nfiammati infiammar sì Augusto,
> che ' lieti onor tornaro in tristi lutti.[12]

veritatem, vel odire Deum, quam non sperare consequi gloriam ab ipso. Sed si comparetur desperatio ad alia duo peccata ex parte nostra, sic desperatio est periculosior, quia per spem revocamur a malis et introducimur in bona prosequenda; et ideo, sublata spe, irrefrenate homines labuntur in vitia, et a bonis laboribus retrahuntur. Unde super illud Proverb. XXIV, "si desperaveris lapsus in die angustiae, minuetur fortitudo tua" dicit Glossa, nihil est execrabilius desperatione, quam qui habet et in generalibus huius vitae laboribus, et, quod peius est, in fidei certamine constantiam perdit'. Et Isidorus dicit, "in libro de summo bono, perpetrare flagitium aliquod mors animae est, sed desperare est descendere in Infernum".' Rarely, however, do the old theologians approach either the substance or intensity of Dante's sense of despair as inauthentic drivenness, as obsessive recourse to the self-consciously inauthentic solution, though Augustine comes close to it when he speaks of desperation as perseverance in impiety: 'in peccatis suis desperata atque impia mentis obstinatione perserverantibus' (*Exp. inc. ep. ad Rom.*); or as the 'piling up' of transgressions: 'et ex ipsa desperatione delicta cumulantes' (*En. in psalm.* cxliv.24; v. 20), etc.

[11] Then I stretched my hand a little forward and plucked a twig from a great thornbush, and its stub cried, "Why do you break me?" And when it had become dark with blood, it began to cry, "Why do you tear me? Have you no spirit of piety? We were men, and now are turned to stocks. Truly your hand ought to be more merciful had we been souls of serpents".

[12] The harlot that never turned her whorish eyes from Caesar's household – the common death and vice of courts – inflamed all minds against me; and they, inflamed, did so inflame Augustus that my glad honours were changed to dismal woes.

Here again, however, Dante intervenes to banish the mists of illusion and of self-deception in favour of an act of self-recognition, of the kind of clear-sightedness which, captive for the most part to mere strategy and to the bad faith thereof, rises up in the critical instant to confront the individual with the truth of what he actually is as an agent of radical undoing – a situation confirmed at the level of style by the tortured substance of sound and syntax:

> L'animo mio, per disdegnoso gusto,
> credendo col morir fuggir disdegno,
> ingiusto fece me contra me giusto.
>
> (*Inf.* XIII.70-71)[13]

Survival at this depth being out of the question, the soul straightaway surfaces to take up the routine psalmody of self-recommendation (the 'Per le nove radici d'esto legno / vi giuro che già mai non ruppi fede / al mio segnor, che fu d'onor sì degno' of lines 73-75),[14] this being the way in hell of pseudo-sanity, of affirming self in the unaffirmability of self. But as Pier della Vigna knows full well (for this is what it means to be in hell) the routine is just that – a routine – the whole thing, therefore, functioning as but a further co-efficient of despair.

As a third and for the moment final instance of this sense in Dante of the ἔσχατος as a matter less of the forthcoming than of the indwelling we may take the case of Guido da Montefeltro in Canto XXVII of the *Inferno*, where again it is a question of Dante's gradually constraining the speaker, and thus by extension the reader, to the truth of his existence as inwardly abiding and thus as forever rising up after the manner of the Leviathan to tax him in conscience. First, then, comes the familiar moment of exoneration, the moment designed to save the subject from the pain and perplexity of self-acknowledgement:

> Io fui uom d'arme, e poi fui cordigliero,
> credendomi, sì cinto, fare ammenda;
> e certo il creder mio venìa intero,
>   se non fosse il gran prete, a cui mal prenda!,
> che mi rimise ne le prime colpe;
> e come e quare, voglio che m'intenda.

---

[13] My mind, in scornful temper, thinking by dying to escape from scorn, made me unjust against my just self. S. Vazzana, 'Il "disdegnoso gusto" di Pier de le Vigne', *L'Alighieri*, n.s. 39, 11 (1998), 91-94.

[14] By the new roots of this tree I swear to you that I never broke faith with my lord, who was so worthy of honour.

> Mentre ch'io forma fui d'ossa e di polpe
> che la madre mi diè, l'opere mie
> non furon leonine, ma di volpe.
>   Li accorgimenti e le coperte vie
> io seppi tutte, e sì menai lor arte,
> chal fine de la terra il suono uscie.
>   Quando mi vidi giunto in quella parte
> di mia etade ove ciascun dovrebbe
> calar le vele e raccoglier le sarte,
>   ciò che pria mi piacëa, allor m'increbbe,
> e pentuto e confesso mi rendei;
> ahi miser lasso! e giovato sarebbe.
>
> (*Inf.* XXVII.67-84)[15]

But then, and again in a manner decisive for any exact understanding of what is going on in the *Inferno*, of Dante's sense of reprobation as a matter of recognition, comes the change of direction, the constraining of the horizontal to the vertical as the axis of ontological intelligence. Impressed, therefore, by the inadequacy of every strategy of the spirit to the business in hand and constrained to what comes next by a sort of grim inevitability, the soul once more settles on the moment of its delivery, on the moment in which, despite every inclination to the contrary (for the inauthentic choice in hell is inauthentic only in the degree to which it is irradiated by a sense of authentic possibility, by a commitment at some level of consciousness to the *what might be* of historical selfhood), it opted and opts still for its annihilation, for its ceasing *to be* in any recognizably human sense of the term:

> Ma come Costantin chiese Silvestro
> d'entro Siratti a guerir de la lebbre,
> così mi chiese questi per maestro
>   a guerir de la sua superba febbre;
> domandommi consiglio, e io tacetti
> perché le sue parole parver ebbre.

---

[15] I was a man of arms and then a corded friar, trusting, so girt, to make amends; and certainly my hope would have come full, but for the high priest – may ill befall him! – who set me back in my first sins; and how and wherefore I would have you hear from me. While I was the form of the flesh and bones my mother gave me, my deeds were not those of the lion, but of the fox. I knew all wiles and covert ways, and plied the art of them so well that to the ends of the earth their sound went forth. When I saw myself come to that part of my life when every man should lower the sails and coil up the ropes, that which before had pleased me grieved me then, and with repentance and confession I turned friar, and – woe is me! – it would have availed.

> E' poi ridisse: "Tuo cuor non sospetti;
> finor t'assolvo, e tu m'insegna fare
> sì come Penestrino in terra getti.
>   Lo ciel poss'io serrare e diserrare,
> come tu sai; però son due le chiavi
> che 'l mio antecessor non ebbe care".
>   Allor mi pinser li argomenti gravi
> là 've 'l tacer mi fu avviso 'l peggio,
> e dissi: "Padre, da che tu mi lavi
>   di quel peccato ov'io mo cader deggio,
> lunga promessa con l'attender corto
> ti farà triunfar ne l'alto seggio".
>
> (*Inf.* XXVII.94-111)[16]

True, with Francis and the pantomimics of the dark angel we are once again on the plane of the horizontal, of the *what happens next* of being under the aspect of eventuality.[17] But the *what happens next* of being under the aspect of eventuality is a function in the *Commedia* of the *what already*

---

[16] But as Constantine sought out Sylvester within Soracte to cure his leprosy, so this one sought me out as the doctor to cure the fever of his pride. He asked counsel of me, and I kept silent, for his words seemed drunken. Then he spoke again, "Let not your heart mistrust. I absolve you here and now, and do you teach me how I may cast Penestrino to the ground. I can lock and unlock heaven, as you know; for which the keys are two, which my predecessor did not hold dear". Thereon the weighty arguments pushed me to where silence seemed to me the worst, and I said, "Father, since you do wash me of that sin into which I must now fall, long promise with short keeping will make you triumph on the high seat".

[17] On the notion of *ius diaboli*, of the devil's right to the body in its sinfulness, Augustine, *Contra sec. Iul. resp.imper. opus* ii.24: 'Necessario quippe sequitur, quia per commixtionem corporum origo progenitis est, si per originem malum in hominibus, per malum ius diaboli in homines, diabolum esse auctorem hominum, a quo est origo nascentium'; *De nupt. et concup.* II.xxvii.44, etc., and also in both Gregory the Great and Bede. See too, however, and in a manner possibly decisive for Dante, Anselm in the *Cur Deus homo* at I.vii: 'Sed et illud quod dicere solemus, Deum scilicet, debuisse prius per justitiam contra diabolum agere, ut liberaret hominem, quam per fortitudinem; ut, cum diabolus eum, in quo nulla mortis erat causa, et qui Deus erat, occideret, juste potestatem, quam super peccatores habebat, amitteret; alioquin injustam violentiam fecisset illi, quoniam juste possidebat hominem, quem non ipse violenter attraxerat, sed idem homo se sponte ad illum contulerat, non video quam vim habeat', with this later in the same chapter: 'Et puto illos, qui diabolum aliquam opinantur habere in possidendo homine justitiam, ad hoc inde adduci, quia vident hominem diaboli vexationi subjacere juste, et Deum hoc juste permittere: et idcirco putant diabolum illam juste inferre'. Otherwise, Jude 9: 'Cum Michael Archangelus cum diabolo disputans altercaretur de Moysi corpore, non est ausus iudicium inferre blasphemiae: sed dixit: Imperet tibi dominus'. A. McGrath, *Iustitia Dei. A History of the Christian Doctrine of Justification: The Beginnings to the Reformation* (Cambridge: Cambridge University Press, 1986), pp. 58 ff.

is of that being, the eventual, in respect of the existential, constituting but a marker, a place-holder, a means of accessibility in respect of its otherwise dark substance. Never, in other words, is the ἔσχατος present to the individual as a matter merely of denouement or of foreclosure. On the contrary, it subsists as the 'infinitely contentful' character of the moment, as that whereby, in and through a turning back of self upon the instant as apt both to signify and to signify ultimately, he is once again summoned into his own presence in the unnegotiability of that presence.

3. One of the remarkable things about the *Commedia*, or, more exactly, about Dante's cast of characters in the *Commedia*, is their continuing preoccupation with the past, with the situation which, though now behind them, continues to fill them with misgiving; so, for example, as bearing on the city as the first of the three great medieval estates, and on this as a cause for melancholy, these lines (97-111) from *Paradiso* XV:

> Fiorenza dentro da la cerchia antica,
> ond' ella toglie ancora e terza e nona,
> si stava in pace, sobria e pudica.
>   Non avea catenella, non corona,
> non gonne contigiate, non cintura
> che fosse a veder più che la persona.
>   Non faceva, nascendo, ancor paura
> la figlia al padre, che 'l tempo e la dote
> non fuggien quinci e quindi la misura.
>   Non avea case di famiglia vòte;
> non v'era giunto ancor Sardanapalo
> a mostrar ciò che 'n camera si puote.
>   Non era vinto ancora Montemalo
> dal vostro Uccellatoio, che, com' è vinto
> nel montar sù, così sarà nel calo.[18]

while as bearing on the empire as the second of them, these (lines 85-97) from *Purgatorio* XVI:

> Esce di mano a lui che la vagheggia
> prima che sia, a guisa di fanciulla

---

[18] Florence, within her ancient circle from which she still takes the tierce and nones, abode in peace, sober and chaste. There was no necklace, no coronal, no embroidered gowns, no girdle that was more to be looked at than the person. Not yet did the daughter at her birth cause fear for the father, for the time and the dowry did not outrun due measure on this side and that. Houses empty of family there were none, nor had Sardanapalus arrived yet to show what could be done in the chamber. Not yet was Montemalo surpassed by your Uccellatoio, which, as it had been passed in the uprising, so shall it be in the fall.

> che piangendo e ridendo pargoleggia,
>   l'anima semplicetta che sa nulla,
> salvo che, mossa da lieto fattore,
> volontier torna a ciò che la trastulla.
>   Di picciol bene in pria sente sapore;
> quivi s'inganna, e dietro ad esso corre,
> se guida o fren non torce suo amore.
>   Onde convenne legge per fren porre;
> convenne rege aver, che discernesse
> de la vera cittade almen la torre.
>   Le leggi son, ma chi pon mano ad esse?[19]

and on the Church as the third of them, these (lines 40-57) from *Paradiso* XXVII:

> Non fu la sposa di Cristo allevata
> del sangue mio, di Lin, di quel di Cleto,
> per essere ad acquisto d'oro usata;
>   ma per acquisto d'esto viver lieto
> e Sisto e Pïo e Calisto e Urbano
> sparser lo sangue dopo molto fleto.
>   Non fu nostra intenzion ch'a destra mano
> d'i nostri successor parte sedesse,
> parte da l'altra del popol cristiano;
>   né che le chiavi che mi fuor concesse,
> divenisser signaculo in vessillo
> che contra battezzati combattesse;
>   né ch'io fossi figura di sigillo
> a privilegi venduti e mendaci,
> ond' io sovente arrosso e disfavillo.
>   In vesta di pastor lupi rapaci
> si veggion di qua sù per tutti i paschi:
> o difesa di Dio, perché pur giaci?[20]

---

[19] From his hands, who fondly loves it before it exists, comes forth after the fashion of a child that sports, now weeping, now laughing, the little simple soul, which knows nothing, save that, proceeding from a glad maker, it turns eagerly to what delights it. First it tastes the savour of a trifling good; there it is beguiled and runs after it, if guide or curb bend not its love. Wherefore it was needful to impose law as a bridle, it was needful to have a ruler who could discern at least the tower of the true city. Laws there are, but who puts his hand to them?

[20] The spouse of Christ was not nurtured on my blood and that of Linus and of Cletus, to be employed for gain of gold; but for gain of this happy life Sixtus and Pius and Calixtus and Urban shed their blood after much weeping. It was not our purpose that one part of the Christian people should sit on the right of our successors, and one part on the left, nor that the keys which were committed to me should become the ensign on

At every point the pattern is the same, the soul in its election living out still the agony of the historical instant, the blasphemous substance of what was and still is under the conditions of time and space. How are we to account for this situation? By way (*a*) of an anthropology and ethic committed as of the essence to the intrinsic dignity of the human project in its power to moral and ontological self-implementation; (*b*) of a secure sense of history as the whereabouts of that self-implementation, and (*c*) of total seriousness on both counts. And with this we are back to our main theme, for in the degree to which Dante takes seriously the greatness and the locatedness of the human project he is committed willy nilly to an immanent eschatology, to an eschatology which, though by no means indifferent to its expectational aspect, turns upon the historical instant and the 'contentfulness' thereof as the whereabouts of ultimate self-interpretation. Its expectational aspect, everywhere dominant as a paradigm of consciousness, is in this sense but the forward projection of something more dreadful, of an immanent absolute empowered from within to devastate the spirit.

a banner of warfare on the baptized; nor that I should be made a figure on a seal to sold and lying privileges, whereat I often blush and flash. Rapacious wolves, in shepherd's garb, are seen from here above in all the pastures. O defence of God, wherefore does thou still lie still?

Two Dantes or One? An Essay in Transcendence and Theatricality

Dante was attached, simultaneously, to Christianity and to paganism. This was not a half-way position, nor a wavering between two conceptions of life according to mood or circumstance. The attachment to paganism was more like that which a man may feel to his youth, except that paganism was a stage in the history of Dante's race, not of himself individually. Yet there is a sense in which the pagan 'object' of his attachment was not something past and done with, existing only in history or legend or works of art; rather it was a permanent part of himself, an *alter ego*; it was that second self which his imagination took into the Other World in the form of Virgil and which, once it had assumed this form, was allowed to take charge of, to guide and govern the Christian protagonist of the resulting poem.[1]

1. Introduction: *ego, alter ego* and the problem of authorial intentionality – a preliminary response. 2. Piety, Peripateticism and sin as unreason: 'The Theology of the *Inferno*'. 3. Irreconcilability in the depths: 'The Two Dantes'. 4. Two Dantes or one?: dimensionality, decorum and the comprehensive geometry of the text.

Kenelm Foster's tripartite essay on the two Dantes, published in 1977, represents a point of arrival in respect of a lifelong meditation on the issues it raises, on, as he himself saw it, the co-presence in Dante of orders of philosophical and theological concern never quite reconciled

---

[1] Kenelm Foster, O.P., 'The Two Dantes (I)', in *The Two Dantes* (London: Darton, Longman and Todd, 1977), p. 156.

one with the other or brought home to a unified and internally consistent spirituality. Encouraged as he was by the massive and massively erudite initiative of Bruno Nardi and of Etienne Gilson, responsible between them for rescuing Dante from those who would see in him a more or less fully professed Thomist,[2] and coming to Dante as he did from the point of view of one committed by profession to the Thomist way in philosophy and theology, he was more than ordinarily sensitive to what in Dante amounts to the difficulty of his particular kind of bi-culturalism, to his living out at one and the same time the exigencies both of a Christian and a Peripateticizing conscience. But for all his insight and tact in seeing and setting up the question, Kenelm's sense of the alterity of it all – certainly if by this we mean the survival into the *Commedia* of distinct and mutually irreducible egos, of a Christian and of a pagan ego – is open to question; for decisive as the idea is for the moments of Dante's meditation represented by the *Convivio* and the *Monarchia* as committed to the resolution of high-level issues in the areas of moral philosophy and of political theology, there are forces at work in the *Commedia* tending to soften and ultimately to liquidate the kind of alternativism which Kenelm Foster sees as a dominant feature even here of Dantean spirituality. On the one hand, then, there are the *theological* forces whereby each successive emphasis in the areas both of moral and of natural philosophy is rendered transparent to the innermost reasons of the text as a product of Christian piety, while on the other hand there are the *theatrical* forces whereby those same emphases, distributed among the poem's players such that each only ever speaks in character, serve merely to confirm its consistency

---

[2] Kenelm on Nardi and Gilson, on Dante and Thomism, and on his own sense of the 'humanistic' problem in Dante: 'This question of the continuity of the *Comedy* with the minor works was a good deal debated by Dante scholars in the 1940s and '50s. As I had occasion to write some years ago and feel able to repeat today, "after Nardi's and Gilson's work in the 1930s it had become evident that Dante could no longer be called a Thomist without very considerable qualifications; and in particular that the *Convivio* and the *Monarchia* show clear traces of a certain dualism – in assertions, more or less explicit, of the independence of philosophy from theology and of the civil power from the Church, and of the twofold 'final end' of man ... The question then arose whether this dualism persisted into the *Comedy*, and if so precisely to what effect; the result being ... to concentrate attention on the contrasted symbols of Virgil and Beatrice, and more generally to raise the issue of the 'humanism' or otherwise of the *Comedy*". This was written when I was still inclined to date the *Monarchia* before the *Comedy*: yet I would still maintain that there is a fundamental difference ... between the *Comedy* and the two other works taken together. This seems to me clear even supposing that the *Monarchia* belongs to the last decade of the poet's life and that *doctrinally* there is agreement between it and the *Comedy* where both works touch on the same themes'. (ibid., pp. 163-64; the reference here is to his piece entitled 'Dante Studies in England, 1921-64', *Italian Studies* 20 (1965), 7).

at the level of authorial intentionality. Now Kenelm, whose inclination was always to turn back upon the leading proposition with a view to its further refinement, would himself have gone along with this, for his too was a sense both of the maturity of the *Commedia* in its bringing home of each subsequent inflexion of the spirit to its depth-dimensionality and of its decorum, its proportioning of each subsequent intervention in the text to the properties of personality. But this, when it comes to the valedictory statement, is not what he chooses to emphasize. Rather, it is a question as far as the *Commedia* is concerned of irresolution and of the melancholy thereof, of a work which, for all its perspectivization both of the moral and the political issues upon which it touches, remains less than equal to the restiveness of its cultural premises.

2. One of Kenelm's earliest accounts of the rationalist or (as he himself used to say) the 'humanistic' component of Dante's thought tending even in the *Commedia* to subsist over against its theological component comes in his essay 'The Theology of the *Inferno*' published in 1957 as part of the volume entitled *God's Tree: Essays in Dante and Other Matters*, an initiative predating the *Two Dantes*, therefore, by twenty years.[3] Setting out to explore the theological programme of the *Inferno*, but also to call into question its status as a stable expression of the Catholic mind, the essay begins by noting that Dante's genius in the *Commedia* can be admired in the wrong way; for Dante, Kenelm maintains, was not really a theologian at all. Enamoured as he was of theology, and given to searching her somewhat after the manner of a lover, he was first and foremost a maker of images, his, therefore, as far as theology is concerned, being something closer to 'usage' – Gilson's 'usage défini' – than to anything more professional or systematic:

> Again, his great intellect can be admired in the wrong way: Dante did not put the *Summa theologiae* into verse, for he could not possibly have put it into prose. The epitaph composed by Giovanni di Virgilio, "Theologus Dantes" etc., cannot, as M. Gilson has said, be taken *à la lettre*. It might be less misleading to deny that Dante was a theologian; it is safer to call him a magnificent amateur. Essentially he was a poet, a maker of images, using doctrine poetically, searching it as a lover. His speculative enthusiasm was superbly pure and strong, but it ran in certain directions. So Dante's teaching remains a selection, as it were, within the doctrinal materials at his disposal. Of these, as Gilson says, he made a certain *usage défini*. (pages 50-51)

---

[3] *God's Tree. Essays on Dante and Other Matters* (London: Blackfriars Publications, 1957), with 'The Theology of the *Inferno*' at pp. 50-66.

The passage is problematic. It is problematic in respect (*a*) of the 'for he could not possibly have put it into prose' formula with which it begins (for it is a question here, not of power, but of preference, not of Dante's being unable to pursue the theological project in the way Thomas had, but of his not wishing to), and (*b*) of its sense of Dante as but a 'magnificent amateur' in theology, a way of putting it which, whether or not acceptable at the time of *God's Tree*, smacks nowadays of a certain cultural 'incorrectness', a certain lack of tact when it comes to our now revised sense of poetry and the theological project.[4] True, Dante was no Thomas, the *Commedia* lacking the power of the great *summae* to systematic awareness, to an orderly statement of the theological situation in its totality. But by the same token Thomas was no Dante, the great *summae* lacking the power of the *Commedia* to engender a sense of the ontological agony and ecstasy of it all, to take us into 'the deepest places of human self-destruction and despair as well as the highest places of courage and salvation',[5] at which point 'magnificent amateurism' as a way of describing Dante's intervention commends itself only for its inadequacy to the business in hand. Be that as it may, however, the way is now open, Kenelm thinks, for a critique of his sense of moral evil in the *Inferno*; for Dante's, he says, was everywhere a tendency, and a none too healthy one at that, to rely on reason alone as the way of getting to grips with this issue:

> This need for clear knowledge was of course innate in Dante; but it was also in this case in line with his principles. He thought that he could pretty thoroughly know evil, and this in virtue of his human reason alone – aided of course by Aristotle's. The mind of Aristotle, indeed, had explored most of the manifestations of human vice. In Dante's view (it seems) the *Inferno*, considered simply as a lecture on human depravity, did not say very much more than the *Nicomachean Ethics*. He does not seem perhaps to have very keenly appreciated the enormous difference that Christianity had in fact made: he sees his *Inferno* mainly as an outline of human evil drawn by human wit. Unlike the *Paradiso* it contains, as he presents it, little that cannot be understood. It unveils iniquity. (p.51)

Evil, then, as envisaged by Dante in the *Inferno*, appears to be no more than an affront to right reason, to the customary co-ordinates of Peripatetic consciousness, with the result, Kenelm goes on, that the

---

[4] Recently on the relationship in Dante of the idea and the image, F. Livi, *Dante e la teologia. L'immaginazione poetica nella 'Divina Commedia' come interpretazione del dogma*, (Rome: Casa Editrice Leonardo da Vinci, 2008); V. Montemaggi and M. Treherne (eds), *Dante's 'Commedia'. Theology as Poetry* (Notre Dame, Ind.: University of Notre Dame Press, 2010).

[5] Paul Tillich, *The Courage To Be* (Collins: Glasgow, 1962; originally 1952), p. 128.

sinners in Dante's hell 'would be sinners in any world that is human at all':

> For my present purpose, however, the chief interest of Limbo is that it points to the very natural or rational character of the *Inferno* as a whole. For, as a vice is understood in terms of the contrary virtue, so it is the virtue of the great pagans in Dante's Limbo which implicitly (though I do not say the poet intended this) sets the standard by which most of the other inhabitants of Hell have failed to live, and, failing, have incurred damnation. I say 'most' of these, because the Heretics and Simonists, at least, are exceptions; they are Christian sinners, in the sense that their sins presuppose a Christian world. But most of the damned appear to have sinned against the norm of reason, the *regula rationis*, rather than against that *regula divinae legis* which St Thomas distinguished from it. They would be sinners in any world that is human at all. (p.54)

Again, the passage, is problematic, for quite apart from the propriety of – at any rate without ado – talking about 'sin' in anything other than a specifically Christian context, the question arises as to how far it can be thought of as a matter merely of irrationality or of unreasonableness. Irrationality and unreasonableness enter into it, but the term 'sin' connotes something both more and other than this, something closer to dividedness, and thus to Godlessness, at the point of willing, by which stage Aristotle and the *Ethics* have been left far behind. And this, as his essay goes on, is Kenelm's own sense of it, evil, he says, amounting to nothing but ingratitude in respect of the goodness which is God:

> Love then is the reflection in creatures of the divine Unity and also the response to the divine Goodness reflected in creatures. The same God is reflected, from our point of view, twice over; and the one reflection (that of Unity) appears as tending to the other (that of Goodness). And since it is one God who is twice reflected, these two reflections – love derived from Unity and goodness derived from the Good – are ultimately the same; and it will be equally true to say that love pursues goodness and goodness pursues love: in short, that love loves love. That is why, in the last resort, the violation of goodness (i.e. evil) is the refusal of a lover, is *ingratitude*.' (p.62; italics original).

This notwithstanding, however, his even so remains a 'humanistic' account of what is going on in the *Inferno*, an account turning less on the notion of dividedness in the depths than on that of unreason on the surface, at which point the tragedy of it all – the tragedy of unreason as but a consequence of man's first disobedience – disappears from view.

3. This, then, is where Kenelm begins in the 'The Two Dantes' essays of 1977, his sense of the intractability of it all, of Dante's entertaining in one and the same moment both the pagan and the pious, having if anything sharpened in the meantime. The opening sequence of the first essay, unsurpassed in the Dante literature of the English-speaking world for its quiet combination of tact and precision, sets up the question. Dante's, Kenelm says, was a living-out in his own person of the great phases of world history, his capacity for rejoicing in its successive moments, however, issuing in a spirituality never wholly at one with itself, never wholly settled in point of root intentionality. Reproduced in part at the head of this essay, the passage in question is worth reading over in full:

> Dante was attached, simultaneously, to Christianity and to paganism. This was not a half-way position, nor a wavering between two conceptions of life according to mood or circumstance. The attachment to paganism was more like that which a man may feel to his youth, except that paganism was a stage in the history of Dante's race, not of himself individually. Yet there is a sense in which the pagan 'object' of his attachment was not something past and done with, existing only in history or legend or works of art; rather it was a permanent part of himself, an *alter ego*; it was that second self which his imagination took into the Other World in the form of Virgil and which, once it had assumed this form, was allowed to take charge of, to guide and govern the Christian protagonist of the resulting poem. Because the hero of the *Divine Comedy* is a Christian the poem is Christian, but through two-thirds of it the hero is guided by a pagan. And even 'guided' is too weak a term; Virgil in the poem is the hero's 'leader', 'master', 'teacher', 'lord'. Above all he is Dante's 'father' – 'my sweet father', 'sweet and dear father', 'my more than father'. Seldom in literature has the filial sentiment, blending reverence and affection, been so finely expressed as in this relationship which carries the central narrative line through so much of the great poem. And it is of its essence that the father here is a pagan, the son a Christian; simultaneously so close and so separated. (page 156)

Wedded in one and the same moment both to Christianity and to paganism, the latter subsisting as an *alter ego* or alternative presence in the world, Dante's was a simultaneous commitment (*a*) to the need for grace as that whereby man as man comes home to God as the beginning and end of his happiness, and (*b*) to the possibility even so of his affirming himself, albeit within certain clearly defined limits, by way of the ordinary processes of seeing, understanding and choosing, each of these things, however, – the grace-theological and the moral-philosophical – forever vying one with the other and seeking the upper hand. At once a principle and a product of this situation, Kenelm thinks, is his treatment of the noble pagans of antiquity, of those who, knowing not the Christ, are nonetheless confirmed in a state, not of atrocious, but of attenuated suffering, in the melancholy of unfulfilled because unfulfillable yearning.[6] How, then, are

[6] In addition to the commentaries on *Inferno* IV and on the Dantean limbo, C. Grabher, 'Il Limbo dantesco e il nobile castello', *Studi danteschi* 29 (1950), 41-60; A. Camilli, 'La teologia del Limbo dantesco', *Studi danteschi* 30 (1951), 209-14; F. Montanari, ad voc. 'Limbo', in the *Enciclopedia dantesca*, 6 vols (Rome: Istituto della Enciclopedia Italiana, 1970-78), vol. 3, pp. 651-54; F. Forti, 'Il Limbo e i Megalopsicoi della "Nicomachea"', in *Magnanimitade. Studi su un tema dantesco* (Bologna, Pàtron, 1977), pp. 9-48; G. Padoan, 'Il Limbo dantesco', in *Il pio Enea, l'empio Ulisse: Tradizione classica e intendimento medievale in Dante* (Ravenna: Longo, 1977), pp. 103-24 (originally in *Lettere Italiane* 21 (1969), 4, 369-88); A. A. Iannucci, 'Limbo: the Emptiness of Time', *Studi Danteschi* 52 (1979-80), 69-128; idem, 'Il limbo dei bambini', in *Sotto il segno di Dante. Scritti in onore di Francesco Mazzoni*, ed. L. Coglievina and D. De Robertis (Florence: Le Lettere, 1998), pp. 153-164; idem, 'Dante's Limbo: at the Margins of Orthodoxy', in *Dante and the Unorthodox: The Aesthetics of Transgression*, ed. by J. L. Miller (Waterloo (Ontario-Canada): Wilfrid Laurier University Press, 2005), pp. 63-82; F. Giardinazzo, 'La passione dell'intelligenza nel limbo dantesco', in *Cercare il volume. Studi danteschi* (Rimini: Guaraldi,1998), pp. 89-112; M. P. Stocchi, 'Canto IV. A Melancholy Elysium', in *Lectura Dantis. Inferno. A Canto-by-Canto Commentary*, ed. by A. Mandelbaum et al. (Berkeley: University of California Press, 1998), pp. 50-62; F. Tateo, 'Figure della didattica e canoni della cultura antica nel limbo dantesco', in *Studi sulla tradizione classica per Mariella Cagnetta*, ed. L. Canfora (Rome and Bari: Laterza, 1999), pp. 507-24 (subsequently 'Gli antichi a confronto (*If.* IV)' in *Simmetrie dantesche* (Bari: Palomar, 2001), pp. 13-34); G. C. Alessio, 'Il canto IV dell' Inferno', in *Regnum celorum violenza pate. Dante e la salvezza dell'umanità. Letture Dantesche Giubilari, Vicenza, October 1999 - June 2000*, ed. G. Cannavò (Montella, Avellino: Accademia Vivarium Novum, 2002), pp. 37-56. On Dante and pagan salvation, F. Ruffini, 'Dante e il problema della salvezza degli infedeli', *Studi danteschi* 14 (1930), 79-92; B. Quilici, *Il destino dell'infidele virtuoso nel pensiero di Dante* (Florence: Ariani, 1936); G. Busnelli, 'La colpa del "non fare" degl'infedeli negativi', *Studi danteschi* 23 (1938), 79-97; C. Filosa, 'La "virtù" dei romani nel giudizio di S. Agostino e di Dante', in *Atti del congresso internazionale di Studi Danteschi, Roma 8-10 aprile 1965* (Florence: Le Monnier, 1965), pp. 195-210; G. Rizzo, 'Dante and the Virtuous Pagans', in W. De Sua and G. Rizzo (eds), *A Dante Symposium in Commemoration of the 700th Anniversary of the Poet's Birth (1265-1321)* (Chapel Hill: University of North Carolina Press, 1965), pp. 115-40; G. Cambon, 'Dante's Noble Sinners: Abstract Examples or Living Characters?', in *Dante's Craft. Studies in Language and Style* (Minneapolis: University of Minnesota Press, 1969), pp. 67-79; T. O'H. Hahn, 'I "gentili" e "un uom nasce a la riva / de l'Indo" (*Par.* XIX, vv.70 sqq.)', *L'Alighieri. Rassegna bibliografica dantesca* 18 (1977), 2, 3-8; D. Thomson, 'Dante's Virtuous Romans', *Dante Studies* 96 (1978), 145-62; R. Morghen, 'Dante tra l'"umano" e la storia della salvezza', in *L'Alighieri. Rassegna bibliografica dantesca* 21 (1980), 1, 18-30; N. Iliescu, 'Will Virgil be saved?', *Mediaevalia* 12 (1986), 93-114 and as 'Sarà salvo Virgilio?' in *Dante. Summa medievalis. Proceedings of the Symposium of the Center for Italian Studies, SUNY Stony Brook*, ed. by C. Franco and L. Morgan (Stony Brook (N.Y.): Forum Italicum, 1995), pp. 112-33; M. Allan, 'Does Dante hope for Vergil's Salvation?', *Modern Language Notes* 104 (1989), 1, 193-205; M. Picone, 'La "viva speranza" di Dante e il problema della salvezza dei pagani virtuosi. Una lettura di *Paradiso* 20', *Quaderni di Italianistica* 10

we to account for this situation? Can it be a question, Kenelm wonders, of implicit faith, of the kind of faith which, lacking any specifically Christian content, is nonetheless sustained by a sense of the providentiality of it all and of what this might mean by way of a presiding deity?[7] No, he says,

(1989), 1-2, 251-68; idem, '*Auctoritas* classica e salvezza cristiana: una lettura tipologica di *Purgatorio* XXII', in *Studi in memoria di Giorgio Varanini* (Pisa: Giardini, 1992), vol. I (*Dal Duecento al Quattrocento*), pp. 379-95; T. Barolini, 'Q: Does Dante hope for Vergil's Salvation?', *Modern Language Notes* 105 (1990), 138-44 and 147-49 (subsequently in *Dante and the Origins of Italian Literary Culture* (New York: Fordham University Press, 2006), pp. 151-57); G. Cremascoli, 'Paganesimo e mondo cristiano nel commento a Dante di Benvenuto da Imola', in P. Palmieri and C. Paolazzi, *Benvenuto da Imola, lettore degli antichi e dei moderni* (Ravenna: Longo, 1991), pp. 111-25; B. D. Schildgen, 'Dante and the Indus', *Dante Studies* 111 (1993), 177-93; eadem, 'Dante's Utopian Political Vision, the Roman Empire, and the Salvation of Pagans', *Annali d'Italianistica* 19 (2001), 51-69; G. Muresu, 'Le "vie" della redenzione (*Paradiso* VII)', *Rassegna della letteratura italiana* 98 (1994), 1-2, 5-19 (and in *Il richiamo dell'antica strega. Altri saggi di semantica dantesca* (Roma: Bulzoni, 1997), pp. 203-24; M. L. Colish, 'The Virtuous Pagan. Dante and Christian Tradition', in W. Caferro and D. G. Fisher (eds), *The Unbounded Community. Papers in Christian Ecumenism in Honor of Jaroslov Pelikan* (New York: Garland, 1996), pp. 43-91 (and in *The Fathers and Beyond. Church Fathers between Ancient and Medieval Thought* (Aldershot: Ashgate, 2008), pp. 1-40); P. Boitani, 'Cristianesimo e tradizione pagana', in *Lo spazio letterario del Medioevo* (Rome: Salerno, 1999-2005), vol. 2 (*Il Medioevo volgare*), pp. 181-204 (subsequently as 'Tradizione classica e tradizione cristiana', in *Letteratura europea e medioevo volgare* (Bologna: Il Mulino, 2007), pp. 21-43); N. Cacciaglia, '"Per fede e per opere" (una lettura del tema della salvezza nella *Divina Commedia*)', in *Critica Letteraria* 30 (2002), 2-3, 265-274 (also in *Annali dell'Università per Stranieri di Perugia* 29 (2002), 123-131); G. Cannavò (ed.), *Regnum celorum vïolenza pate. Dante e la salvezza dell'umanità. Letture Dantesche Giubilari, Vicenza, October 1999 - June 2000* (above), with A. M. Chiavacci Leonardi, 'La salvezza degli infedeli: il canto XX del *Paradiso*' at pp. 193-203; B. Martinelli, 'Canto XIX', in *Lectura Dantis Turicensis. Paradiso*, ed. G. Güntert and M. Picone (Florence: Cesati, 2002), pp. 281-305 (revised with the title 'La fede in Cristo. Dante e il problema della salvezza (*Paradiso* XIX)', *Rivista di Letteratura Italiana* 20 (2002), 2, 11-39 and in *Dante. L'"altro viaggio"* (Pisa: Giardini, 2007), pp. 289-319); G. Inglese, 'Il destino dei non credenti. Lettura di *Paradiso* XIX', *La Cultura. Rivista trimestrale di filosofia letteratura e storia* 42 (2004), 2, 315-29; A. Lanza, 'Giustizia divina e salvezza dei 'senza fede', in *Dante eterodosso* (Bergamo: Moretti Honegger, 2004), pp. 113-24; C. O'Connell Baur, *Dante's Hermeneutics of Salvation. Passages to Freedom in the 'Divine Comedy'* (Toronto, Buffalo and London: University of Toronto Press, 2007). More generally on the soteriological issue, M. Frezza, *Il problema della salvezza dei pagani da Abelardo al Seicento* (Naples: Fiorentino, 1962); R. V. Turner, '"Descendit ad Inferos". Medieval Views on Christ's Descent into Hell and the Salvation of the Ancient Just', *Journal of the History of Ideas* 27 (1966), 173-94.

[7] Thomas, *ST* at IIa IIae.2.7 ad 3: 'Ad tertium dicendum quod multis gentilium facta fuit revelatio de Christo, ut patet per ea quae praedixerunt. Nam Iob XIX dicitur, "scio quod redemptor meus vivit". Sibylla etiam praenuntiavit quaedam de Christo, ut Augustinus dicit. Invenitur etiam in historiis Romanorum quod tempore Constantini Augusti et Irenae matris eius inventum fuit quoddam sepulcrum in quo iacebat homo auream laminam habens in pectore in qua scriptum erat, "Christus nascetur ex virgine et credo in eum. O sol, sub Irenae et Constantini temporibus iterum me videbis". Si qui tamen

this will not do, for given the notion of implicit faith as a gift to theologians in moments such as this, Dante seems not to have heard of it:

> Now it had always been accepted in the Church that the Old Testament was the record of the first stage in God's self-revelation to mankind; and, by the same token, of a kind of inchoate faith in the Christ to come on the part of the pious Jews. And this reading of the Bible was expressed theologically by speaking of faith in Christ as passing through stages of gradually increasing explicitness. Foreshadowings of Christianity were also looked for in the records of paganism, though less seriously and systematically. Still, since Dante himself looked in that direction for 'prophecies' of Christ – taking the Sibylline oracles, for example, to be such, as so many medieval Christians did – one might expect to find some suggestion in the *Comedy* that pagans too might be saved by an implicit faith in Christ analogous to that of the Hebrew patriarchs and prophets. But it is hard to find even a hint of this. Indeed, apart from the Jewish heroes and heroines whom Virgil saw being led out of Limbo by Christ in person after his Passion, there seems to be no certain case of merely implicit faith in Christ in the whole *Comedy*. (p. 177)[8]

---

salvati fuerunt quibus revelatio non fuit facta, non fuerunt salvati absque fide mediatoris. Quia etsi non habuerunt fidem explicitam, habuerunt tamen fidem implicitam in divina providentia, credentes Deum esse liberatorem hominum secundum modos sibi placitos et secundum quod aliquibus veritatem cognoscentibus ipse revelasset, secundum illud Iob XXXV, "qui docet nos super iumenta terrae".' Thus with reference to Cornelius in Acts 10:4, ibid. IIa IIae.10.4 ad 3: 'Ad tertium dicendum quod per infidelitatem non corrumpitur totaliter in infidelibus ratio naturalis, quin remaneat in eis aliqua veri cognitio, per quam possunt facere aliquod opus de genere bonorum. De Cornelio tamen sciendum est quod infidelis non erat, alioquin eius operatio accepta non fuisset Deo, cui sine fide nullus potest placere. Habebat autem fidem implicitam, nondum manifestata Evangelii veritate. Unde ut eum in fide plene instrueret, mittitur ad eum Petrus.' William of Ockham, in the *Dialogus* (pt 1, bk 4, ch. 3), has: 'Hoc per exemplum de Cornelio centurione de quo habetur Actuum 10 c. patere videtur. Qui antequam de Christo fidem haberet explicitam fuit fidelis quia iustus et timens Deum et per consequens fidem habuit saltem implicitam. Et ita fides implicita sufficit ad hoc quod aliquis sit catholicus et fidelis', etc.

[8] See too p. 185: 'The conclusion then seems clear, that while Dante allows in principle for the salvation of pagans, he represents this, in his poem, as extremely exceptional; not necessarily so, perhaps, in respect of the *number* of pagans who might be saved, but certainly in respect of the *way* they may be saved. For this way must be by an explicit faith in Christ; which, in the two cases described by Dante, required the working of miracles. Thus the episode would seem to show that for Dante grace and the faith that lays hold of it was emphatically not available to all men through the ordinary workings of Providence; or at least it had nothing of that "normality" which we nowadays tend to attribute to it by extending to the utmost the concept of implicit faith. Medieval theology possessed this concept, but did little with it; Dante seems hardly aware of it.' G. Whatley, 'The Uses of Hagiography: the Legend of Pope Gregory and the Emperor Trajan in the Middle Ages', *Viator* 15 (1984), 25-63.

If not, then, of implicit faith, can it be a question of negative unbelief, of the kind of unbelief proper to those knowing no better? No, says Kenelm, neither will this do, Virgil, anxious as he is to confirm the collective innocence of the noble pagans (the 'ei non peccaro' of *Inf.* IV.34),[9] admitting as far as he personally is concerned to an element of recalcitrance, to his having rebelled against the law of God (the 'perch' i' fu' ribellante a la sua legge' of *Inf.* I.125). How, therefore, given the disqualification both of implicit faith and of negative unbelief as ways around the problem of pagan righteousness and reprobation, are we to account for Dante's position here, for his concern to separate out the noble spirits of antiquity and to make a special case of them? The answer, Kenelm thinks, lies deep within him, for piety, in Dante, is always challenged by paganism, by a counter-commitment to Aristotle – not Peter, Paul, Augustine, Bernard, Thomas or even Christ himself, but Aristotle – as spokesman for properly human happiness here and now; so, for example, to look back for a moment to the *Convivio*, these lines from Book IV (vi.7-16), secure in their sense of the *Ethics* as a point of arrival in the area of moral philosophy:

> Veramente Aristotile, che Stagirite ebbe sopranome, e Zenocrate Calcedonio, suo compagnone, [per lo studio loro], e per lo 'ngegno [eccellente] e quasi divino che la natura in Aristotile messo avea, questo fine conoscendo per lo modo socratico quasi e academico, limaro e a perfezione la filosofia morale redussero, e massimamente Aristotile. E però che Aristotile cominciò a disputare andando in qua e in lae, chiamati furono – lui, dico, e li suoi compagni – Peripatetici, che tanto vale quanto 'deambulatori'. E però che la perfezione di questa moralitade per Aristotile terminata fue, lo nome de li Academici si spense, e tutti quelli che a questa setta si presero Peripatetici sono chiamati; e tiene questa gente oggi lo reggimento del mondo in dottrina per tutte parti, e puotesi appellare quasi cattolica oppinione. Per che vedere si può, Aristotile essere additatore e conduttore de la gente a questo segno.
>
> (*Conv.* IV.vi.15-16)[10]

---

[9] [Now, before you go farther, I will have you know] that they did not sin. *Purg.* VII.7-9 and 25-36: '"Io son Virgilio; e per null' altro rio / lo ciel perdei che per non aver fé". / Così rispuose allora il duca mio. / ... / "Non per far, ma per non fare ho perduto / a veder l'alto Sol che tu disiri / e che fu tardi per me conosciuto. / Luogo è là giù non tristo di martìri, / ma di tenebre solo, ove i lamenti / non suonan come guai, ma son sospiri. / Quivi sto io coi pargoli innocenti / dai denti morsi de la morte avante / che fosser da l'umana colpa essenti; / quivi sto io con quei che le tre sante / virtù non si vestiro, e sanza vizio / conobber l'altre e seguir tutte quante"'.

[10] However, it was Aristotle (surnamed the Stagirite) and his noted companion Xenocrates of Chalecedon, who, thanks to the unique – one might say divine – intelligence

while as far as the *Commedia* is concerned, these from *Inferno* IV, no less complete in their commitment to the philosopher as the master of those who know and thus, once again, as the guide to a certain kind of properly human happiness:

> Poi ch'innalzai un poco più le ciglia,
> vidi 'l maestro di color che sanno
> seder tra filosofica famiglia.
>   Tutti lo miran, tutti onor li fanno:
> quivi vid' ïo Socrate e Platone,
> che 'nnanzi a li altri più presso li stanno.
>
> (*Inf.* IV.130-35)[11]

Now Thomas, Kenelm notes, is more circumspect, the *Ethics* for him pointing to a species of happiness, not sufficient unto itself and thus qualitatively distinct in respect of what comes next, but merely proportionate to our circumstances here and now. Not so, however, Dante, who, inclined as he was to read with a dash of enthusiasm, saw in it a recipe for perfect happiness – or for perfect happiness, at any rate, of a certain sort – this side of death. True, there is more to come, but what awaits us in the next life must be something other than what we have or can have in this life, something not merely *human* but *more than human* in kind – a notion which, taken up in the *Convivio* and the *Monarchia* for the purposes of resolving a set of 'high-level' concerns in the areas of moral philosophy and political theology, subsists both into the Dantean limbo and into the fabric generally of the first canticle of the *Commedia*. With this, then, we are home, Dante, even here, being captive to an antique but still powerfully insistent habit of mind. True, he is no Boethius of Dacia with, in the *De summo bono*, his state-of-the-art essay

---

with which nature had endowed Aristotle, refined moral philosophy and brought it to perfection through pursuing their study of this end by much the same method as Socrates and the Academics; in this, Aristotle played the major role. Since he began to hold public disputations during which he walked up and down, he and his companions were called Peripatetics, or 'people who walk around'. Since it was Aristotle who brought this doctrine to its final perfection, the name 'Academics' was eclipsed, and all who adhered to this school of thought were called Peripatetics. Today, the teaching of this group holds sway everywhere, and may almost be said to be the universal opinion. It is evident, therefore, that Aristotle has directed and led people to the goal we have been discussing. Cf. *Conv.* II.v.7: 'Queste oppinioni sono riprovate per false nel secondo De Celo et Mundo da quello glorioso filosofo al quale la natura più aperse li suoi segreti ...', etc.

[11] When I raised my eyes a little higher, I saw the Master of those who know, seated in a philosophic family. All look to him, all do him honour. There, nearest to him and in front of the rest, I saw Socrates and Plato.

on the Aristotelian 'model man'.¹² But neither is he a Thomas Aquinas, with, in the *Prima secundae*, his no less state-of-the-art meditation on the referability of each and every righteous inflexion of the spirit to a prior movement of grace as its point of departure;¹³ for Dante's, even into the

---

¹² p. 219, with, a little further down on that page: 'Now, probably neither of these texts I have glanced at – almost certainly not the *De Summo Bono* – would have met with Dante's entire approval; not even when writing the *Convivio*. But they are, I think, extremely indicative of a temper, an approach, a way of thinking about and formulating the situation of man on earth without which neither *Convivio* IV, nor *Monarchia* III.xv, nor the Dantean Limbo would in fact have been possible. What had emerged here and there in the West was the conception of a humanist ethic based more or less exclusively on the "natural order" – of an area of human activity that would be self-contained and autonomous; virtually independent of grace whether *elevans* or *sanans*. It was against just such a conception that the Augustinian Petrarch was later fiercely to react; but in the meantime it had deeply affected the Aristotelian Dante.' For the *De summo bono* of Boethius of Dacia, M. Grabmann, *Mittelalterlisches Geistesleben: Abhandlungen zur Geschichte der Scholastik und Mystik* (München: Hueber, 1936), vol. 2, pp. 200-24, and, for the *Quaestio de felicitate* of James of Pistoia, *Medioevo e Rinascimento. Studi in onore di B. Nardi* (Florence: Sansoni, 1955), vol. 2, pp. 427-63. E. Gilson, 'Boèce de Dacie et la double vérité', *Archives d'histoire doctrinale et littéraire du moyen âge* 22 (1955), 81-99, and on James of Pistoia, P. O. Kristeller, 'A Philosophical Treatise from Bologna dedicated to Guido Cavalcanti: Magister Jacobus de Pistorio and his "Questio de felicitate"', *Medioevo e Rinascimento* (above), vol. 1, pp. 425-63. More generally, M. Grabmann, 'L'aristotelismo italiano al tempo di Dante con particolare riguardo all'Università di Bologna', *Rivista di filosofia neoscolastica* 38 (1946), 260-77; C. I. Ermatinger, 'Averroism in the Early Fourteenth Century', *Medieval Studies* 16 (1954), 35-56; A. Maier, 'Die Bologneser Philosophen des 14. Jahrhunderts', *Studi e memorie per la Storia dell'Università di Bologna*, new series, 1 (1956), 299-312; M. Corti, *Dante a un nuovo crocevia* (Florence: Sansoni, 1982).

¹³ *ST* Ia IIae.109.2 resp.: 'natura hominis dupliciter potest considerari, uno modo, in sui integritate, sicut fuit in primo parente ante peccatum; alio modo, secundum quod est corrupta in nobis post peccatum primi parentis. Secundum autem utrumque statum, natura humana indiget auxilio divino ad faciendum vel volendum quodcumque bonum, sicut primo movente, ut dictum est. Sed in statu naturae integrae, quantum ad sufficientiam operativae virtutis, poterat homo per sua naturalia velle et operari bonum suae naturae proportionatum, quale est bonum virtutis acquisitae, non autem bonum superexcedens, quale est bonum virtutis infusae. Sed in statu naturae corruptae etiam deficit homo ab hoc quod secundum suam naturam potest, ut non possit totum huiusmodi bonum implere per sua naturalia. Quia tamen natura humana per peccatum non est totaliter corrupta, ut scilicet toto bono naturae privetur; potest quidem etiam in statu naturae corruptae, per virtutem suae naturae aliquod bonum particulare agere, sicut aedificare domos, plantare vineas, et alia huiusmodi; non tamen totum bonum sibi connaturale, ita quod in nullo deficiat. Sicut homo infirmus potest per seipsum aliquem motum habere; non tamen perfecte potest moveri motu hominis sani, nisi sanetur auxilio medicinae. Sic igitur virtute gratuita superaddita virtuti naturae indiget homo in statu naturae integrae quantum ad unum, scilicet ad operandum et volendum bonum supernaturale. Sed in statu naturae corruptae, quantum ad duo, scilicet ut sanetur; et ulterius ut bonum supernaturalis virtutis operetur, quod est meritorium. Ulterius autem in utroque statu indiget homo auxilio divino ut ab ipso moveatur ad bene agendum' – notable for its sense of autonomy as stretching, strictly speaking, only to matters of moral

Commedia, is a separating out of these things, a distinction between them for the purpose of recognizing and of rejoicing in their *perseitas*, this, in fact, being Kenelm's point of arrival in these essays, the point-towards-which of his troubled meditation:

> From all the above, in any event, we may conclude, I think, that Dante shows a marked tendency, through the *Convivio* and the *Monarchia* and even in the *Comedy*, to reduce to a minimum the conceivable contacts between human nature and divine grace; even if we are persuaded, by the evidence adduced in the last few pages, or on other grounds, that he did allow a bare possibility of such contact for all adult human beings. And that tendency, with its consequences, is what I have taken as characteristic of the 'other', the *second* Dante implied in the title of this essay. And perhaps it reveals an important defect, from the Christian point of view, in this great Christian's thinking about man: an over-readiness to conceive of moral virtue in isolation from Charity, 'the first and greatest commandment'. After all, a certain practice and cult of moral virtue is quite compatible with the radical perversity of indifference to God. But Christianity requires that the moral virtues themselves be offered to God as a way – as *the* way – of cooperating with his grace. In this perspective the natural virtues themselves, ordered under Charity ('the mother of the virtues'), become as it were organs of grace, are no longer just humanly 'acquired' but divinely 'infused'. Guided by this insight St Thomas could take over the whole achievement of Aristotle, as a philosophical moralist, while giving it an entirely new setting and direction. In Dantean terms this means the difference between Limbo and the *Purgatorio*; in which we see repentant man recovering, under

---

indifference ('building houses, planting vines, and the like'); *De ver.* 24.14 passim, etc. On Dante and Thomas, B. Nardi, *Nel mondo di Dante* (Rome: Edizioni di Storia e Letteratura, 1944); idem, *Saggi e note di critica dantesca* (Milan: Ricciardi, 1966); idem, *Saggi di filosofia dantesca*, 2nd edn (Florence: La Nuova Italia, 1967); idem, *Dante e la cultura medievale*, ed. P. Mazzantini with an introduction by T. Gregory (Rome: Laterza, 1983, originally Bari: Laterza, 1942); idem, *Dal 'Convivio' alla 'Commedia': sei saggi danteschi*, with a preface by O. Capitani (Rome: Nella sede dell'Istituto, 1992, originally 1960); E. Gilson, *Dante and Philosophy*, trans. D. Moore (New York: Harper and Row, 1963; originally *Dante et la philosophie* (Paris: Vrin, 1939), second edn 1953). In Kenelm himself, see especially *The Mind in Love*, Aquinas Society of London 25 (London: Blackfriars, 1956, and in J. Freccero (ed.), *Dante. A Collection of Critical Essays* (Englewood Cliffs, N.J.: Prentice Hall, 1965), pp. 43-60; 'The Tact of St Thomas', in *God's Tree: Essays on Dante and Other Matters* (London: Blackfriars, 1957), pp. 141-49; 'Religion and Philosophy in Dante', in *The Mind of Dante* (Cambridge: Cambridge University Press, 1965), pp. 47-78; 'Tommaso d'Aquino', in the *Enciclopedia dantesca*, 6 vols (Rome: Istituto della Enciclopedia Italiana, 1970-78), vol. 5, pp. 626-49; *Dante e San Tommaso* (Rome: Casa di Dante, 1975; lecture of 17 November, 1974 at the Casa di Dante in Rome).

grace, the lost or diminished natural virtues, but only in preparation for something that is utterly beyond their own range, a love-union with the Infinite. In the *Purgatorio* Aristotelianism is integrated into Christianity; in the Dantean Limbo it is not. (pp. 252-53)

In the event, the passage is as troubling as it is troubled; for in the degree to which Dante was himself aware of the tensions at work deep within him (a situation confirmed in the course of his encounter with Beatrice in the earthly paradise), then his courage in seeking to address and as far as may be to resolve this situation by way of the fresh mechanism of the *Commedia* – by way of what we have described and shall describe again as the twofold theologism and theatricality of the text – is all the more impressive, all the more likely to confirm us in a sense of his having at last come of age as a theological spirit. How far Kenelm himself was persuaded of this I cannot be sure, for I remember his asking me a shade anxiously what, soon after its publication, I thought of the *Two Dantes* volume, to which I replied then as I would reply now that I was much impressed by it. But how far this was anxiety in respect of precisely this issue, as distinct from matters arising from the book generally, I cannot say.

4. What, then, are we to make of the two Dantes thesis, of Kenelm's account of Dantean spirituality – by which we mean the mature spirituality of the *Commedia* – as, if not captive to, then at any rate detained by its pagan component? The first thing to say is that there can be no underestimating, still less any denying, what Kenelm describes as the 'humanistic' element of that spirituality, just as there can be no denying the way in which, in key moments both of natural- and of moral-philosophical clarification (Virgil's account of the structure of hell in Canto XI of the *Inferno* for example), this element subsists into the *Commedia*. But by the same token there can be no passing over either (*a*) the way in which Dante is careful to bring home the moral and metaphysical moments of the argument to their theological ground, to what actually matters about them in respect of the soul's journey into God, or (*b*) the care with which he distributes the alternative voice with a view to its neutralization as a principle of instability in the poem. Taking, then, the first, of these things we may say that while there is much to be said for seeing and interpreting hell in terms of its unreasonableness, there can be no question of its being exhausted by this, for unreason, within the economy of the text generally, points on to something more serious than itself, namely to the the truth of separation from self and from God as the ground of its sinfulness and root of its effrontery, at which point its theological substance moves clearly into view. Now for Kenelm too unreason as a high-level inflexion of the spirit

points on to something more serious than itself, namely, to ingratitude and lovelessness. But for all his discerning in the depths of unreason its status as a matter of impiety, he remains unwilling to develop his sense of this first canticle of the poem in terms of its specifically Christian content, preferring instead to look in the direction of its Peripatetic component, of its accountability, less to the gospels, than to the Philosopher; so, for example, these lines from his introduction to the 1961 Warwick Chipman translation of the *Inferno*, oddly reluctant in its endorsement of the 'religious' as distinct from the philosophical substance the text:

> And the sin he encounters on his way is, I repeat, largely sin against the light of reason alone, apart from any 'higher' considerations. It is wrongdoing very much on the human level and in the give and take of ordinary social discourse. A strong social emphasis marks the *Inferno*; and, since the poet was deeply involved in politics and his world was that of the medieval commune, the more or less self-governing city-state, a strong political emphasis too. It is true that all wrong-doing, however social or political its circumstances, had for Dante a deep religious significance. Since human nature is God's creation, to injure man is to offend God. And certainly the *Inferno* could only have been written by a believing Christian. Nevertheless the measure of right and wrong that governs, immediately, the greater part of it is a rational, not a specifically Christian, measure; it is drawn from moral philosophy (especially Aristotle) rather than from the Gospels.[14]

Now the *Inferno* – the *Inferno*, perhaps, more than either the *Purgatorio* or the *Paradiso* – is a canticle of layered consciousness, both of surface and of deep awareness, and there can be no gainsaying the presence of Aristotle at the first of these levels, at the point of moral-philosophical elucidation. And neither can there be any gainsaying Dante's preoccupation in the *Inferno* with the socially detrimental character of sin as a matter of separation in the depths, with its power, not only to destroy the sinner, but, in destroying him, to separate out one man from another and thus to shatter the unity of the Spirit and the bond of peace. Unreason, therefore, both in itself and as a matter of social annihilation is everywhere in the text and everywhere decisive for its interpretation. But – and this now is the point – layered as it is in consciousness, and this in such a way as to free the text for the development of this or that discrete emphasis, each layer of awareness, within the economy of the whole, remains transparent

---

[14] W. Chipman (trans), *Inferno* (London, New York and Toronto: Oxford University Press, 1961), p. xiii.

to the others, invoking them as it does so for the purposes of a statement ultimately one in conception. Each, in other words, susceptible as it is to development in its own right and on its own terms, coalesces with the others to form a single and ultimately undifferentiated stratum of awareness, a movement of the spirit comprehending in a single sweep both its surface and its deep reasons, herein precisely lying the triumph of the *Commedia* as testimony to its inner consistency, to an overcoming in Dante of everything in him making for alternativism at the point of ultimate concern.

But that is not all, for in addition to the transparency of every surface emphasis in the text to the theological substance by which it is indwelt and in terms of which it stands ultimately to be interpreted, there is the kind of theatricality operative on the plane of the horizontal and responsible for ensuring over against the heterodox and thus disruptive voice the unity of what fundamentally is being said in the poem. Given, in other words, what amounts in the *Commedia* to its decorum, to Dante's distribution of the discordant voice, then the claim to moral innocence voiced by Virgil in *Inferno* IV or *Purgatorio* VII and all this implies by way of antique righteousness need not worry us; for Virgil, in insisting in the way he does upon his sinlessness, says what Virgil *would* say, indeed the only thing he *can* say. Now here again we have to be careful, for Kenelm, himself alert to the nature of the text as drama, is as sensitive as any to the particularity of the Virgilian utterance, to Virgil's speaking out of the properties of personality as reconstructed by Dante in his poem; so, for example, from the Chipman translation of the *Inferno* mentioned a moment ago, these nicely calibrated remarks on the difference as far as the Dantean Virgil is concerned between *knowing* Christianity and merely *knowing of* it or *about* it:

> This 'Virgil' believes in God. He knows that an original goodness glows through all creation; moreover he knows how creatures can deny and dishonour that Goodness and besmirch and violate its effects, particularly the noblest effect of which man has experience, his own rational nature. Virgil even knows something of the fall of the angels. "Behold Dis", he says at the end, pointing to Satan; and we can suppose that he, like his pupil, knew that it was through pride that "he who was so fair ... raised his brow against his Maker". He is aware too of the Church even if, in the great ecclesiastical Canto XIX, he will tactfully step aside and leave that unforgettable indictment of clerical materialism to flow from Catholic lips. But Virgil only knows *of* the Christian revelation, he has not personally received it; and though familiar with the topography of Hell, there is something about

damnation itself that always escapes him. No wonder; never having known God incarnate, how can he understand a condition which is only definable as the consequence of a rejection of that God?[15]

to which, from the *Two Dantes*, we might add these on Virgil's particular kind of piety in the poem, piety yes, but piety at a remove, lived out at a distance from the real thing:

> Virgil's own kind of piety is a fact entwined in the narrative of the *Inferno* and *Purgatorio*, more or less visible as the occasion requires. It is always in character; never Christian, always at a certain remove, like his discernment of those points of doctrine which he has to leave to Beatrice to instruct Dante in.[16]

Kenelm's too, therefore, is a sense of Dante's decorum, of his proceeding by way of what might reasonably be expected of his characters. But – and this now is the point – for all his discerning in this respect, he is not averse to lifting that same Virgil from the context in which Dante has so carefully placed him with a view to fashioning from him an *alter ego* or alternative self functioning in the poem as a principle of disruption, as tending, not merely to differentiate, but to damage and ultimately to destroy its consistency as a specifically Christian utterance. True, by the time we reach purgatory there is something of a recovery, a fresh sense of how one thing stands to be integrated with another, the Aristotelian with the Christian and the pagan with the pious. But by the time we reach purgatory we are a good third of the way into it, our sense of the shape and structure of the poem having long since crystallized. Now it may be that neither transparency nor theatricality, taken alone, is enough to do anything about this, transparency coming in degrees, and theatricality never above privileging one party in particular as spokesman for the author. Taken together, however, they are just about invincible, for operative as they are on the planes respectively of the vertical and of the horizontal they comprehend absolutely the space they describe, every contingency in the area of thought and expression. Operative as they are on the twin axes of awareness, they carry all before.

---

[15] *Inferno* (previous note), p. xiv.
[16] *The Two Dantes* (note 1 above), p. 244.

Complementarity and Coalescence:
Dante and the Sociology of Authentic Being

> S'io era corpo, e qui non si concepe
> com' una dimensione altro patio,
> ch'esser convien se corpo in corpo repe,
> accender ne dovria più il disio
> di veder quella essenza in che si vede
> come nostra natura e Dio s'unio.
>
> (*Par.* II.37-42)[1]

1. Introduction: the social dimension of the *Inferno* and a moment of misgiving. 2. The New Testament perspective: Pauline and Johannine collectivity. 3. The sociology of estrangement: self-denial and social denial. 4. The sociology of emergence: co-presence, co-immanence and the revised dimensionality of being.

Kenelm Foster, not far into his preliminary meditation on the theology of the *Inferno*, has this to say about its social aspect, its sense of sin as civic:

> In fact, there is generally a very human quality about the *Inferno*, not unconnected, I think, with the strong social and political emphasis that has often been remarked in it. Most of the damned have violated human nature in some way, in themselves or in their fellow men; and the deeper damnations are reserved for the sinners against their fellows. In the circles of 'frode' – if one excepts Satan himself – all the sins punished are sins against one's neighbour. I fancy that Ezra Pound said somewhere that the damned in the lower circles of *Inferno* were all 'damned for money'. This, if he said it, was an exaggeration, but certainly the lower circles of Malebolge and Cocito are malevolently anti-social, although this aspect is not everywhere stressed by the poet, and in one case – Canto XIX – the society in question is 'supernatural'

---

[1] If I was body (and here we conceive not how one bulk could brook another, which must be if body enters body), the more should longing enkindle us to see that essence wherein we behold how our nature and God united themselves. I am grateful to the President and staff of the John Cabot American University in Rome where, by their kind invitation, this paper was first delivered.

– the Church. The phrase Charles Williams applied to Geryon, the symbol of Deceit, might indeed be applied to all that lower Hell into which Geryon carried Dante (canto XVII): it is 'the City infernalized'.[2]

This, as far as it goes, is unexceptionable, many and possibly most of the sins punished in hell having about them the nature of injury, of doing down the next man. But for all that, there is a sense in the *Inferno* in which every dysfunctionality on the surface of things, including every specifically social dysfunctionality, is reducible to dysfunctionality in the depths, to the kind of dysfunctionality whereby, having established himself at the centre of his own universe, the individual cannot but live in a state of resentment with regard to the next man, with regard, that is to say, to all those who have similarly established themselves at the centre of *their* universe. Strictly speaking, therefore, the social emphases of the *Inferno*, prominent as they are in the text and decisive for its overall interpretation, stand to be referred to something both prior and more profound than themselves, to the tragic substance of self as divided in the forum of conscience. Short of this, of a referral of dividedness in the open forum to dividedness in the innermost reaches of personality, the root cause of every instance of antagonism on the surface remains hidden from view, obscured by its mere phenomenology or showing forth. That said, however, there is no denying the social character of Dante's discourse in the *Inferno* and thus the possibility of seeing and setting this up as an object of enquiry in its own right, especially in that it is here, at the point of being under the aspect of collectivity, that we discover some of his most radiant emphases in the area of moral philosophy and theology.

2. In proposing the social aspect of the *Commedia* as an object of enquiry in its own right, we need for a moment to look back to the New Testament as a point of departure; for the New Testament, if not systematically then even so unmistakably, commends two kinds of collectivity or social configuration, the one Pauline and the other Johannine in origin. On the one hand, then, there is Paul's sense of the common life as a matter of complementarity, each individual facilitating that life by bringing to it what he or she does best, the substance of his or her genius or vocation; so, for example, as a classic instance of his anthropomorphism, of his sense of the indispensability of each member of the body of Christ to the proper operation of the whole, these lines from I Corinthians 12, an essay in functionality as a matter of *co*-functionality, in collectivity as a matter of cooperation:

---

[2] Kenelm Foster, O.P., *God's Tree. Essays on Dante and Other Matters* (London: Blackfriars, 1957), pp. 54-55.

Vos autem estis corpus Christi et membra de membro, et quosdam quidem posuit Deus in ecclesia primum apostolos, secundo prophetas, tertio doctores, deinde virtutes exin gratias curationum, opitulationes, gubernationes, genera linguarum. Numquid omnes apostoli, numquid omnes prophetae, numquid omnes doctores, numquid omnes virtutes, numquid omnes gratiam habent curationum, numquid omnes linguis loquuntur, numquid omnes interpretantur?

(I Cor. 12:27-30)[3]

Uppermost in Paul's mind as he considers the nature and the mechanism of the common life are two things: first, the importance of the individual's seeking and living out his or her proper calling, as but part of the body of Christ; and, following on from this, the possibility of defining the relationship between one man and another in terms of the kind of proximity whereby the one is present to the other as an extrinsic principle of his well-being. Self, in other words, comes alongside and engages with the other-than-self as part of what it means to be in Christ, a notion which, though less than adequate to all this might mean for Paul, nonetheless gives satisfactory expression to one aspect of it, to how Christian neighbourliness might be usefully understood.

But there is in the New Testament a further model of the collective life, one which, while both acknowledging the Pauline model, deepens it in favour of something closer to coalescence than to contiguity as a way of developing this issue, to a sense of collectivity as involving the occupation by the many of one and the same spiritual space. Each individual, in other words, is present to his or her neighbour, not only nor even primarily as a fellow labourer, but as an inward and abiding presence, as a principle of being operative from out of the recesses of being. Fundamental here are the farewell discourses of Christ prior to his passion as recorded in the fourth gospel, discourses designed by way of a series of immanences to confirm in circumstances of faith the co-inherence both of man and God and of man and man as party to a common undertaking. First, then, and as quickened by a sense of imminent catastrophe, there is Christ's sense of his being in the Father, of the Father's being in him, and of this as the

---

[3] Now you are Christ's body, and each of you a limb or organ of it. Within our community God has appointed, in the first place apostles, and in the second place prophets, thirdly teachers; then miracle workers, then those who have gifts of healing, or ability to help others or power to guide them, or the gift of ecstatic utterance of various kinds. Are all apostles? all prophets? all teachers? Do all work miracles? Have all gifts of healing? Do all speak in tongues of ecstasy? Can all interpret them? (*REB*). Eph. 4:11-12: 'Et ipse dedit quosdam quidem apostolos, quosdam autem prophetas, alios vero evangelistas, alios autem pastores et doctores ad consummationem sanctorum in opus ministerii in aedificationem corporis Christi', etc.

basis of his messianic status; so, for example, John 10:37-38 and 14:10-11: 'Si non facio opera Patris mei, nolite credere mihi; si autem facio, et si mihi non vultis credere operibus, credite ut cognoscatis et credatis quia in me est Pater et ego in Patris ... non credis quia ego in Patre et Pater in me? Est verba quae ego loquor vobis a me ipso non loquor, Pater autem in me manens, ipse facit opera. Non creditis quia ego in Patre et Pater in me est.'[4] To the fore, then, in this second moment of the gospel meditation is an emphasis on the mutual indwellingness of the One who sends and of the one who is sent, this in turn determining the relationship one with another of those naming the name; for in the degree to which a man names the name he not only indwells the Christ, in turn to be indwelt by him, but he indwells all those professing the Christ, again to be indwelt by them:

> Non pro his autem rogo tantum, sed pro eis qui credituri sunt per verbum eorum in me, ut omnes unum sint sicut tu, Pater, in me et ego in te ut et ipsi in nobis unum sint, ut mundus credat quia tu me misisti. Et ego claritatem quam dedisti mihi dedi eis ut sint unum sicut nos sumus, ego in eis et tu in me ut sint consummati in unum ...
>
> (John 17:20-22)[5]

Here, therefore, in the Johannine phase of the argument, it is a question, less of complimentarity, than of co-immanence as the form of collective consciousness, of how one man might be said to enter into the humanity of another there to shape and substantiate it from deep within itself.

3. Coming now to Dante, these models of collective being, the Pauline model of contiguity and the Johannine model of co-inherence, bring us to one of the most luminous aspects of his spirituality in the *Commedia*, to his rejoicing in the rich configuration of man's collective life in the Spirit. Let us begin, however, if only because this is where Dante himself begins, at the opposite end, with the kinds of tension and antagonism tending to undermine and ultimately to destroy complementarity and mutual

---

[4] If I am not acting as my Father would, do not believe me. But if I am, accept the evidence of my deeds, even if you do not believe me, so that you may recognize and know that the Father is in me, and I in the Father ... Do you not believe that I am in the Father and the Father in me; I am not myself the source of the words I speak to you; it is the Father who dwells in me doing his own work. Believe me when I say that I am in the Father and the Father in me.

[5] But it is not for these alone that I pray, but for those also who through their words put their faith in me; may they all be one: as you, Father, are in me, and I in you, so also may they be in us, that the world may believe that you sent me. The glory which you gave me I have given to them, that they may be one as we are one; I in them and you in me, may they be perfectly one.

immanence thus understood as models of man's being together as man. Dante's, then, with Aristotle's, is a sense of the psychosomatic structure of man's presence in the world, the rational part of his nature constituting the *species intelligibilis* or intelligible and operative principle of the whole. But there is a difference, for happy as he is to talk with Aristotle and the Aristotelians about human nature in terms of the specification of the whole by way of the *psyche* rather than of the *soma*, he is happier, whenever the opportunity presents itself, to proceed in affective categories, to discuss the whole thing in terms of the complexity of properly human loving. Man as man, then, loves variously: like the stones he cleaves to the ground, like the plants he seeks out the goodness of the soil and the sunlight as conditions of his proper well-being, like the animals he craves the pleasure of eating, sleeping and procreating, and like the angels he yearns for an uncluttered act of intellection, for an orderly understanding both of self and of the world beyond self; so, for example, as testimony to a uniform pattern of thought in Dante, and indeed to a uniform pattern of rejoicing, these lines from Book III of the *Convivio*, a hymn to the openness of being in general and of human being in particular to celebration under the aspect of its multiple affectivity:

> Onde è da sapere che ciascuna cosa, come detto è di sopra, per la ragione di sopra mostrata ha 'l suo speziale amore. Come le corpora simplici hanno amore naturato in sé a lo luogo proprio, e però la terra sempre discende al centro; lo fuoco ha [amore a] la circunferenza di sopra, lungo lo cielo de la luna, e però sempre sale a quello. Le corpora composte prima, sì come sono le minere, hanno amore a lo luogo dove la loro generazione è ordinata, e in quello crescono e acquistano vigore e potenza; onde vedemo la calamita sempre da la parte de la sua generazione ricevere vertù. Le piante, che sono prima animate, hanno amore a certo luogo più manifestamente, secondo che la complessione richiede; e però vedemo certe piante lungo l'acque quasi c[ontent]arsi, e certe sopra li gioghi de le montagne, e certe ne le piagge e dappiè monti: le quali se si transmutano, o muoiono del tutto o vivono quasi triste, disgiunte dal loro amico. Li animali bruti hanno più manifesto amore non solamente a li luoghi, ma l'uno l'altro vedemo amare. Li uomini hanno loro proprio amore a le perfette e oneste cose. E però che l'uomo, avvegna che una sola sustanza sia, tuttavia [la] forma, per la sua nobilitade, ha in sé e la natura [d'ognuna di] queste cose, tutti questi amori puote avere e tutti li ha.
>
> (*Conv.* III.iii.2-5)[6]

---

[6] It should be explained here that, as was said above, for the reason given there, every being has a love specific to it. Just as simple bodies have an inborn love for the place proper to them – so that earth always descends to the centre, while fire has an inborn love

But if man as man loves by way of the many impulses proper to his complex nature, then how are these impulses to be organized, fitted in with one another within the economy of the whole? By way, Dante thinks, of their bringing home to the kind of love given with the act itself of existence and inclining the individual to seek out God as the beginning and end of all seeking, herein alone lying the ground and legitimacy of his every affective inflexion of the spirit. The key passages here, the first of them touching on the species of human loving precisely as such and the second of them on the gathering in of one kind of love to another, run as follows:

> "Né creator né creatura mai"
> cominciò el, "figliuol, fu sanza amore,
> o naturale o d'animo; e tu 'l sai.
>   Lo naturale è sempre sanza errore,
> ma l'altro puote errar per malo obietto
> o per troppo o per poco di vigore.
>   Mentre ch'elli è nel primo ben diretto,
> e ne' secondi sé stesso misura,
> esser non può cagion di mal diletto;
>   ma quando al mal si torce, o con più cura
> o con men che non dee corre nel bene,
> contra 'l fattore adovra sua fattura.
>   Quinci comprender puoi ch'esser convene
> amor sementa in voi d'ogne virtute
> e d'ogne operazion che merta pene"
> ...
>   Però, là onde vegna lo 'ntelletto
> de le prime notizie, omo non sape,
> e de' primi appetibili l'affetto,
>   che sono in voi sì come studio in ape
> di far lo mele; e questa prima voglia

for the circumference above us bordering the heaven of the Moon, and therefore always rises upwards towards that – so primary compound bodies, such as minerals, have a love for the place suited to their generation; in that place they grow, and from it they derive their vigour and power. That is why, as we observe, the magnet always receives power from the quarter in which it was generated. Plants, which are the primary form of animate life, even more clearly have a love for certain places, in accordance with what their constitution requires; so we see some deriving pleasure, as it were, when alongside water, others when on the ridges of mountains, others when on slopes and on foothills; if they are transplanted, they either die completely or live a sad life, as it were, like beings separated from their friends. Human beings have their specific love for what is perfect and just. And since the human being, despite the fact that his whole form constitutes a single substance in virtue of its nobility, has a nature that embraces all these features, he can have all these loves, and indeed does have them.

merto di lode o di biasmo non cape.
Or perché a questa ogn' altra si raccoglia,
innata v'è la virtù che consiglia,
e de l'assenso de' tener la soglia.
Quest' è 'l principio là onde si piglia
ragion di meritar in voi, secondo
che buoni e rei amori accoglie e viglia.
Color che ragionando andaro al fondo,
s'accorser d'esta innata libertate;
però moralità lasciaro al mondo.

(*Purg.* XVII. 91-102 and XVIII.55-69)[7]

---

[7] He began: "Neither creator nor creature, my son, was ever without love, either natural or of the mind, and this you know. The natural is always without error; but the other may err either through an evil object, or through too much or too little vigour. While it is directed on the primal good, and on secondary goods observes right measure, it cannot be the cause of sinful pleasure. But when it turns awry to evil, or speeds to good with more zeal, or with less, than it ought, against the creator works his creature. Hence you can comprehend that love must needs be the seed in you of every virtue and of every action deserving punishment ... Therefore, whence comes the intelligence of the first cognitions man does not know, nor whence the affection for the first objects of desire, which exist in you even as zeal in the bee for making honey; and this primal will admits no deserving of praise or blame. Now in order that to this will every other will may be conformed, there is innate in you the faculty that counsels and that ought to hold the threshold of consent. This is the principle wherefrom is derived the reason of desert in you, according as it garners and winnows good and evil loves. Those who in their reasoning went to the root of the matter took note of this innate liberty, and accordingly bequeathed ethics to the world." Thomas on natural and elective love (*dilectio naturalis* and *dilectio electiva*), *ST* Ia.60.2 resp.: 'in Angelis est quaedam dilectio naturalis et quaedam electiva. Et naturalis dilectio in eis est principium electivae, quia semper id quod pertinet ad prius, habet rationem principii; unde, cum natura sit primum quod est in unoquoque, oportet quod id quod ad naturam pertinet, sit principium in quolibet. Et hoc apparet in homine et quantum ad intellectum, et quantum ad voluntatem. Intellectus enim cognoscit principia naturaliter, et ex hac cognitione causatur in homine scientia conclusionum, quae non cognoscuntur naturaliter ab homine, sed per inventionem vel doctrinam. Similiter in voluntate finis hoc modo se habet, sicut principium in intellectu, ut dicitur in II Physic. Unde voluntas naturaliter tendit in suum finem ultimum, omnis enim homo naturaliter vult beatitudinem. Et ex hac naturali voluntate causantur omnes aliae voluntates, cum quidquid homo vult, velit propter finem. Dilectio igitur boni quod homo naturaliter vult sicut finem, est dilectio naturalis, dilectio autem ab hac derivata, quae est boni quod diligitur propter finem, est dilectio electiva.' O. Ciacci, 'La teoria dell'amore: Canto XVII del *Purgatorio*', in *Nuove interpretazioni dantesche* (Perugia: Volumina, 1974), pp. 75-95; K. Foster, O.P., 'The Human Spirit in Action: *Purgatorio* XVIII', in *The Two Dantes* (London: Darton, Longman and Todd, 1977), pp. 107-119; B. Nardi, 'Filosofia dell'amore nei rimatori italiani del Duecento e in Dante', in *Dante e la cultura medievale*, ed. P. Mazzantini (Bari: Laterza, 1983, originally 1942), pp. 9-79; G. Morgan, 'Natural and Spiritual Movements of Love in the Soul: an Explanation of *Purgatorio* XVIII. 16-39', *Modern Language Review* 80 (1985), 2, 320-29; S. F. Di Zenzo, 'La dottrina dell'amore nel *Purgatorio* dantesco', *Avallon* 18 (1988), 99-114; C. Fordyce, 'Il

Man as man, Dante suggests, knows himself in two kinds of loving. He knows himself in the kind of *connatural* loving given with the act itself of existence and calling him from beforehand into the presence of God as the first and final cause of all loving ('amore naturale'), and he knows himself in the kind of *contingent* loving generated by his encounter with the world around him ('amore d'animo'), his task as a creature of moral accountability being to gather in the latter to the former as the principle of his proper well-being, this gathering in of the one to the other being the province of free will, of that faculty of the rational soul empowered to decisive intervention. Only in the degree to which he is successful in this, in bringing home occasional to essential loving, will he know himself in the integrity and intelligibility of his presence in the world and in his acceptability in the sight of God. Short of this, he knows himself, and is known to his maker, only under the aspect of effrontery. But that is not all, for in the moment of his disinclination to bring home one species of loving to another, the next man, inasmuch as he is known to him at all, is known to him by way only of intimidation, as forever looking to see him off as a competitor and an intruder, at which point the social aspect of it all – sin under the aspect of savagery – moves into view; so, for example, the cases of the avaricious and of the prodigal in Canto VII of the *Inferno* and of the counterfeiters in Canto XXX, each of whom, divided against self in the recesses of self, lives at enmity with the world beyond self, the crisis of collectivity being in this sense nothing but the crisis of personality writ large:

> Qui vid' i' gente più ch'altrove troppa,
> e d'una parte e d'altra, con grand' urli,
> voltando pesi per forza di poppa.
>   Percotëansi 'ncontro; e poscia pur lì
> si rivolgea ciascun, voltando a retro,
> gridando: "Perché tieni?" e "Perché burli?"
> ...
>   E l'un di lor, che si recò a noia
> forse d'esser nomato sì oscuro,
> col pugno li percosse l'epa croia.
>   Quella sonò come fosse un tamburo;
> e mastro Adamo li percosse il volto

problema di amore e libero arbitrio nella *Commedia* di Dante', *Romance Review* 4 (1994), 1, 35-51; S. Wenzel, 'Dante's Rationale for the Seven Deadly Sins (*Purgatorio* XVII)' in *Dante. The Critical Complex*, 8 vols, ed. R. Lansing (New York and London, 2003), vol. 3, pp. 227-31 (and in *Elucidations. Medieval Poetry and its Religious Backgrounds* (Louvain and Paris: Walpole and Peeters, 2010), pp. 113-19; originally 1965).

> col braccio suo, che non parve men duro,
> dicendo a lui: "Ancor che mi sia tolto
> lo muover per le membra che son gravi,
> ho io il braccio a tal mestiere sciolto"

(*Inf.* VII.26-30 and XXX.100-108)[8]

Both psychologically and socially, then, it is a question of hostility. Ranged over against self in the forum of conscience and forever living out the fragility of this situation, the individual impressed by a sense of his vulnerability in the world only ever knows his neighbour in a spirit of resentment, of, at best, inconvenience and, at worst, menace, herein, in the a-sociology of the *Inferno*, in its sense of being as but a matter of over-againstness, lying the twofold substance and sadness of it all.

4. What, then, of being in its authenticity, of being as gathered on the plane of loving? In circumstances of *in*authentic being communication gives way as we have seen to communicationlessness. Established at the centre of his universe, the individual neither knows nor is known by the next man, preferring instead to subsist as a stranger to every kind of creative communion. But in circumstances of authentic being, of being as transparent to its own innermost reasons, a new species of collectivity emerges, repudiation giving way to recognition as a habit of mind, to a sense of the next man as present to self, less as an impediment, than as a means of affirmation. To take, then, the Pauline model of contiguity, of being as a matter of being *alongside*, we have first of all the Charles Martel passage of *Paradiso* VIII, a passage for all its soaring substance alert to the notion of being and becoming in man as a matter of *civic* being and becoming, of the individual's bringing what he is and what he has by way of the unprecedented and unparalleled properties of personality to the collective enterprise:

> Ond' elli ancora: "Or dì: sarebbe il peggio
> per l'omo in terra, se non fosse cive?".
> "Sì", rispuos' io; "e qui ragion non cheggio".
> "E puot' elli esser, se giù non si vive
> diversamente per diversi offici?

---

[8] Here I saw far more people than elsewhere, both on the one side and on the other, howling loudly, rolling weights, which they pushed with their chest; they clashed together, and then right there each wheeled round, rolling back his weight, shouting, "Why do you hoard?" and "Why do you squander?" ... And one of them, who took offence perhaps at being named so darkly, with his fist struck him on his stiff paunch; it sounded like a drum; and Master Adam struck him in the face with his arm, which seemed no less hard, saying to him, "Though I am kept from moving by the weight of my limbs, which are heavy, I have a free arm for such a need".

Non, se 'l maestro vostro ben vi scrive".

Sì venne deducendo infino a quici;
poscia conchiuse: "Dunque esser diverse
convien di vostri effetti le radici:

 per ch'un nasce Solone e altro Serse,
altro Melchisedèch e altro quello
che, volando per l'aere, il figlio perse.

 La circular natura, ch'è suggello
a la cera mortal, fa ben sua arte,
ma non distingue l'un da l'altro ostello.

 Quinci addivien ch'Esaù si diparte
per seme da Iacòb; e vien Quirino
da sì vil padre, che si rende a Marte.

 Natura generata il suo cammino
simil farebbe sempre a' generanti,
se non vincesse il proveder divino.

 Or quel che t'era dietro t'è davanti:
ma perché sappi che di te mi giova,
un corollario voglio che t'ammanti.

 Sempre natura, se fortuna trova
discorde a sé, com' ogne altra semente
fuor di sua regïon, fa mala prova.

 E se 'l mondo là giù ponesse mente
al fondamento che natura pone,
seguendo lui, avria buona la gente.

 Ma voi torcete a la religïone
tal che fia nato a cignersi la spada,
e fate re di tal ch'è da sermone;
onde la traccia vostra è fuor di strada".

(*Par.* VIII.115-48)[9]

---

[9] Whereupon he again, "Now say, would it be worse for man on earth if he were not a citizen?" "Yes," I replied, "and here I ask for no proof". "And can it be that, unless men below live in diverse ways for diverse duties? Not if your master writes well of this for you." Thus he came deducing far as here, then he concluded, "Therefore the roots of your works must be diverse, so that one is born of Solon and another Xerxes, one Melchizidek and another he who flew through the air and lost his son. Circling nature, which is a seal on mortal wax, performs its arts well, but does not distinguish one house from another. Whence it happens that Esau differs in the seed from Jacob, and Quirinus comes from so base a father that he is ascribed to Mars. The begotten nature would always make its course like its begetters did not divine provision overrule. Now that which was behind you is before you; but, that you may know that I delight in you, I will have a corollary cloak you round. Ever does Nature, if she find fortune discordant with herself, like any kind of seed out of its proper region, come to ill result. And if the word there below would give heed to the foundation which Nature lays, and followed it, it would have

Eloquent as this is, however, in respect of alongsidedness as a model of collective being, it is only with Thomas, a little further down the line, that we glimpse something of its refined and indeed rapturous substance; for with Thomas it is a question, not simply of citizenship, but of companionship, of a species of co-presencing apt by way of those same properties of personality to confirm each alike in a sense of the fullness and incontrovertibility of his own presence in the world, in the deep substance of his own humanity:

> Tu vuo' saper di quai piante s'infiora
> questa ghirlanda che 'ntorno vagheggia
> la bella donna ch'al ciel t'avvalora.
> Io fui de li agni de la santa greggia
> che Domenico mena per cammino
> u' ben s'impingua se non si vaneggia.
> Questi che m'è a destra più vicino,
> frate e maestro fummi, ed esso Alberto
> è di Cologna, e io Thomas d'Aquino.
> Se sì di tutti li altri esser vuo' certo,
> di retro al mio parlar ten vien col viso
> girando su per lo beato serto.
> Quell' altro fiammeggiare esce del riso
> di Grazïan, che l'uno e l'altro foro
> aiutò sì che piace in paradiso.
> L'altro ch'appresso addorna il nostro coro,
> quel Pietro fu che con la poverella
> offerse a Santa Chiesa suo tesoro.
> La quinta luce, ch'è tra noi più bella,
> spira di tale amor, che tutto 'l mondo
> là giù ne gola di saper novella:
> entro v'è l'alta mente u' sì profondo
> saver fu messo, che, se 'l vero è vero,
> a veder tanto non surse il secondo.
> Appresso vedi il lume di quel cero
> che giù in carne più a dentro vide
> l'angelica natura e 'l ministero.
> Ne l'altra piccioletta luce ride

its people good. But you wrest to religion one born to girt on the sword, and you make a king one that is fit for sermons, so that your track is off the road". On the specificity, well-nigh, of this or that instance of properly human being in its historical instantiation, *DVE* I.iii.1: 'Cum igitur homo non nature instinctu, sed ratione moveatur, et ipsa ratio vel circa discretionem vel circa iudicium vel circa electionem diversificetur in singulis, adeo ut fere quilibet sua propria specie videatur gaudere, per proprios actus vel passiones, ut brutum anirnal, neminem alium intelligere opinamur.'

> quello avvocato de' tempi cristiani
> del cui latino Augustin si provide.
>   Or se tu l'occhio de la mente trani
> di luce in luce dietro a le mie lode,
> già de l'ottava con sete rimani.
>   Per vedere ogne ben dentro vi gode
> l'anima santa che 'l mondo fallace
> fa manifesto a chi di lei ben ode.
>   Lo corpo ond' ella fu cacciata giace
> giuso in Cieldauro; ed essa da martiro
> e da essilio venne a questa pace.
>   Vedi oltre fiammeggiar l'ardente spiro
> d'Isidoro, di Beda e di Riccardo,
> che a considerar fu più che viro.
>   Questi onde a me ritorna il tuo riguardo,
> è 'l lume d'uno spirto che 'n pensieri
> gravi a morir li parve venir tardo:
>   essa è la luce etterna di Sigieri,
> che, leggendo nel Vico de li Strami,
> silogizzò invidïosi veri.
>
> (*Par.* X.91-138)[10]

Here, then, patient demonstration (the 'Sì venne deducendo infino a quici' of VIII.121) gives way to something closer to concelebration as a

---

[10] You wish to know what plants these are that enflower this garland, which amorously circles round the fair lady who strengthens you for heaven. I was of the lambs of the holy flock which Dominic leads on the path where there is good fattening if they do not stray. He that is next beside on the right was my brother and my master, and he is Albert of Cologne, and I, Thomas of Aquino. If thus of all the rest you would be informed, come, following my speech with your sight. The next flaming comes from the smile of Gratian, who served the one and the other court so well that it pleases in paradise. The other who next adorns our choir was that Peter who, like the poor widow, offered his treasure to Holy Church. The fifth light, which is the most beautiful among us, breathes with such love that all the world there below thirsts to know tidings of it. Within it is the lofty mind to which was given wisdom so deep that, if the truth be true, there never rose a second of such full vision. At its side behold the light of that candle which, below in the flesh, saw deepest into the angelic nature and its ministry. In the next little light smiles that defender of the Christian times of whose discourse Augustine made use. If now you are bringing your mind's eye from light to light after my praises, you are already thirsting for the eighth. Therewithin, through seeing every good, the sainted soul rejoices who makes the fallacious world manifest to any who listen well to him. The body from which it was driven lies down below in Cieldauro, and he came from martyrdom and exile to this peace. See, flaming beyond, the glowing breath of Isidore, of Bede, and of Richard who in contemplation was more than man. This one from whom your look returns to me is the light of a spirit to whom, in his grave thoughts, it seemed that death came slow. It is the eternal light of Siger who, lecturing in Straw Street, demonstrated invidious truths.

mode of existence, Thomas's, whatever else it is, being an ode to friendship as the way of properly human affirmation. Fully and unambiguously himself, in other words, and operating from out of a space wholly his own, one individual comes alongside another to reassure him in respect both of the distinctiveness and the decisiveness of his presence – of the presence of each alike – in the world as party to the common undertaking and the universal hymn of praise.

But that is not all, for the argument stands now to be developed in terms of the way in which, operating as it does from out of his own space, each of those party to the universal proclamation may be said to operate from out of the same space, from out of a consummate act of indwelling. The model is Trinitarian, Dante's Trinitarianism having about it both a processional and a perichoretic aspect. First, then, on the processional side, there is his sense of the Son's issuing from the Father by way of filiation or of begottenness, and of the Spirit's issuing from the Father and the Son together by way of spiration or of a species of breathing-forth; so, for example, these two passages from *Paradiso* X (lines 1-6 and 49-51), the former, in its attentiveness to the *filioque* (to the doctrine of the Spirit's proceeding from both the Father and the Son), recalling the Augustine of the *De trinitate*, and the latter, more attuned to issues of filiation and spiration, the Thomas of the *Summa theologiae*:

> Guardando nel suo Figlio con l'Amore
> che l'uno e l'altro etternalmente spira,
> lo primo e ineffabile Valore
>   quanto per mente e per loco si gira
> con tant' ordine fé, ch'esser non puote
> sanza gustar di lui chi ciò rimira.
>
> ...
>
> Tal era quivi la quarta famiglia
> de l'alto Padre, che sempre la sazia,
> mostrando come spira e come figlia.[11]

---

[11] Looking upon his Son with the love which the one and the other eternally breathe forth, the primal and ineffable power made everything that revolves through the mind or through space with such order that he who contemplates it cannot but taste of him ... Such was here the fourth family of the exalted Father who ever satisfies it, showing how he breathes forth and how he begets.

Most recently on the *filioque* (Augustine, *De trin.* XV.v.29; 45; Anselm, *Pros.* xxiii, etc.), A. Riaud, *Le Filioque: origine et rôle de la troisième personne de la Trinité* (Paris: Fraternités du Saint-Esprit, 1989); R. Simon, *Das Filioque bei Thomas von Aquin: eine Untersuchung zur dogmengeschichtlichen Stellung, theologischen Struktur und ökumenischen Perspektive der thomanischen Gotteslehre* (Frankfurt am Main and New York: P. Lang, 1994); P. Gemeinhardt, *Die Filioque-Kontroverse zwischen Ost- und Westkirche im Frühmittelalter* (Berlin and New York: Walter de Gruyter, 2002); D. Ngien, *Apologetic for Filioque in Medieval*

On the perichoretic side, by contrast, there his sense of the mutual indwelling or 'inseatedness' of the three Persons of the Trinity, a model open to contemplation under the aspect, less now of extensivity, than of intensivity or co-dimensionality;[12] so, for example, again from the *Paradiso*,

Theology (Bletchley and Waynesboro, GA: Paternoster, 2005). Thomas on filiation and spiration, *ST* Ia.28.4 resp.: 'Processio autem verbi dicitur generatio secundum propriam rationem qua competit rebus viventibus. Relatio autem principii generationis in viventibus perfectis dicitur paternitas; relatio vero procedentis a principio dicitur filiatio. Processio vero amoris non habet nomen proprium ... Sed vocatur relatio principii hujus processionis spiratio.' On the procession of the Spirit from the Father by way of the Son, *ST* Ia.36. 2-3, and on the procession of the Spirit from the Son, *ScG* IV.xxiv-xxv. Notable among the finer points of Dantean Trinitarianism are (*a*) its appropriation of creative power in the *Par.* X.1-6 passage to the Father (the 'con tant' ordine fé' of line 5; cf. Thomas, *ST* Ia.45.6 ad 2: 'patri attribuitur et appropriatur potentia, quae maxime manifestatur in creatione; et ideo attribuitur patri creatorem esse. Filio autem appropriatur sapientia, per quam agens per intellectum operatur, et ideo dicitur de Filio per quem omnia facta sunt. Spiritui Sancto autem appropriatur bonitas, ad quam pertinet gubernatio, deducens res in debitos fines, et vivificatio'); (*b*) its sense of the dispositive role of the Spirit in respect of the Word as a principle of creation (the 'Però se 'l caldo amor la chiara vista / de la prima virtù dispone e segna, / tutta la perfezione quivi s'acquista' of *Par.* XIII.79-81); and (*c*) its linking of divine subsistence with the splendour of the Son in particular (the Idea or $\lambda \acute{o} \gamma o \varsigma$) as the in-and-through-which of the creative initiative (the 'Ciò che non more e ciò che può morire / non è se non splendor di quella idea / che partorisce, amando, il nostro Sire' of *Par.* XIII.52-54, for which the 'Qui cum sit splendor gloriae, et figura substantiae ejus, portansque omnia verbo virtutis suae' of Heb. 1:3). In respect of the first and third of these emphases, Thomas, *ST* Ia.46.3 resp.: 'Sicut enim principium effectivum appropriatur patri, propter potentiam, ita principium exemplare appropriatur filio, propter sapientiam, ut sicut dicitur, omnia in sapientia fecisti, ita intelligatur Deum omnia fecisse in principio, idest in filio; secundum illud apostoli ad Coloss. I, in ipso, scilicet filio, condita sunt universa.'

[12] For the terminology ($\pi \varepsilon \rho \iota \chi \acute{\omega} \rho \eta \sigma \iota \varsigma$), Gregory Nazianzen, *Epistula* ci.6; xxii.4; Pseudo-Cyril, *De sacro. trin.* xxiv; John of Damascus *De fide ortho.* i.14, etc. On the notion of perichoresis as dance (a pseudo-etymology), Hilary, *De trin.* ix.69. Historically and dogmatically, A. Deneffe, 'Perichoresis, circumincessio, circuminsessio,' in *Zeitschrift für katholische Theologie* 47 (1923), 497-532; D. F. Stramara Jr, 'Gregory of Nyssa's Terminology for Trinitarian Perichoresis', *Vigiliae Christianae* 52 (1998), 3, 257-63; R. Cross, 'Perichoresis, Deification, and Christological Predication in John of Damascus', *Medieval Studies* 62 (2000), 69-124. For an up-to-date implementation of the idea, E. L. Simmons, 'Quantum *Perichoresis*: Quantum Field Theory and the Trinity', *Theology and Science* 4 (2006), 2, 137-50. As part of a more general synthesis, J. Macquarrie, *Principles of Christian Theology*, rev. edn (London: SCM Press, 1966), pp. 174ff.; J. N. D. Kelly, *Early Christian Doctrines*, 5th edn (London: Adam and Charles Black, 1977), pp. 263ff.; T. F. Torrance, *The Trinitarian Faith: The Evangelical Theology of the Ancient Catholic Church* (Edinburgh: T. & T. Clark, 1988); idem, *Trinitarian Perspectives: Towards Doctrinal Agreement* (Edinburgh: T. & T. Clark, 1994), especially pp. 32-33, 93ff. and 121-23; C. Gunton, *The Promise of Trinitarian Theology*, 2nd edn (Edinburgh: T. & T. Clark, 1997); P. S. Fiddes, *Participating in God: A Pastoral Doctrine of the Trinity* (London: Darton, Longman and Todd, 2000), pp. 71ff. More generally still on Trinitarian theology, E. J. Fortman, *The Triune God: A Historical Study of the Doctrine of the Trinity* (London: Hutchinson, 1972); D. Brown,

these passages from Cantos XXIV and XXXIII (139-41 and 124-26 respectively), the first a meditation on the grammar of Trinitarianism, and the second on the notion of inseatedness (the 'in te sidi' of XXXIII.124) and on this as a matter of love and laughter:

> e credo in tre persone etterne, e queste
> credo una essenza sì una e sì trina,
> che soffera congiunto 'sono' ed 'este'.
> ...
> O luce etterna che sola in te sidi,
> sola t'intendi, e da te intelletta
> e intendente te ami e arridi![13]

Dante's, then, to go by the rapt emphases of *Paradiso* XXXIII, is a privileging of essence over economy as a way of seeing and celebrating the three-in-oneness of the Godhead, this in turn encouraging him in the most resplendent of his social formulations in the *Commedia*, in what amounts to his last word on the nature of one man's being with another at the point of emergence; for to be with the next man at the point of emergence is to be, not so much *with* him, as *within* him, as, somewhat after the manner of the Persons themselves of the Godhead, indwelling and indwelt one by the other. This at any rate is the implication, indeed the substance, of Dante's initiative in the ninth canto of the *Paradiso* when, proceeding once again neologistically

The Divine Trinity (London: Duckworth, 1985), especially pp. 272ff.
    Otherwise on the Trinity in Dante: *Inf.* III.4-6: 'Giustizia mosse il mio alto fattore; / fecemi la divina podestate, / la somma sapienza e 'l primo amore', with reference to the *opus ad extra* of the Trinity as a principle of cosmic organization; *Par.* XXXIII.115-20: 'Ne la profonda e chiara sussistenza / de l'alto lume parvermi tre giri / di tre colori e d'una contenenza; / e l'un da l'altro come iri da iri / parea reflesso, e 'l terzo parea foco / che quinci e quindi igualmente si spiri', with reference to the annular imagery of, especially, Joachim of Fiore (L. Tondelli (ed.), *Il libro delle figure dell'abate Gioachino da Fiore*, 2nd edn (Turin: Società editrice internazionale, 1990)). G. Busnelli, 'Dalla luce del cielo della luna alla trina luce dell'Empireo', *Studi danteschi* 27 (1943), 95-116; M. Apollonio, 'Una meditazione trinitaria', in *Dante. Storia della Commedia* (Milan: Vallardi, 1951), pp. 182-90; G. Fallani, *Dante poeta teologo* (Milan: Marzorati, 1965), pp. 211-25; idem, ad voc. 'Trinità', in the *Enciclopedia dantesca*, 6 vols (Rome: Istituto della Enciclopedia Italiana, 1970-78), vol. 5, pp. 718-21; P. Priest, *Dante's Incarnation of the Trinity* (Ravenna: Longo, 1982); V. Crupi, 'Dal *Paradiso* di Dante: l'impronta trinitaria nella creazione', *Nuova Umanità* 135-36 (2001), 433-63 (subsequently in *Saggi danteschi* (Cosenza: Luigi Pellegrini, 2003), pp. 33-68, with 'La Trinità nell'esegesi dantesca' in the same volume, pp. 69-105); G. Montanari, 'Terza parte; saggio teologico. Una terzina da rivedere: *Par.* XXXIII, 124-126 sulla Trinità?', in *Socrate, Cristo, Dante e la Bibbia: saggi di filologia estetica e sull'ebraismo fondamento della cultura* (Ravenna: Girasole, 2002), pp. 93-123.

[13] And I believe in three eternal persons, and these I believe to be one essence, so one and so threefold as to comport at once with *are* and *is* ... O light eternal, who alone abidest in thyself, and, known to thyself and knowing, lovest and smilest on thyself!

(the 'com' a lo re che 'n suo voler ne 'nvoglia' of *Par.* III.84 or the 'D'i Serafin che più s'india' of IV.28), he speaks of the kind of 'inhimming', 'inyouing' and 'inmeing' whereby one instance of being in its blessedness may be said to indwell another, a way of thinking and of speaking designed, not so much to liquidate otherness as a property of historical selfhood, as to confirm the radical nature of one man's presence to another in the moment of self-actualization. In the moment of self-actualization, Dante maintains, one man is present to another, not merely as a companion or fellow breaker of bread, but as an immanently operative principle of being and becoming, at which point diversity gives way to identity as a principle of social intelligence, as a way of conceiving and articulating the dialectic in human experience of *being in self* and *being with another*, of Selbstsein and Mitsein:

> "Dio vede tutto, e tuo veder s'inluia",
> diss' io, "beato spirto, sì che nulla
> voglia di sé a te puot' esser fuia.
>   Dunque la voce tua, che 'l ciel trastulla
> sempre col canto di quei fuochi pii
> che di sei ali facen la coculla,
>   perché non satisface a' miei disii?
> Già non attendere' io tua dimanda,
> s'io m'intuassi, come tu t'inmii".
>
> (*Par.* IX.73-81)[14]

Thus Trinitarianism once again encourages and facilitates, as Trinitarianism always, does a rethinking of the social issue in human experience; for if on the one hand there is a sense in which to be as man is to stand alone in respect of that which matters alone (this being the point of Dante's preference for the first-person singular in the *Commedia*), there is also a sense in which that same being both knows and is known by way of its brooking no dimensionality, no impediment to the mutual informing of self and the other-than-self in the moment of affirmation.

---

[14] "God sees all, and into him your vision sinks, blessed spirit", I said, "so that no wish may steal itself from you. Why then does your voice, which ever gladdens heaven – together with the singing of those devout fires that make themselves a cowl with six wings – not satisfy my longings? Surely I should not wait for your request, were I in you, even as you are in me". Cf. *Par.* XXII.124-29: "'Tu se' sì presso a l'ultima salute", / cominciò Bëatrice, "che tu dei / aver le luci tue chiare e acute; / e però, prima che tu più t'inlei, / rimira in giù, e vedi quanto mondo / sotto li piedi già esser ti fei".

Dante and the Protestant Principle

> Cum essem parvulus, loquebar ut
> parvulus, sapiebam ut parvulus,
> cogitabam ut parvulus. Quando factus
> sum vir, evacuavi quae erant parvuli.
>
> (I Cor. 13:11)[1]
>
> La maggiore parte de li uomini vivono
> secondo senso e non secondo ragione, a
> guisa di pargoli.
>
> (*Conv.* III.iv.3)[2]

1. Introduction: Protestantism and the protestant principle – preliminary considerations. 2. The Dantean protest: patterns of sacramentalism (Dante, grace and the historical encounter) and superintendence (Dante, episcopacy and self-episcopacy). 3. Conclusion: ecclesiality, existentiality and the whereabouts of the Dantean protest.

The first thing to say, lest the reader be tempted to pass by on the other side, is that what follows in this essay has nothing to do with fashioning from Dante a protestant in anything like the most obvious sense of the term, with making of him a sixteenth-century reformer *avant la lettre*.[3] On the contrary, it is a question of looking beneath and beyond protestantism in any of its historical manifestations to discern as far as may be something of what Paul Tillich – attuned as he was to the restiveness of Christianity vis-à-vis its own formalities – used to call the protestant principle; so, for example, this from the *Protestant Era* on the

---

[1] When I was a child, I spake as a child, I understood as a child, I thought as a child; but when I becam a man, I put away childish things (*AV*).

[2] The greater part of mankind live according to sense rather than reason, like children.

[3] On protestant readings and appropriations of Dante, E. Moore, 'Dante as a Religious Teacher', in *Studies in Dante. Second Series (Miscellaneous Essays)* (Oxford: Clarendon Press, 1899; reprint 1968), pp. 1-78 (especially pp. 7-8); A. Valensin, *Le Christianisme de Dante* (Paris: Aubier, 1954), pp. 15-16. See too M. Caesar (ed.), *Dante. The Critical Heritage* (London and New York: Routledge, 1989).

distinction to be drawn between the institutional expression of the idea and the idea itself, the idea by which the institution is at once authorized from deep within itself and by which it is called to account:

> Protestantism has a principle that stands beyond all its realizations. It is the critical and dynamic source of all protestant realizations, but it is not identical with any of them. It cannot be confined by a definition. It is not exhausted by any historical religion; it is not identical with the structure of the Reformation or early Christianity or even with a religious form at all. It transcends them as it transcends any cultural form. On the other hand, it can appear in all of them; it is a living, moving, restless power in them; and this is what it is supposed to be in a special way in historical protestantism. The protestant principle, in name derived from the protest of the 'protestants' against decisions of the Catholic majority, contains the divine and human protest against any absolute claim made for a relative reality, even if this claim is made by a protestant church. The protestant principle is the judge of every religious and cultural reality, including the religion and culture which calls itself 'protestant'.
>
> The protestant principle, the source and judge of protestantism, is not to be confused with the 'Absolute' of German idealism or with the 'Being' of ancient and recent philosophy. It is not the highest ontological concept derived from an analysis of the whole of being; it is the theological expression of the true relation between the unconditional and the conditioned or, religiously speaking, between God and man. As such, it is concerned with what theology calls 'faith', namely, the state of mind in which we are grasped by the power of something unconditional which manifests itself to us as the ground and judge of our existence. The power of grasping us in the state of faith is not a being beside others, not even the highest; it is not an object among objects, not even the greatest; but it is a quality of all beings and objects, the quality of pointing beyond themselves and their finite existence to the infinite, inexhaustible, and unapproachable depth of their being and meaning. The protestant principle is the extension of this relationship. It is the guardian against the attempts of the finite and conditioned to usurp the place of the unconditional in thinking and acting. It is the prophetic judgment against religious pride, ecclesiastical arrogance, and secular self-sufficiency and their destructive consequences.[4]

---

[4] Paul Tillich, *The Protestant Era*, trans. J. L. Adams (London: Nisbet, 1951), pp. 239-40; cf., idem, *Systematic Theology, Part II. Being and God* (London: SCM Press, 1978; originally 1951), p. 227: 'The Protestant principle is the restatement of the prophetic principle as an attack against a self-absolutizing and, consequently, demonically distorted church.'

to which, as similarly alert to the ideal transparency of the historically conditional in the life of the Church to the eternally unconditional, and to this as the main business of theology, we may add these lines – more than ever Tillichian in their combination of power and precision – from his *Theology of Culture*:

> The criterion of every concrete expression of our ultimate concern is the degree to which the concreteness of the concern is in unity with its ultimacy. It is the danger of every embodiment of the unconditional element, religious and secular, that it elevates something conditioned, a symbol, an institution, a movement as such to ultimacy. This danger was well known to the religious leaders of all types, and the whole work of theology can be summed up in the statement that it is the permanent guardian of the unconditional against the aspiration of its own religious and secular appearances.[5]

Thus to live with the protestant principle is to review in respect of their power to new life every received and accredited emphasis in the areas of moral, social, cultural and – as the encompassing of all these things – religious concern. In all these areas, Tillich thinks, it is a question of rethinking every settled habit of mind in respect of its accountability to the agapeic and thus subversive substance of the gospel kerygma, its extraordinary capacity for turning things on their head. This, then, is what Tillich has in mind when he speaks of the protestant principle. What he has in mind is the kind of discerning originating with Christ himself and present to his Church as that whereby it is saved from the demonic possibilities of its own historical forms.

2. Given the challenge mounted by Christianity to each of its successive solutions in the historical order, where, then, is the 'protest' in Dante? In reply to this, we cannot, alas, look to his critique of the contemporary

---

[5] *The Theology of Culture*, ed. R. C. Kimball (London, Oxford and New York: Oxford University Press, 1980; originally 1959), p. 29. Similarly in *The Protestant Era* cit. (previous note), p. 246: 'In the power of the protestant principle, protestantism must fight not only against other ideologies but also against its own. It must reveal the "false consciousness" wherever it hides. It must show how the "man-made God" of Catholicism was in the interest of the feudal order, of which the medieval church was part; how the ideology of Lutheranism was in the interest of the patriarchal order, with which Lutheran orthodoxy was associated; how the idealistic religion of humanistic protestantism is in the interest of a victorious *bourgeoisie*. The creation of these ideologies – religiously speaking, idols – representing man's will to power, occurs unconsciously. It is not a conscious falsification or a political lie. If this were the case, ideologies would not be very dangerous. But they are dangerous precisely because they are unconscious and are therefore objects of belief and fanaticism. To reveal these concrete ideologies is one of the most important functions of the protestant principle, just as it was one of the main points in the attack of the prophets on the religious and social order of their times.'

Church in what appears to him to be its lovelessness, for this is a critique inaugurated and sustained, not from *beyond*, but from *within*, his general ecclesiology, from out of a prior and settled sense of what the Church actually is.[6] What, then, for Dante, is the Church? The Church, he thinks, is nothing but the continuing presence of Christ to us under the conditions of time and space, its responsibility, therefore, being that of caring for the flock by way (*a*) of a faithful proclamation of the gospel message, and (*b*) of an integral administration of the keys as the power to discernment and to absolution made over to Peter by Christ in the Matthean commission; thus on the life of Christ as the intelligible form of the Church and on the role of the pope as pastor, this passage (xv.2-3) from the third book of the *Monarchia*:

> Ad evidentiam autem minoris sciendum quod natura Ecclesie forma est Ecclesie: nam, quamvis natura dicatur de materia et forma, per prius tamen dicitur de forma, ut ostensum est in *Naturali auditu* [*Physics* II. i]. Forma autem Ecclesie nichil aliud est quam vita Cristi, tam in dictis quam in factis comprehensa: vita enim ipsius ydea fuit et exemplar militantis Ecclesie, presertim pastorum, maxime summi, cuius est pascere agnos et oves.[7]

while on the integral preaching of the word, these lines (103-17) from *Paradiso* XXIX:

---

[6] On Dante's critique of the contemporary Church, G. Cattani, 'Il sacro zelo di San Pier Damiani a sostegno del sacro zelo di Dante nell'invettiva religiosa della *Commedia* (*Par.* c. XXI)', in *San Pier Damiani. Atti del Convegno di studi nel IX centenario della morte* (Florence: Società Torricelliana di Scienze e Lettere, 1973), pp. 43-59; K. Foster, O.P., 'The Canto of the Damned Popes, *Inferno* XIX', in *The Two Dantes and Other Studies* (London: Darton, Longman and Todd, 1977), pp. 86-106; A. Comollo, 'Il topos della corruzione della Chiesa nella *Commedia* e negli autori cattolici del tempo', in *Il dissenso religioso in Dante* (Florence: Olschki, 1990), pp. 79-104 (with a number of essays bearing on this subject); E. Airava, 'I papi buoni e cattivi nella *Divina Commedia*', *Settentrione. Rivista di Studi Italo-Finlandesi*, n.s. 3 (1996), 115-26; A. Lanza, 'I falsi pastori della Chiesa di Roma', in *Dante all'inferno. I misteri eretici della Commedia* (Rome: Tre Editori. 1999), pp, 143-55; N. Enright, 'Dante and the Scandals of a Beloved Church', *Logos. A Journal of Catholic Thought and Culture* 7 (2004), 4, 17-36; R. Imbach, 'Zum Heil der Welt, die übel lebt. Dantes Kirchenkritic und ihre Bedeutung', in *Die Kirchenkritic der Mystiker. Prophetie aus Gottesfahrung. I. Mittelalter*, ed. M. Delgado et al. (Fribourg-Stuttgart: Academic Press Fribourg-Kohlhammer, 2004), pp. 273-83; I. Castiglia, 'La lupa e l'orsa. L'invettiva contro il "clericus carnalis" nel Canto XIX dell'*Inferno*', *Dante. Rivista internazionale di studi su Dante Alighieri* 7 (2010), 35-55.

[7] To clarify the minor premiss it must be borne in mind that the church's nature is the form of the church; for although 'nature' is used with reference to matter and to form, nonetheless it refers first and foremost to form, as is shown in the Physics. Now the 'form' of the church is simply the life of Christ, including both his words and his deeds; for his life was the model and exemplar for the church militant, especially for the pastors, and above all for the supreme pastor, whose task is to feed the lambs and the sheep.

> Non ha Fiorenza tanti Lapi e Bindi
> quante sì fatte favole per anno
> in pergamo si gridan quinci e quindi:
>   sì che le pecorelle, che non sanno,
> tornan del pasco pasciute di vento,
> e non le scusa non veder lo danno.
>   Non disse Cristo al suo primo convento:
> 'Andate, e predicate al mondo ciance';
> ma diede lor verace fondamento;
>   e quel tanto sonò ne le sue guance,
> sì ch'a pugnar per accender la fede
> de l'Evangelio fero scudo e lance.
>   Ora si va con motti e con iscede
> a predicare, e pur che ben si rida,
> gonfia il cappuccio e più non si richiede.[8]

and, on the power of the keys and Peter's injunction to admit the contrite in spirit, these (lines 115-29) from *Purgatorio* IX:

> Cenere, o terra che secca si cavi,
> d'un color fora col suo vestimento;
> e di sotto da quel trasse due chiavi.
>   L'una era d'oro e l'altra era d'argento;
> pria con la bianca e poscia con la gialla
> fece a la porta sì, ch'i' fu' contento.
>   "Quandunque l'una d'este chiavi falla,
> che non si volga dritta per la toppa",
> diss' elli a noi, "non s'apre questa calla.
>   Più cara è l'una; ma l'altra vuol troppa
> d'arte e d'ingegno avanti che diserri,
> perch' ella è quella che 'l nodo digroppa.
>   Da Pier le tegno; e dissemi ch'i' erri
> anzi ad aprir ch'a tenerla serrata,
> pur che la gente a' piedi mi s'atterri."[9]

---

[8] Florence has not so many Lapos and Bindos as fables such as these that are shouted the year long from the pulpits on every side; so that the poor sheep, who know naught, return form the pasture fed with wind – and not seeing the harm does not excuse them. Christ did not say to his first company, "Go and preach idle stories to the world", but he gave them the true foundation; and that alone sounded on their lips, so that to fight for kindling of the faith they made shield and lance of the gospel. Now men go forth to preach with jests and with buffooneries, and so there be only a good laugh, the cowl puffs up and nothing more is asked.

[9] Ashes, or earth that is dug out dry, would be of one colour with his vesture, and from beneath it he drew two keys, the one of gold and the other of silver. First with the white

Here, though, we need to be careful, for committed as it is to the care of Peter and to those standing in the line of Petrine descent, the Church as but the body of Christ in its continuing presence to us is committed to one whose authority is not that of Christ himself, but of a delegate and appointee. On the one hand, then, these passages from the *Monarchia* (III.iii.7 and III.vii.4-8) on equivalence and non-equivalence in the area of proper authority:

> Summus nanque Pontifex, domini nostri Iesu Cristi vicarius et Petri successor, cui non quicquid Cristo sed quicquid Petro debemus, zelo fortasse clavium, necnon alii gregum cristianorum pastores, et alii quos credo zelo solo matris Ecclesie promoveri, veritati quam ostensurus sum de zelo forsan ut dixi non de superbia contradicunt ... Et si quis instaret de vicarii equivalentia, inutilis est instantia; quia nullus vicariatus, sive divinus sive humanus, equivalere potest principali auctoritati: quod patet de levi. Nam scimus quod successor Petri non equivalet divine auctoritati saltem in operatione nature: non enim posset facere terram ascendere sursum, nec ignem descendere deorsum per offitium sibi commissum. Nec etiam possent omnia sibi commicti a Deo, quoniam potestatem creandi et similiter baptizandi nullo modo Deus commictere posset, ut evidenter probatur, licet Magister contrarium dixerit in quarto. Scimus etiam quod vicarius hominis non equivalet ei, quantum in hoc quod vicarius est, quia nemo potest dare quod suum non est. Auctoritas principalis non est principis nisi ad usum, quia nullus princeps se ipsum auctorizare potest; recipere autem potest atque dimictere, sed alium creare non potest, quia creatio principis ex principe non dependet. Quod si ita est, manifestum est quod nullus princeps potest sibi substituere vicarium in omnibus equivalentem: qua re instantia nullam efficaciam habet.[10]

and then with the yellow he did so to the gate that I was content. "Whenever one of these keys fails so that it does not turn rightly in the lock", he said to us, "this passage does not open. The one is more precious; but the other requires great skill and wisdom before it will unlock, for this is the one that disentangles the knot. From Peter I hold them, and he told me to err rather in opening than in keeping shut, if but the people prostrate themselves at my feet". Otherwise on the power of the keys, *Mon.* III.i.5: 'et queritur utrum auctoritas Monarche romani, qui de iure Monarcha mundi est, ut in secundo libro probatum est, inmediate a Deo dependeat an ab aliquo Dei vicario vel ministro, quem Petri successorem intelligo, qui vere claviger est regni celorum'; *Inf.* XIX.100-105; XXVII.100-105; *Par.* XXIII.136-39; XXIV. 34-39; XXVII.46-51; XXXII.124-26, etc. P. Armour, *The Door of Purgatory. A Study of Multiple Symbolism in Dante's 'Purgatorio'* (Oxford: Clarendon Press, 1983), pp. 76-99; C. Ross, 'Canto IX. The Ritual Keys', in *Lectura Dantis. Purgatorio*, ed. A. Mandelbaum et al. (Berkeley, Los Angeles and London: University of California Press, 2008), pp. 85-94.

[10] For the supreme Pontiff, the vicar of our Lord Jesus Christ and Peter's successor, to whom we owe not what is due to Christ but what is due to Peter, perhaps motivated by a zealous concern for the keys, and with him other shepherds of the Christian flock and

while on the other, these (III.xvi.10 and 15) from the final moments of the book on the status of imperial no less than of papal office as a product of divine intentionality:

> Propter quod opus fuit homini duplici directivo secundum duplicem finem: scilicet summo Pontifice, qui secundum revelata humanum genus perduceret ad vitam ecternam, et Imperatore, qui secundum phylosophica documenta genus humanum ad temporalem felicitatem dirigeret ... Sic ergo patet quod auctoritas temporalis Monarche sine ullo medio in ipsum de fonte universalis auctoritatis descendit: qui quidem fons, in arce sue simplicitatis unitus, in multiplices alveos influit ex habundantia bonitatis.[11]

It is, then, from out of a sense of the Church thus understood, as that whereby man is confirmed in his ultimate happiness in and through God's provision for him by way of the Christ and of those commissioned by the Christ in expectation of his coming again, that Dante embarks on his litany of indictment; so, for example, the 'I' non so s' i' mi fui qui troppo folle' passage of *Inf.* XIX.88-105 on clerical greed and on the blasphemy thereof:

> others who I believe act only out of zealous concern for Mother Church: these people oppose the truth I am about to demonstrate – perhaps, as I said, out of zealous concern and not out of pride ... And if anyone were to base an objection on a vicar's being equivalent, the objection has no force, for no vicariate, human or divine, can be equivalent to the primary authority; and this is easy to see. For we know that Peter's successor is not the equivalent of divine authority at least as regards the workings of nature, for he could not make earth rise nor fire descend by virtue of the office entrusted to him. Nor could all things be entrusted to him by God, since God certainly could not entrust to him the power to create and the power to baptize, as is quite apparent, although Peter Lombard expressed the contrary opinion in his fourth book. We also know that a man's vicar, in as much as he is his vicar, is not equivalent to him, because no one can give away what does not belong to him. A prince's authority belongs to a prince only as something for his use, for no prince can confer authority on himself; he can accept it and renounce it, but he cannot create another prince, for the creation of a prince is not dependent on a prince. If this is the case, it is clear that no prince can appoint a vicar to take his place who is equivalent to him in all things; thus the objection has no force.

[11] It is for this reason that man had need of two guides corresponding to his twofold goal: that is to say the supreme Pontiff, to lead mankind to eternal life in conformity with revealed truth, and the Emperor, to guide mankind to temporal happiness in conformity with the teachings of philosophy ... Thus it is evident then that the authority of the temporal monarch flows down into him without any intermediary from the fountainhead of universal authority; this fountainhead, though one in the citadel of its own simplicity of nature, flows into many streams from the abundance of his goodness. On the precise relationship of imperial and philosophical authority as twin co-efficients in respect of the happiness of this life (the 'secundum phylosophica documenta' of III.xvi.10), J. Took, '"Diligite iustitiam qui iudicatis terram": Justice and the Just Ruler in Dante', in *Dante and Governance*, ed. J. R. Woodhouse (Oxford: Oxford University Press, 1997), pp. 137-51.

> Io non so s'i' mi fui qui troppo folle,
> ch'i' pur rispuosi lui a questo metro:
> "Deh, or mi dì: quanto tesoro volle
>
> Nostro Segnore in prima da san Pietro
> ch'ei ponesse le chiavi in sua balìa?
> Certo non chiese se non 'Viemmi retro'.
>
> Né Pier né li altri tolsero a Matia
> oro od argento, quando fu sortito
> al loco che perdé l'anima ria.
>
> Però ti sta, ché tu se' ben punito;
> e guarda ben la mal tolta moneta
> ch'esser ti fece contra Carlo ardito.
>
> E se non fosse ch'ancor lo mi vieta
> la reverenza de le somme chiavi
> che tu tenesti ne la vita lieta,
>
> io userei parole ancor più gravi;
> ché la vostra avarizia il mondo attrista,
> calcando i buoni e sollevando i pravi".[12]

or the 'tosto libere fien de l'avoltero' passage of *Par*. IX.133-42 on the Church's desertion the Nazarene in favour of the decretalists:

> Per questo l'Evangelio e i dottor magni
> son derelitti, e solo ai Decretali
> si studia, sì che pare a' lor vivagni.
>
> A questo intende il papa e ' cardinali;
> non vanno i lor pensieri a Nazarette,
> là dove Gabrïello aperse l'ali.
>
> Ma Vaticano e l'altre parti elette
> di Roma che son state cimitero
> a la milizia che Pietro seguette,
> tosto libere fien de l'avoltero.[13]

---

[12] I do not know if here I was overbold, in answering him in just this strain: "Pray now tell me how much treasure did our Lord require of St Peter before he put the keys into his keeping? Surely he asked nothing save 'Follow me'. Nor did Peter or the others take gold or silver of Matthias when he was chosen for the office which the guilty soul had lost. Therefore stay right here, for you are justly punished; and guard well the ill-got gain that made you bold against Charles. And were it not that reverence for the great keys which you held in the glad life even now forbids it to me, I would use yet harder words, for your avarice afflicts the world, trampling down the good and exalting the poor."

[13] For this the gospel and the great doctors are deserted, and only the decretals are studied, as may be seen from their margins. Thereon the pope and the cardinals are intent. Their thoughts go not to Nazareth whither Gabriel spread his wings. But the Vatican and the other chosen parts of Rome which have been the burial place for the soldiery that followed Peter shall soon be free from this adultery.

or the 'il luogo mio, il luogo mio, il luogo mio' passage of *Par.* XXVII.16-27 on the stench of ecclesiastical corruption:

> La provedenza, che quivi comparte
> vice e officio, nel beato coro
> silenzio posto avea da ogne parte,
>   quand' ïo udi': "Se io mi trascoloro,
> non ti maravigliar, ché, dicend' io,
> vedrai trascolorar tutti costoro.
>   Quelli ch'usurpa in terra il luogo mio,
> il luogo mio, il luogo mio, che vaca
> ne la presenza del Figliuol di Dio,
> fatt' ha del cimitero mio cloaca
> del sangue e de la puzza; onde 'l perverso
> che cadde di qua sù, là giù si placa".[14]

For Dante, then, papacy, piracy and profligacy – indeed papacy, piracy and prostitution (the 'puttana sciolta' passage of *Purg.* XXXII.148-60)[15] – flow one into the other, reinforcing as they do so their joint capacity for scandalizing the pious spirit. But – and this now is the point – Dante's, for all the strength of its indictment, is a discourse contained by, rather than challenging, his ecclesiology, his sense of the Church in its hierocracy, its apostolicity and its sacramentality. None of this is at stake. What is at stake is not the idea, but the practicality of it all, the maladministration by those entrusted with it, of Christ's substance and legacy.

If not here, then, where *is* the Dantean protest, that element of restiveness and of rethinking marking him out as a Christian poet and prophet? The answer is twofold, Dante's being a sense (*a*) of the cultural encounter generally, as distinct from the ecclesiastical encounter in particular, as a channel of grace, and (*b*) of episcopacy as, whatever else it is, a matter of *self*-episcopacy, of self-oversight on the plane of properly human being and doing, these things between them making for an opening-out of the

---

[14] The providence which there assigns turn and office had imposed silence on the blessed choir on every side, when I heard, "If I change colour, marvel not, for, as I speak, you shall see all these change colour. He who on earth usurps my place, my place, my place, which in the sight of the Son of God is vacant, has made my burial-ground a sewer of blood and of stench, so that the perverse one who fell from here above takes comfort there below".

[15] [Secure, like a fortress on a high mountain, there appeared to me] an ungirt harlot [sitting upon it, with eyes quick to rove around]. The passage in its entirety runs as follows: 'Sicura, quasi rocca in alto monte, / seder sovresso una puttana sciolta / m'apparve con le ciglia intorno pronte; / e come perché non li fosse tolta, / vidi di costa a lei dritto un gigante; / e basciavansi insieme alcuna volta. / Ma perché l'occhio cupido e vagante / a me rivolse, quel feroce drudo / la flagellò dal capo infin le piante; / poi, di sospetto pieno e d'ira crudo, / disciolse il mostro, e trassel per la selva, / tanto che sol di lei mi fece scudo / a la puttana e a la nova belva.'

ecclesiastical upon the existential, upon existence itself, in all the myriad determinacy of existence, as enlisted and empowered as a means of divine purposefulness. To take then, the first of these things – the status of the cultural encounter generally, as distinct from the ecclesiastical encounter in particular, as a means of grace – we may begin by noting that references in the *Commedia* to the sacraments, even to the sacraments of baptism and the eucharist, are few and far between and, as often as not, either allusive or parodistic;[16] so, for example, as regards baptism, the 'cleansing with the reed' episode of *Purg.* I.94-99 and 130-36 or the Lethe and Eunoè episodes of *Purg.* XXXI.91-105 and XXXIII.127-45, and, as regards the eucharist, the cases of Ugolino and of Lucifer, each alike suggestive of the substance and significance of the sacrament in question, but at an imaginative remove, indirectly rather than in any sense systematically. How, then, are we to account for this situation? By way not so much of the attenuated importance of these things in a discourse of anagogical inspiration (the sacramental phase of the religious life now slipping into the past), but of a preoccupation in Dante with the encounter itself, in all the incarnational intensity of the encounter, as a means of grace and principle of salvation. This at any rate, or something close to it, is the implication of the Virgilian and the Beatrician moment of the text, each alike present to him as soteriologically significant; on the one hand, then, as regards the Virgilian moment, these lines (40-54) from Canto XXX of the *Purgatorio*, secure in their sense of the salvific substance of it all, of the encounter itself as the way of emergence:

> Tosto che ne la vista mi percosse
> l'alta virtù che già m'avea trafitto
> prima ch'io fuor di püerizia fosse,
> volsimi a la sinistra col respitto
> col quale il fantolin corre a la mamma
> quando ha paura o quando elli è afflitto,
> per dicere a Virgilio: 'Men che dramma
> di sangue m'è rimaso che non tremi:

---

[16] To the fore among Dante's references to baptism, *Inf.* IV.31-36 and *Par.* XXV.1-12 on baptism as the 'portal of faith' (*Inf.* IV.36), *Par.* XXXII.76-84 on baptism as confirmation of being in Christ, and *Par.* XX.127-29 on the baptism of grace preceding baptism proper by a thousand years ('Quelle tre donne li fur per battesmo / che tu vedesti da la destra rota, / dinanzi al battezzar più d'un millesmo'). On marriage, after Matt. 22:30 and in addition (but metaphorically) to the *Neque nubent* of *Purg.* XIX.136-38, *Inf.*, XIX.1-4, *Par.* X.139-44, XI.55-66 and XXXI.1-3. On ordination, and apart from the 'sommo officio' and 'ordini sacri' moment of *Inf.* XXVII.85-93 (itself scarcely systematic), the crowning and mitring moment of *Purg.* XXVII ult. (but see below on this passage). P. Armour, *The Door of Purgatory. A Study of Multiple Symbolism in Dante's 'Purgatorio'* (note 9 above), pp. 5 ff.; E. Ardissino, 'La storia dell'eterno e il rinnovamento battesimale del poeta', in *Tempo liturgico e tempo storico nella "Commedia" di Dante* (Città del Vaticano: Libreria Editrice Vaticana, 2009), pp. 89-108.

conosco i segni de l'antica fiamma'.
Ma Virgilio n'avea lasciati scemi
di sé, Virgilio dolcissimo patre,
Virgilio a cui per mia salute die'mi;
né quantunque perdeo l'antica matre,
valse a le guance nette di rugiada,
che, lagrimando, non tornasser atre.[17]

while on the other, and as far now as the Beatrician moment of his experience is concerned, these (lines 70-93) from Canto XXXI of the *Paradiso*, similarly committed to the status of the encounter, in all the particularity of the encounter, as the in-and-through-which of new life:

Sanza risponder, li occhi sù levai,
e vidi lei che si facea corona
reflettendo da sé li etterni rai.
Da quella regïon che più sù tona
occhio mortale alcun tanto non dista,
qualunque in mare più giù s'abbandona,
quanto lì da Beatrice la mia vista;
ma nulla mi facea, ché süa effige
non discendëa a me per mezzo mista.
"O donna in cui la mia speranza vige,
e che soffristi per la mia salute
in inferno lasciar le tue vestige,

---

[17] As soon as on my sight the lofty virtue smote that had already pierced me before I was out of my boyhood, I turned to the left with the confidence of a little child that runs to his mother when he is frightened or in distress, to say to Virgil, "Not a drop of blood is left in me that does not tremble: I know the tokens of the ancient flame". But Virgil had left us bereft of himself, Virgil sweetest father, Virgil to whom I gave myself for my salvation; nor did all that our ancient mother lost keep my dew-washed cheeks from turning dark again with tears. See too as regards the soteriological significance of the Virgilian moment of his experience in the case now of Statius, the 'Per te poeta fui, per te cristiano' moment of *Purg*. XXII.55-75:"'Or quando tu cantasti le crude armi / de la doppia trestizia di Giocasta", / disse 'l cantor de' buccolici carmi, / "per quello che Clïò teco lì tasta, / non par che ti facesse ancor fedele / la fede, sanza qual ben far non basta. / Se così è, qual sole o quai candele / ti stenebraron sì, che tu drizzasti / poscia di retro al pescator le vele?". / Ed elli a lui: "Tu prima m'invïasti / verso Parnaso a ber ne le sue grotte, / e prima appresso Dio m'alluminasti. / Facesti come quei che va di notte, / che porta il lume dietro e sé non giova, / ma dopo sé fa le persone dotte, / quando dicesti: 'Secol si rinova; / torna giustizia e primo tempo umano, / e progenïe scende da ciel nova'. / Per te poeta fui, per te cristiano: / ma perché veggi mei ciò ch'io disegno, / a colorare stenderò la mano'". T. Barolini, *Dante's Poets. Textuality and Truth in the* Comedy (Princeton, N.J.: Princeton University Press, 1984), especially pp. 256-69; G. Brugnoli, 'Statius christianus', *Italianistica* 17 (1988), 1, 9-15; C. Kallendorf and H. Kallendorf, '"Per te poeta fui, per te cristiano" (*Purg*. 22.73). Statius as Christian, from "Fact" to "Fiction"', *Deutsches Dante-Jahrbuch* 77 (2002), 61-72; P. M. Clogan, 'Dante and Statius: Revisited', *Medievalia et Humanistica* 35 (2009), 77-101.

> di tante cose quant' i' ho vedute,
> dal tuo podere e da la tua bontate
> riconosco la grazia e la virtute.
> Tu m'hai di servo tratto a libertate
> per tutte quelle vie, per tutt' i modi
> che di ciò fare avei la potestate.
> La tua magnificenza in me custodi,
> sì che l'anima mia, che fatt' hai sana,
> piacente a te dal corpo si disnodi".
> Così orai; e quella, sì lontana
> come parea, sorrise e riguardommi;
> poi si tornò a l'etterna fontana.[18]

Now grace, as nothing other than the extrinsication or outpouring of the love-substance of the Godhead, everywhere abounds in the *Commedia*, and everywhere abounds as the prior and perpetual condition of man's proper homecoming as man, as that whereby, in and through the love-solicitude of the Father, he lays hold of the deiformity or Godlikeness to which he is called from beforehand. But within the economy of the *Commedia* as an account of the 'indiarsi' or in-Godding of self as the final cause of every significant inflexion of the spirit, grace thus understood, as nothing but the overflowing of divine goodness in ever new channels of creative and recreative concern, is mediated as much by the encounter as by the forms and formularies of the Church, at which point ecclesiology gives way to something closer to a theology of culture as a way of seeing and setting up the soteriological issue. Emphatically, nothing is lost here ecclesiologically, for Dante's, in the *Commedia*, is a rejoicing both in the unspeakable sweetness of the liturgical moment and in the refined substance of prayer under the aspect both of praise and of intercession.[19] But for all that, the journey into

---

[18] Without answering I lifted up my eyes and saw her where she made for herself a crown as she reflected the eternal rays. From the region which thunders most high no mortal eye is so distant, were it plunged most deep within the sea, as there from Beatrice was my sight. But to me it made no difference, for her image came down to me unblurred by aught between. "O lady in whom my hope is strong, and who for my salvation did endure to leave in hell your footprints, all those things which I have seen I acknowledge the grace and the virtue to be from your power and your excellence. It is you who have drawn me from bondage into liberty by all those paths, by all those means by which you had the power so to do. Preserve in me your great munificence, so that my soul which you have made whole, may be loosed from the body, pleasing unto you." So did I pray; and she, so distant as she seemed, smiled and looked on me, then turned again to the eternal fountain.

[19] J. C. Barnes, 'Vestiges of the Liturgy in Dante's Verse', in *Dante and the Middle Ages*, ed. J. C. Barnes and C. Ó Cuilleanáin (Dublin: Irish Academic Press, 1995), pp. 231-270; E. Alberione, 'Liturgie della speranza nel *Purgatorio* dantesco', in *Purgatorio* (Milan: San Fedele, 1996), pp. 54-67; R. L. Martinez, 'L'"amoroso canto". Liturgy and Vernacular

God is existentially rather than ecclesially conceived, effected by way, not of the strange semiosis of the sacrament, but of the sacredness of the event itself in all its power to persuade from out of its innermost recesses.

But with what amounts to a sense in Dante of the salvific status of the encounter generally we are still in the foothills where his version of the protest is concerned, for more impressive still is his fashioning from the idea of episcopacy something closer to *self*-episcopacy as the goal of moral and ontological aspiration. Now this too needs careful statement, for if on the one hand to be as man is to be in and through the power properly one's own to moral self-determination, then there can, on the other, be no dispensing with the kind of episcopal oversight whereby self is encouraged and sustained from beyond self as a pilgrim spirit; so, for example, these lines from *Paradiso* V (73-78) with their commitment, not only to Scripture, but to pastoral care as the way of salvation:

> Siate, Cristiani, a muovervi più gravi:
> non siate come penna ad ogne vento,
> e non crediate ch'ogne acqua vi lavi.
>   Avete il novo e 'l vecchio Testamento,
> e 'l pastor de la Chiesa che vi guida;
> questo vi basti a vostro salvamento.[20]

or these (lines 13-18) from the next canto on the place of the priest and above all of the Pope as pastor to the perplexed:

Lyric in Dante's *Purgatorio*', *Dante Studies* 127 (2009), 93-127; idem, 'Place and Times of the Liturgy from Dante to Petrarch', in *Petrarch and Dante. Anti-dantism, Metaphysics, Tradition*, ed. Z. G. Barański (Notre Dame: Notre Dame University Press, 2009), pp. 320-370. On prayer and prayerfulness, E. Auerbach, 'La preghiera di Dante alla Vergine (*Par*. XXXIII) ed antecedenti elogi', in *Studi su Dante* (Milan: Feltrinelli, 1984), pp. 273-308; N. Costanzo, 'I versi 1-21 della preghiera alla Vergine. Ipotesi di rilettura', in *L'Alighieri. Rassegna bibliografica dantesca* 28 (1987), 2, 26-47 (and in *Curiosità del ritmo poetico* (Pasian di Prato: Campanotto, 2003), pp. 31-65); A. Vallone, '*Par*. XXXIII: la preghiera, l'uso della scuola e l'insufficienza della parola', in *Cultura e mxemoria in Dante* (Naples: Guida, 1988), pp. 59-119; F. Salsano, 'Nella preghiera alla Vergine un percorso melodico. Considerazioni sul Canto XXXIII del *Paradiso*', in *L'Osservatore Romano*, 8 dicembre (1991), p. 3 (with a revised version entitled 'Canto XXXIII', in *Lecturae Dantis* (Ravenna: Longo 2003), pp. 242-53); G. Barberi Squarotti, 'La preghiera alla Vergine: Dante e Petrarca', *Filologia e Critica* 20 (1995), 2-3, 365-74 (subsequently in *Il tragico cristiano da Dante ai moderni* (Florence: Olschki, 2003), pp. 87-95); P. A. Perotti, 'La preghiera alla Vergine (*Par*. XXXIII.1-39)', in *L'Alighieri. Rassegna bibliografica dantesca* 36 (1995), 6, 75-83; R. Migliorini Fissi, 'La preghiera alla Vergine (*Paradiso* XXXIII, vv. 1-39)', in *Archivio Perugino-Pievese*, 3 (2000), 1, 115-33; R. Scrivano, 'Superbia, umiltà e preghiera in *Purgatorio* XI', in *Esperienze Letterarie* 31 (2006), 3, 3-19.

[20] Be graver, you Christians, in moving. Be not like a feather to every wind, and think not that every water may cleanse you. You have the New Testament and the Old, and the shepherd of the Church, to guide you.

> E prima ch'io a l'ovra fossi attento,
> una natura in Cristo esser, non piùe,
> credea, e di tal fede era contento;
>   ma 'l benedetto Agapito, che fue
> sommo pastore, a la fede sincera
> mi dirizzò con le parole sue.[21]

or these from the *Monarchia* at III.xv.3 on feeding the sheep as the very stuff of the Church Militant:

> Forma autem Ecclesie nichil aliud est quam vita Cristi, tam in dictis quam in factis comprehensa : vita enim ipsius ydea fuit et exemplar militantis Ecclesie, presertim pastorum, maxime summi, cuius est pascere agnos et oves.[22]

Everywhere, then, it is a question of priestly oversight, of a species of superintendency designed in response to the gospel imperative to ensure the well-being of Christ's flock, to exercise, in short, a duty of care and compassion. But – and this now is what matters – for all the indispensability of shepherding thus understood to any kind of ultimate homecoming, there can be no question of Dante's privileging the heteronomous over the autonomous component of human experience under the conditions of time and space, the regulative over the self-regulative component, for herein – in the power of self to self-governance – lies the ground and guarantee of man's likeness to God as a creature of self-understanding and of self-determination; hence the following passage from Canto XXVII of the *Purgatorio* designed precisely to confirm and celebrate the entry of the soul into its own company, there to rejoice in the completeness of its regal and episcopal sufficiency:

> "Quel dolce pome che per tanti rami
> cercando va la cura de' mortali,
> oggi porrà in pace le tue fami".
>   Virgilio inverso me queste cotali
> parole usò; e mai non furo strenne
> che fosser di piacere a queste iguali.
>   Tanto voler sopra voler mi venne

---

[21] And before I had put my mind to this work, one nature and no more I held to be in Christ, and with that faith I was content; but the blessed Agapetus, who was the supreme pastor, directed me to the true faith by his words.

[22] Now the form of the Church is simply the life of Christ, including both his words and his deeds; for his life was the model and exemplar for the Church Militant, especially for the pastors, and above all for the supreme pastor, whose task is to feed the lambs and the sheep. John 21:15-17.

> de l'esser sù, ch'ad ogne passo poi
> al volo mi sentia crescer le penne.
>   Come la scala tutta sotto noi
> fu corsa e fummo in su 'l grado superno,
> in me ficcò Virgilio li occhi suoi,
>   e disse: "Il temporal foco e l'etterno
> veduto hai, figlio; e se' venuto in parte
> dov' io per me più oltre non discerno.
>   Tratto t'ho qui con ingegno e con arte;
> lo tuo piacere omai prendi per duce;
> fuor se' de l'erte vie, fuor se' de l'arte.
>   Vedi lo sol che 'n fronte ti riluce;
> vedi l'erbette, i fiori e li arbuscelli
> che qui la terra sol da sé produce.
>   Mentre che vegnan lieti li occhi belli
> che, lagrimando, a te venir mi fenno,
> seder ti puoi e puoi andar tra elli.
>   Non aspettar mio dir più né mio cenno;
> libero, dritto e sano è tuo arbitrio,
> e fallo fora non fare a suo senno:
>   per ch'io te sovra te corono e mitrio".
>
>   (*Purg.* XXVII.115-42)[23]

Predictable as this is as a point of arrival in respect of what amounts in the first two canticles of the *Commedia* to a song of descents and of ascents on the part of the ontically anxious subject, it comes as a shock to see it in black and white, Dante's in this sense being a radical internalization of every authoritarian structure in the Church, a fashioning from observance and obedience something closer to an inner discipline of the Spirit. If, then, princes and prelates have their part to play in facilitating the process of

---

[23] "That sweet fruit which the care of mortals goes seeking on so many branches, this day shall give your hungering peace." Such were Virgil's words to me, and never were there gifts that could be equal in pleasure to these. Such wish upon wish came to me to be above, that at every step thereafter I felt my feathers growing for the flight. When all the stair was sped beneath us and we were on the topmost step, Virgil fixed his eyes on me and said, "The temporal fire and the eternal you have seen, my son, and are to come to a part where I of myself discern no farther onward. I have brought you here with understanding and with art. Take henceforth your own pleasure for your guide. Forth you are from the steep ways, forth from the narrow. See the sun that shines on your brow, see the tender grass, the flowers, the shrubs, which here the earth of itself alone produces; till the beautiful eyes come rejoicing which weeping made me come to you, you may sit or go among them. No longer expect a word or sign from me. Free, upright, and whole is your will, and it would be wrong not to act according to its pleasure; wherefore I crown and mitre you over yourself".

properly human being and becoming, dereliction by way either of vacancy or of violence making for catastrophe in the lives of those subject to them, there can, he thinks, be no delivering of self to anything other than its proper power to self-actualization, anything other than this, Dante must have thought, making less for the meat than for the milk of the moral and religious life, for something closer to the adolescent than to the adult as a disposition of the spirit.

3. The first thing to say when it comes to Dante and the protestant principle is that there can be no question of fashioning from him a proto-protestant, a crypto-protestant or any other kind of protestant in any historically determinate sense of the word, Dante's being an understanding of the religious situation generally and of the ecclesiological situation in particular predating both in the letter and in the spirit those of the great divide. On the contrary, both in its sacramentalism and in its sacerdotalism (neither, however, figuring prominently on his horizon of concern) his sense of the Church in respect of what it is and what it does remains a product of contemporary consciousness in all the, as far as he is concerned, unexceptionality of that consciousness. But for all that, and entirely without prejudice to the indispensibility of the rites and observances of the moral and religious life to its stable pursuit and orderly implementation, his is a thinking through of that life in terms, less of its ecclesiality, than of its existentiality, of its rootedness in, and transparency to a consummate act of specifically human being. Thus those same rights and observances, functional in the highest degree as that whereby the spirit knows itself in the rhythm of its journey into God, stand at last to be referred to something at once more profound and more primordial than themselves, at which point the protest – as indispensible to the life of the spirit as its forms and formularies – once again moves into view.

The Courage of the *Commedia*

"Or va, ch'un sol volere è d'ambedue:
tu duca, tu segnore e tu maestro".
Così li dissi; e poi che mosso fue,
intrai per lo cammino alto e silvestro.

(*Inf.* II.139-42)[1]

1. Paul Tillich, *The Courage To Be*, and species of ontological anxiety: the anxiety of death and fate – the anxiety of guilt and condemnation – the anxiety of meaninglessness. 2. A further distinction: the *courage to be as part* and the *courage to be as oneself*. 3. Dante and the *courage to be as part* (*civitas*, *imperium* and *ecclesia*). 4. Dante and the *courage to be as oneself*: the moment of acknowledgement (*Inferno*), the moment of alignment (*Purgatorio*), and the moment of actualization (*Paradiso*). 5. Conclusion: the courage of the pilgrim and the courage of the poet.

In his book *The Courage To Be*, Paul Tillich identifies three forms of ontological anxiety, of the kind of anxiety which, transcending the merely circumstantial, rises up from the depths to constitute the dominant mood of existence. First comes the kind pertaining to being – by which we mean this or that instance of specifically human being – as it contemplates non-being as its polar counterpart. This, Tillich calls the *anxiety of fate and of death*, an order of anxiety engendered by the rhythm of unpredictability in human experience and confirmed in its power to terrify by the prospect sooner rather than later of ceasing to be.[2] Courage as the *courage to be*

---

[1] "Now on, for a single will is in us both; you are my leader, you my master and my teacher." So I said to him, and when he moved on, I entered along the deep and savage way. What follows is the revised version of a lecture by the same title delivered in University College London on 25 April, 2007 as the twelfth Alan Marre Maccabaeans Centenary Lecture in the Humanities. I am grateful to René Weiss, Professor of English in University College London and (at that time) Chair of the Maccabaeans Lectureship Committee for his kindness to me on that occasion.

[2] Paul Tillich, *The Courage To Be* (Glasgow: Collins, 1977; originally 1952), pp. 52-53: 'The threat of non-being to man's ontic self-affirmation is absolute in the threat of death, relative in the threat of fate. But the relative threat is a threat only because in its background stands the absolute threat. Fate would not produce inescapable anxiety without death behind it. And death stands behind fate and its contingencies not only

enters into this situation as that whereby the individual seeks even so to affirm self in the fundamental intelligibility and thus in the fundamental security of self, thus offsetting as far as may be those forces operative both from within and from beyond making by way of fear for a tearing down, as distinct from a building up, of historical selfhood. This, Tillich notes, was what Plato had in mind when in attempting to identify the dynamic element in human experience, he settled upon its thymotic or spirited component (θυμος) as dwelling somewhere between reason and desire and quickening the whole in respect of its proper finality.[3] It was what Aristotle had in mind when it came to the notion of bravery as a matter, not merely of military, but of moral concern, of a man's readiness 'to endure or fear the right things, for the right purpose, in the right manner, and at the right time', all this making for a nobility of spirit.[4] And it was what the Stoics

in the last moment when one is thrown out of existence but in every moment within existence. Non-being is omnipresent and produces anxiety even where an immediate threat of death is absent. It stands behind the experience that we are driven, together with everything else, from the past toward the future without a moment of time which does not vanish immediately. It stands behind the insecurity and homelessness of our social and individual existence. It stands behind the attacks on our power of being in body and soul by weakness, disease and accidents. In all these fate actualizes itself, and through them the anxiety of non-being takes hold of us. We try to transform the anxiety into fear and to meet courageously the objects in which the threat is embodied. We succeed partly, but somehow we are aware of the fact that it is not these objects with which we struggle that produce the anxiety but the human situation as such. Out of this the question arises: Is there a courage to be, a courage to affirm oneself in spite of the threat against man's ontic self-affirmation?' Dante on the death as the far limit of significant activity, *Purg.* XXXIII.54: 'del viver ch'è un correr a la morte'.

[3] Plato, *Republic* IV.xv (440c-e): Ἀληθῆ , ἔφη. Τί δὲ ὅταν ἀδικεῖσθαί τις ἡγῆται; οὐκ ἐν τούτῳ ζεῖ τε καὶ χαλεπαίνει καὶ συμμαχεῖ τῷ δοκοῦντι δικαίῳ καί, διὰ τὸ πεινῆν καὶ διὰ τὸ ῥιγοῆν καὶ πάντα τὰ τοιαῦτα πάσχειν, ὑπομένων καὶ νικᾷ καὶ οὐ λήγει τῶν γενναίων, πρὶν ἂν ἢ διαπράξηται ἢ τελευτήσῃ ἢ ὥσπερ κύων ὑπὸ νομέως ὑπὸ τοῦ λόγου τοῦ παρ' αὑτῷ ἀνακληθεὶς πραϋνθῇ; Πάνυ μὲν οὖν, ἔφη, ἔοικε τούτῳ ᾧ λέγεις καίτοι γ' ἐν τῇ ἡμετέρᾳ πόλει τοὺς ἐπικούρους ὥσπερ κύνας ἐθέμεθα ὑπηκόους τῶν ἀρχόντων ὥσπερ ποιμένων πόλεως. Καλῶς γάρ, ἦν δ' ἐγώ, νοεῖς ὃ βούλομαι λέγειν. ἀλλ' ἢ πρὸς τούτῳ καὶ τόδε ἐνθυμῇ; Τὸ ποῖον; Ὅτι τοὐναντίον ἢ ἀρτίως ἡμῖν φαίνεται περὶ το θυμοειδοῦς. τότε μὲν γὰρ ἐπιθυμητικόν τι αὐτὸ ᾠόμεθα εἶναι, νῦν δὲ πολλοῦ δεῖν φαμεν, ἀλλὰ πολὺ μᾶλλον αὐτὸ ἐν τῇ τῆς ψυχῆς στάσει τίθεσθαι τὰ ὅπλα πρὸς τὸ λογιστικόν.'

[4] Aristotle, *Nic. Eth.* III.vii (1115b16-24): 'ὁ μὲν οὖν ἃ δεῖ καὶ οὗ ἕνεκα ὑπομένων καὶ φοβούμενος, καὶ ὡς δε καὶ ὅτε, ὁμοίως δὲ καὶ θαρρῶν, ἀνδρεῖος κατ' ἀξίαν γάρ, καὶ ὡς ἂν ὁ λόγος, πάχει καὶ πράττει ὁ ἀνδρεῖος. τέλος δὲ πάσης ἐνεργείας ἐστὶ τὸ κατὰ τὴν ἕξιν, καὶ τῷ ἀνδρείῳ δὲ ἡ ἀνδρεία καλόν. τοιοῦτον δὴ καὶ τὸ τέλος ὁρίζεται γὰρ ἕκαστον τῷ τέλει. καλοῦ δὴ ἕνεκα ὁ ἀνδρεῖος ὑπομένει καὶ πράττει τὰ κατὰ τὴν ἀνδρείαν.' Thomas, ad loc. (III.xv, n. 6): 'Dicit ergo primo, quod ille qui sustinet quae oportet sustinere et fugit per timorem ea quae oportet vitare, et facit hoc eius gratia cuius oportet et eo modo quo oportet et quando oportet, vocatur fortis. Qui

had in mind when, sensitive to the challenge mounted by fate and death to the integrity and intelligibility of this or that act of specifically human being, they looked to the kind of self-sufficiency whereby the individual remains equal to the vicissitudes of the world as ranged over against him.[5] Courage thus understood, clearly, falls well short of the kind of courage whereby the guilt of estrangement is taken into self as the condition of its liquidation, Stoic courage in this sense being a matter, less of recognition than of resolve, of standing in the λόγος as a reply to the threat to existence everywhere mounted by existence. But for all that, it is ontological in kind, attuned to the problematics, not merely of right doing, but of right being as an object of concern.

But if the dominant species of anxiety in the ancient world is the anxiety of fate and of death, this, though never eclipsed as the deepest and most insistent form of ontological apprehension in human experience, is overlaid in successive periods of western sensibility by the *anxiety of guilt and condemnation* characteristic of the high Middle Ages and the early modern world, and by the *anxiety of meaninglessness* characteristic

---

etiam similiter audet quae oportet, et cuius gratia et cetera. Et huius rationem assignat dicens quod quia fortis et virtuosus patitur per timorem et operatur per audaciam, secundum quod dignum est et secundum quod recta ratio dictat. Omnis enim virtus moralis est secundum rationem rectam, ut supra habitum est.'

[5] *The Courage To Be* cit. (note 2 above), pp. 23-24: 'The Stoic courage is, in the ontological as well as the moral sense, "courage to be". It is based on the control of reason in man. But reason is not in either the old or the new Stoic what it is in contemporary terminology. Reason, in the Stoic sense, is not the power of "reasoning", of arguing on the basis of experience and with the tools of ordinary or mathematical logic. Reason for the Stoics is the Logos, the meaningful structure of reality as a whole and of the human mind in particular. "If there is", says Seneca, "no other attribute which belongs to man as man except reason, then reason will be his one good, worth all the rest put together". This means that reason is man's true or essential nature, in comparison with which everything else is accidental. The courage to be is the courage to affirm one's own reasonable nature over against what is accidental in us. It is obvious that reason in this sense points to the person in his centre and includes all mental functions. Reasoning as a limited cognitive function, detached from the personal centre, never could create courage. One cannot remove anxiety by arguing it away. This is not a recent psychoanalytical discovery; the Stoics, when glorifying reason, knew it as well. They knew that anxiety can be overcome only through the power of universal reason which prevails in the wise man over desires and fears. Stoic courage presupposes the surrender of the personal centre to the Logos of being; it is participation in the divine power of reason, transcending the realm of passions and anxieties. The courage to be is the courage to affirm our own rational nature, in spite of everything in us that conflicts with its union with the rational nature of being-itself.' Cicero (in the course of his reconstruction of the moral systems of antiquity), *De fin.* III.ix.31: 'Circumscriptis igitur iis sententiis quas posui, et iis si quae similes earum sunt, relinquitur ut summum bonum sit vivere scientiam adhibentem earum rerum quae natura eveniant, seligentem quae secundum naturam et quae contra naturam sint reicientem, id est convenienter congruenterque naturae vivere', etc.

of the modern world. The anxiety of guilt and condemnation is there whenever the individual sensitive to the part he himself has to play in the working out of his historical and eschatological destiny is at the same time possessed by a sense of his perversity, of his both willing and not willing at one and the same time. Impressed to the point of oppressed by his unrighteousness, he stands forever indicted in the forum of conscience and prey to despair.[6] Courage as the *courage to be* enters into this situation as that whereby, embarking on the way of sorrowing and of repentance, the individual delivers himself to grace either as a principle of additional formality (Aquinas) or else as a principle of acceptability in the midst of unacceptibility (Luther), either way the burden of guilt and condemnation finding relief in a movement of faith as the beginning of new life. The anxiety of meaninglessness, by contrast, is there whenever the individual concerned on the plane of self-intelligibility feels unable to discern within

---

[6] *The Courage To Be* cit. (note 2 above), pp. 58-59: 'Non-being threatens from a third side: it threatens man's moral self-affirmation. Man's being, ontic as well as spiritual, is not only given to him but also demanded of him. He is responsible for it; literally, he is required to answer, if he is asked, what he has made of himself. He who asks him is his judge, namely he himself, who, at the same time, stands against him. This situation produces the anxiety which in relative terms is the anxiety of guilt; in absolute terms, the anxiety of self-rejection or condemnation. Man is essentially "finite freedom"; freedom not in the sense of indeterminacy but in the sense of being able to determine himself through decisions in the centre of his being. Man, as finite freedom, is free within the contingencies of his finitude. But within these limits he is asked to make of himself what he is supposed to become, to fulfil his destiny. In every act of moral self-affirmation man contributes to the fulfilment of his destiny, to the actualization of what he potentially is. It is the task of ethics to describe the nature of this fulfilment, in philosophical or theological terms. But however the norm is formulated man has the power of acting against it, of contradicting his essential being, of losing his destiny. And under the conditions of man's estrangement from himself this is an actuality. Even in what he considers his best deed non-being is present and prevents it from being perfect. A profound ambiguity between good and evil permeates everything he does, because it permeates his personal being as such ... The awareness of this ambiguity is the feeling of guilt. The judge who is oneself and who stands against oneself, he who "knows with" (conscience) everything we do and are, gives a negative judgment, experienced by us as guilt.' Thomas on despair as sin, *ST* IIa IIae.20.1 resp.: 'secundum philosophum, in VI Ethic., id quod est in intellectu affirmatio vel negatio est in appetitu prosecutio et fuga, et quod est in intellectu verum vel falsum est in appetitu bonum et malum. Et ideo omnis motus appetitivus conformiter se habens intellectui vero, est secundum se bonus, omnis autem motus appetitivus conformiter se habens intellectui falso, est secundum se malus et peccatum. Circa Deum autem vera existimatio intellectus est quod ex ipso provenit hominum salus, et venia peccatoribus datur; secundum illud Ezech. XVIII, nolo mortem peccatoris, sed ut convertatur et vivat. Falsa autem opinio est quod peccatori poenitenti veniam deneget, vel quod peccatores ad se non convertat per gratiam iustificantem. Et ideo sicut motus spei, qui conformiter se habet ad existimationem veram, est laudabilis et virtuosus; ita oppositus motus desperationis, qui se habet conformiter existimationi falsae de Deo, est vitiosus et peccatum.'

him the still centre of that existence, this too serving both to sustain and to be sustained by a movement of despair.[7] Courage as the *courage to be* enters now as that whereby the acknowledgement of meaninglessness comes in itself to constitute a meaningful act, at which point being, despite every inkling to the contrary, triumphs over non-being as a principle of self-understanding.[8] Here too, therefore, in the context of anxiety as the anxiety of meaninglessness, courage as the *courage to be* breaks through to neutralize everything within the economy of personality making for resignation as a response to the agony of existence.

2. Now, however, the argument is subject to further inflexion, for the idea of courage thus understood — as a matter of the *courage to be* in respect of the anxiety of fate and death, of guilt and condemnation, and of meaninglessness — admits of a further distinction between the *courage to be as part* and the *courage to be as oneself*. By the expression 'courage to be as part', Tillich has in mind the kind of courage whereby the individual alert to the problematics of his existence under the conditions of time and space seeks to assuage his anxiety by way of allegiance to the structures of collective and of institutional consciousness by which he is sustained and reassured in respect of the

---

[7] ibid., pp. 54-55: 'The anxiety of meaninglessness is anxiety about the loss of an ultimate concern, of a meaning which gives meaning to all meanings. This anxiety is aroused by the loss of a spiritual centre, of an answer, however symbolic and indirect, to the question of the meaning of existence.' Further on the place of systematic doubt in the spiritual life, and on the shading off of systematic doubt into existential despair, pp. 55-56: 'Emptiness and loss of meaning are expressions of the threat of non-being to the spiritual life. This threat is implied in man's finitude and actualized by man's estrangement. It can be described in terms of doubt, its creative and its destructive function in man's spiritual life. Man is able to ask because he is separated *from*, while participating *in*, what he is asking about. In every question an element of doubt, the awareness of not having, is implied. In systematic questioning systematic doubt is effective, e.g. of the Cartesian type. This element of doubt is a condition of all spiritual life. The threat to spiritual life is not doubt as an element but total doubt. If awareness of not having has swallowed up the awareness of having, doubt has ceased to be methodological asking and has become existential despair.'

[8] ibid., p. 171: 'The faith which makes the courage of despair possible is the acceptance of the power of being, even in the grip of non-being. Even in the despair about meaning being affirms itself through us. The act of accepting meaninglessness is itself a meaningful act. It is an act of faith. We have seen that he who has the courage to affirm his being in spite of fate and guilt has not removed them. He remains threatened and hit by them. But he accepts his acceptance by the power of being-itself in which he participates and which gives him the courage to take the anxieties of fate and guilt upon himself. The same is true of doubt and meaninglessness. The faith which creates the courage to take them into itself has no special content. It is simply faith, undirected, absolute. It is undefinable, since everything defined is dissolved by doubt and meaninglessness.'

otherwise impossible loneliness of his presence in the world.[9] In fact, Tillich is careful in the course of his argument to distinguish between what he sees as primitive and as developed forms of the *courage to be as part*. Primitive versions – recrudescences of which, he thinks, are discernible in certain kinds of modern totalitarianism – are primitive in the degree to which the collective solution is espoused as a matter of course, there being as yet no developed sense of the problematics of selfhood.[10] Advanced manifestations of this same phenomenon, however, are advanced in the degree to which, albeit within the context of collective consciousness as the means of self-actualization, there is even so some doubt as to the power of that consciousness fully to resolve the sensation of personal anxiety, an element of misgiving thus ruling out unqualified submergence of the private in the collective – a situation discernible, Tillich thinks, in the bourgeois conformism of the modern world. Even so, the fundamental pattern is the same, the *courage to be as part* commending itself as a way of overcoming the sensation of ontological anxiety and thus of drawing its sting. True, without the *courage to be as oneself* as its innermost principle, Tillich says,[11] the *courage to be as part* can never be equal to the problem it seeks to address, for the problem it seeks to address can only ever be resolved by a coming home of self to the deep reasons of self; but in the degree to which the soul in its far-offness is strengthened by the institutions and ideologies which it embraces and by which it is in turn embraced

---

[9] ibid., p. 93: 'The courage to be as part is the courage to affirm one's own being by participation. One participates in the world to which one belongs and from which one is at the same time separated. But participating in the world becomes real through participation in those sections of it which constitute one's own life. The world as a whole is potential, not actual. Those sections are actual with which one is partially identical. The more self-relatedness a being has the more it is able, according to the polar structure of reality, to participate. Man as the completely centred being or as a person can participate in everything, but he participates through that section of the world which makes him a person. Only in the continuous encounter with other persons does the person become and remain a person. The place of this encounter is the community.'

[10] In the context of primitive collectivism, the individual 'affirms himself through the group in which he participates. The potential anxiety of losing himself is not actualized, because the identification with the group is complete. Non-being in the form of the threat of loss of self in the group has not yet appeared' (ibid., p. 95).

[11] ibid., pp. 94-95: 'There is no collective anxiety save an anxiety which has overtaken many or all members of a group and has been intensified or changed by becoming universal. The same is true of what is wrongly called collective courage. There is no entity "we-self" as the subject of courage. There are selves who participate in a group and whose character is partly determined by this participation. The assumed we-self is a common quality of ego-selves within a group. The courage to be as part is like all forms of courage, a quality of individual selves.'

as a means of affirmation, it holds at bay the structures of destruction by which it is threatened both from within and from beyond.

By the expression *courage to be as oneself* Tillich means the kind of courage whereby, anxious in respect of the problematics of historical selfhood, the individual seeks to address this anxiety by way, not now of social, institutional or ideological alignment, but of an encounter with self in the depths. Sensitive to the forces at work within him making by turns for being and for non-being, and yet unwilling either by formation or by conviction, or both, to deliver himself to the collective solution, he looks instead to the interrogation of his own existence as a point of departure, the *courage to be as oneself*, therefore, taking the form of a seeking out of the deep rationality of self as glimpsed across its surface *ir*rationality, across the clutter of high-level consciousness making in the ordinary way of things for distraction, confusion, and self-inexplicability. Tillich, with special reference at this point to the courage of the Enlightenment as, in this respect, exemplary, puts it thus:

> Courage to be as oneself, as this is understood in the Enlightenment, is a courage in which individual self-affirmation includes participation in universal, rational, self-affirmation. Thus it is not the individual self as such which affirms itself but the individual self as the bearer of reason. The courage to be as oneself is the courage to follow reason and to defy irrational authority. In this respect – but only in this respect – it is neo-Stoicism. For the courage to be of the Enlightenment is not a resigned courage to be. It dares not only to face the vicissitudes of fate and the inescapability of death but to affirm itself as transforming reality according to the demands of reason. It is a fighting, daring courage. It conquers the threat of meaninglessness by courageous action. It conquers the threat of guilt by accepting errors, shortcomings, misdeeds in the individual as well as in social life as unavoidable and at the same time to be overcome by education. The courage to be as oneself within the atmosphere of Enlightenment is the courage to affirm oneself as a bridge from a lower to a higher state of rationality.[12]

Courage as the *courage to be as oneself*, therefore, is the courage of being in the structured character of being, herein lying its power to overcome the threat of non-being as its demonic counterpart. Now neither of these forms of courage, Tillich thinks, excludes the other, the *courage to be as part* everywhere bearing deep within itself something of the *courage to be as oneself* and the *courage to be as oneself* everywhere shading off into the

---

[12] ibid, pp. 116-17.

courage to be as part, into the courage of belonging. Nonetheless, as a way of setting up the issue here – namely the interaction of anxiety and courage as paradigms of consciousness – the distinction may be allowed to stand. Both ontologically, in respect of its basic taxonomy, and historically, in respect of its basic phenomenology, it takes us to the heart of the matter.

3. Typically, Tillich thinks,[13] the courage of the Middle Ages was the *courage to be as part*, the courage to affirm self by way of the great power-configurations presiding over human affairs in this period and having about them both a prior and a providential status, a situation which Dante, with his sense of the city, empire and Church – of *civitas*, *imperium*, and *ecclesia* – as part of the pre-ordained pattern of things, reflects perfectly. First, then, comes the city, which, in addition to its function as a means of survival (no one man being equal to the practicalities of his existence), constitutes both a context and a co-efficient of historical selfhood, both the whereabouts and the means of a properly fulfilled humanity; on the one hand, then, and in respect first of all of survival pure and simple, this passage from the *Convivio* at IV.iv.2: 'E sì come un uomo a sua sufficienza richiede compagnia dimestica di famiglia, così una casa a sua sufficienza richiede una vicinanza: altrimenti molti difetti sosterrebbe che sarebbero impedimento di felicitade. E però che una vicinanza [a] sé non può in tutto satisfare, conviene a satisfacimento di quella essere la cittade',[14] while on the other, and as touching now on the idea of the city as the crucible of properly human being and becoming as determined in this or that individual by way of personality and/or vocation, these lines (115-48) from *Paradiso* VIII:

---

[13] ibid., pp. 96-97: 'The courage of the Middle Ages [...] is basically the courage to be as a part. The so-called realistic philosophy of the Middle Ages is a philosophy of participation. It presupposes that universals logically and collectives actually have more reality than the individual. The particular (literally: being a small part) has its power of being by participation in the universal. The self-affirmation expressed, for instance, in the self-respect of the individual is self-affirmation as follower of a feudal lord, or as the member of a guild, or as the student in an academic corporation, or as a bearer of a special function like that of a craft or a trade or a profession. But the Middle Ages, in spite of all primitive elements, is not primitive. Two things happened in the ancient world which separate medieval collectivism definitely from primitive collectivism. One of these was the discovery of personal guilt – called by the prophets guilt before God: the decisive step to the personalization of religion and culture. The other was the beginning of autonomous question-asking in Greek philosophy, the decisive step to the problematization of culture and religion. Both elements were transmitted to the medieval nations by the Church. With them went the anxiety of guilt and condemnation and the anxiety of doubt and meaninglessness.'

[14] And just as the individual for his fulfilment requires the domestic society of a family, so the household requires for its fulfilment to be part of a neighbourhood; it would otherwise be lacking in many ways, and thus be precluded from attaining happiness. Again, a single neighbourhood cannot satisfy all its own needs; for this the city is required.

Ond' elli ancora: "Or dì: sarebbe il peggio
per l'omo in terra, se non fosse cive?".
"Sì", rispuos' io; "e qui ragion non cheggio".
   "E puot' elli esser, se giù non si vive
diversamente per diversi offici?
Non, se 'l maestro vostro ben vi scrive".
   Sì venne deducendo infino a quici;
poscia conchiuse: "Dunque esser diverse
convien di vostri effetti le radici:
   per ch'un nasce Solone e altro Serse,
altro Melchisedèch e altro quello
che, volando per l'aere, il figlio perse.
   La circular natura, ch'è suggello
a la cera mortal, fa ben sua arte,
ma non distingue l'un da l'altro ostello.
   Quinci addivien ch'Esaù si diparte
per seme da Iacòb; e vien Quirino
a sì vil padre, che si rende a Marte.
   Natura generata il suo cammino
simil farebbe sempre a' generanti,
se non vincesse il proveder divino.
   Or quel che t'era dietro t'è davanti:
ma perché sappi che di te mi giova,
un corollario voglio che t'ammanti.
   Sempre natura, se fortuna trova
discorde a sé, com' ogne altra semente
fuor di sua regïon, fa mala prova.
   E se 'l mondo là giù ponesse mente
al fondamento che natura pone,
seguendo lui, avria buona la gente.
   Ma voi torcete a la religïone
tal che fia nato a cignersi la spada,
e fate re di tal ch'è da sermone;
   onde la traccia vostra è fuor di strada".[15]

---

[15] "Now say, would it be worse for man on earth if he were not a citizen?" "Yes", I replied, "and here I ask for no proof". "And can that be, unless men below live in diverse ways for diverse duties? Not if your master writes well of this for you." Thus he came deducing as far as here, then he concluded, "therefore the roots of your work must needs be diverse, so that one is born Solon and another Xerxes, one Melchizedeck and another he who flew through the air and lost his son. Circling nature, which is a seal on the mortal wax performs its art well, but does not distinguish one house from another. Whence it happens that Esau differs in seed from Jacob, and Quirinus comes from so base a father that he is ascribed to Mars. The begotten nature would always make its course like its begetters, did not divine provision overrule. Now that which was behind you is before you; but that you may know

It is then, by way of the special socio-political and cultural complexion of the city that the individual sees and lays hold of the moral and ontological possibilities properly his and his alone, of all that he has it in himself to be and to become, at which point courage as the *courage to be as part* – the courage, that is to say, of affirmation as a matter of allegiance – moves into view.

But that is not all, for no less indispensable to a consummate act of specifically human being is the empire as the ground and guarantee of universal peace.[16] The idea is simple. Man as man, Dante maintains in the *Monarchia*, has a collective as well as a private end, the collective end

that I delight in you, I will have a corollary cloak you round. Ever does nature, if she find fortune discordant with herself, like any kind of seed out of its proper region, come to ill result. And if the world below would give heed to the foundation which nature lays, and followed it, it would have its people good. But you wrest to religion one born to gird on the sword, and you make a king of one that is fit for sermons; so that your track is off the road". Aristotle, *Pol.* I.2; 1252b27-29 ('Quae autem ex pluribus vicis communitas perfects civitas, iam omnis, habens terminum per se sufficientiae'), etc., though see in relation to Dante and Aristotle, A. H. Gilbert, 'Had Dante read the *Politics* of Aristotle', *Publications of the Modern Language Association* 43 (1928), 3, 602-13; L. Minio Paluello, 'Dante's Reading of Aristotle', in *The World of Dante. Essays on Dante and his Times*, ed. C. Grayson (Oxford: Clarendon Press, 1980), pp. 61-80, subsequently in *Luoghi cruciali in Dante*, ed. F. Santi (Spoleto: Centro Italiano di Studi sull'Alto Medioevo, 1993), pp. 29-49, and in *Dante. The Critical Complex*, 8 vols, ed. R. Lansing (New York and London: Routledge, 2003), vol. 3, pp. 35-54. On Dante and the city, E. Peters, '*Pars, parte*: Dante and an Urban Contribution to Political Thought', in H. A. Miskimin et al. (eds), *The Medieval City* (New Haven: Yale University Press, 1977), pp. 113-40; C. Honess, 'Feminine Virtues and Florentine Vices: Citizenship and Morality in *Paradiso* XV-XVII', in J. R. Woodhouse (ed.), *Dante and Governance* (Oxford: Clarendon Press, 1997), pp. 102-20; C. Keen, *Dante and the City* (Stroud: Tempus, 2003). More generally, G. Holmes, 'The Emergence of an Urban Ideology at Florence, c. 1250-1450', *Transactions of the Royal Historical Society* 22 (1973), 111-34; J. K. Hyde, *Society and Politics in Medieval Italy. The Evolution of Civil Life, 1000-1350* (New York and London: St Martin's Press, 1973); D. Waley, *The Italian City-Republics*, 3rd edn (London: Longman, 1988); P. Jones, *The Italian City State. From Comune to Signoria* (Oxford: Clarendon Press, 1997).

[16] Preliminary in respect of an ample bibliography, F. Ercole, *Il pensiero politico di Dante*, 2 vols (Milan: Alpes, 1927-28); F. Battaglia, *Impero, Chiesa e Stati particolari nel pensiero di Dante* (Bologna: Zanichelli, 1944); A. P. D'Entrèves, *Dante as a Political Thinker* (Oxford: Clarendon Press, 1952; repr. 1965); M. Barbi, 'L'ideale politico-religioso di Dante', 'L'Italia nell'ideale politico di Dante' and 'Impero e Chiesa', in *Problemi fondamentali per un nuovo commento alla Divina Commedia* (Florence: Sansoni, 1955), pp. 49-68, 69-89, 91-114; C. T. Davis, *Dante and the Idea of Rome* (Oxford: Clarendon Press, 1957); idem, *Dante's Italy and Other Essays* (Philadelphia: University of Pennsylvania Press, 1984); B. Nardi, 'Il concetto dell'Impero nello svolgimento del pensiero dantesco' and 'Tre pretese fasi del pensiero politico di Dante', in *Saggi di filosofia dantesca*, 2nd edn (Florence: La Nuova Italia, 1967), pp. 215-75 and 276-310; M. Maccarrone, 'Papato e Impero nella *Monarchia*', *Nuove letture dantesche* 8 (1976), 259-332; D. Mancusi-Ungaro, *Dante and the Empire* (New York: Peter Lang, 1987); J. R. Woodhouse (ed.), *Dante and Governance* (previous note).

consisting in the actualization at any given moment of his total capacity for knowing and understanding. But actualization on any scale and with any degree of permanence requires a quiet mind and an untroubled spirit, which is where the emperor comes in, he and he alone being in a position to establish and maintain the peace and quiet necessary to the joint enterprise; on the notion, then, of collective intelligence and of universal peace as its prior and subsistent condition, these lines from not too far into the first book of the *Monarchia*:

> Satis igitur declaratum est quod proprium opus humani generis totaliter accepti est actuare semper totam potentiam intellectus possibilis, per prius ad speculandum et secondario propter hoc ad operandum per suam extensionem. Et quia quemadmodum est in parte sic est in toto, et in homine particulari contingit quod sedendo et quiescendo prudentia et sapientia ipse perficitur, patet quod genus humanum in quiete sive tranquillitate pacis ad proprium suum opus ... liberrime atque facillime se habet. Unde manifestum est quod pax universalis est optimum eorum que ad nostram beatitudinem ordinantur.
>
> (*Mon.* I.iv.1-2)[17]

while on the notion of peace and quiet thus understood as the responsibility

---

[17] Now it has been sufficiently explained that the activity proper to mankind considered as a whole is constantly to actualize the full intellectual potential of humanity, primarily through thought and secondarily through action (as a function and extension of thought). And since what holds true for the part is true for the whole, and an individual human being "grows perfect in judgment and wisdom when he sits at rest", it is apparent that mankind most freely and readily attends to this activity ... in the calm or tranquillity of peace. Hence it is clear that universal peace is the best of those things which are ordained for our human happiness. On the collective actualization of the possible intellect, *Mon.* I.iii 7-8: 'Patet igitur quod ultimum de potentia ipsius humanitatis est potentia sive virtus intellectiva. Et quia potentia ista per unum hominem seu per aliquam particularium comunitatum superius distinctarum tota simul in actum reduci non potest, necesse est multitudinem esse in humano genere, per quam quidem tota potentia hec actuetur; sicut necesse est multitudinem rerum generabilium ut potentia tota materie prime semper sub actu sit; aliter esset dare potentiam separatam, quod est inpossibile.' For the 'sedendo et quiescendo prudentia et sapientia ipse perficitur' motif, Aristotle, *Physics* VII, 3; 247b17-18; Thomas, *ScG* III.xxxvii.7: 'Ad hanc etiam omnes aliae humanae operationes ordinari videntur sicut ad finem. Ad perfectionem enim contemplationis requiritur incolumitas corporis, ad quam ordinantur artificialia omnia quae sunt necessaria ad vitam. Requiritur etiam quies a perturbationibus passionum, ad quam pervenitur per virtutes morales et per prudentiam; et quies ab exterioribus perturbationibus, ad quam ordinatur totum regimen vitae civilis'; *In Eth.* X.vii, lect. xi, n. 4 ult.: 'Haec est enim felicitas speculativa, ad quam tota vita politica videtur ordinata; dum per pacem, quae per ordinationem vitae politicae statuitur et conservatur, datur hominibus facultas contemplandi veritatem.'

of the emperor, this passage from the third book:

> Et cum ad hunc portum vel nulli vel pauci, et hii cum difficultate nimia, pervenire possint, nisi sedatis fluctibus blande cupiditatis genus humanum liberum in pacis tranquillitate quiescat, hoc est illud signum ad quod maxime debet intendere curator orbis, qui dicitur romanus Princeps, ut scilicet in areola ista mortalium libere cum pace vivatur.
>
> (*Mon.* III.xvi.11)[18]

Now imperial jurisdiction, as Dante understands it, is not a moral jurisdiction. On the contrary, imperial writ runs fully and unequivocally only in matters of pure positive law, in all other cases – wherever human law preserves by virtue of its descent from the natural law a moral component – the subject retaining a right of dissent.[19] In the degree, however, to which a man 'grows wise by sitting at rest', imperial power is present to him as a necessary condition of his proper

---

[18] And since none can reach this harbour (or few, and these few with great difficulty) unless the waves of seductive greed are calmed and the human race rests free in the tranquillity of peace, this is the goal which the protector of the world, who is called the Roman Prince, must strive with all his might to bring about: i.e. that life on this threshing-floor of mortals may be lived freely and in peace. On the further and more refined notion of the emperor as emancipator of the spirit, as guaranteeing by way of his universal jurisdiction a free passage in the subject from seeing and understanding to willing and doing, I.xii.3-4 and 9: 'Et ideo dico quod iudicium medium est apprehensionis et appetitus: nam primo res apprehenditur, deinde apprehensa bona vel mala iudicatur, et ultimo iudicans prosequitur sive fugit. Si ergo iudicium moveat omnino appetitum et nullo modo preveniatur ab eo, liberum est; si vero ab appetitu quocunque modo proveniente iudicium moveatur, liberum esse non potest, quia non a se, sed ab alio captivum trahitur [...] Genus humanum solum imperante Monarcha sui et non alterius gratia est: tunc enim solum politie diriguntur oblique – democratie scilicet, oligarchie atque tyrampnides – que in servitutem cogunt genus humanum, ut patet discurrenti per omnes, et politizant reges, aristocratici quos optimates vocant, et populi libertatis zelatores; quia cum Monarcha maxime diligat homines, ut iam tactum est, vult omnes homines bonos fieri: quod esse non potest apud oblique politizantes.'

[19] *Conv.* IV.ix.14-15: 'Queste cose simigliantemente, che de l'altre arti sono ragionate, vedere si possono ne l'arte imperiale; ché regole sono in quella che sono pure arti, sì come sono le leggi de' matrimonii, de li servi, de le milizie, de li successori in dignitade, e di queste in tutto siamo a lo Imperadore subietti, sanza dubbio e sospetto alcuno. Altre leggi sono che sono quasi seguitatrici di natura, sì come constituire l'uomo d'etade sofficiente a ministrare, e di queste non semo in tutto subietti. Altre molte sono, che paiono avere alcuna parentela con l'arte imperiale – e qui fu ingannato ed è chi crede che la sentenza imperiale sia in questa parte autentica –: sì come [diffinire] giovinezza e gentilezza, sovra le quali nullo imperiale giudicio è da consentire, in quanto elli è imperadore: però, quello che è di Dio sia renduto a Dio.' J. Took, '"Diligite iustitiam qui iudicatis terram": Justice and the Just Ruler in Dante', in *Dante and Governance*, ed. J. R. Woodhouse (note 15 above), pp. 137-51.

emergence, at which point courage as the *courage to be as part* once again moves centre stage.

Finally, there is the Church, the gathered community of souls naming the name here below on earth and in heaven.[20] Now here there is a paradox, for not only was Dante among the staunchest critics of the Church in its lovelessnesss,[21] but he spent a great deal of time and energy rescuing the human project from what amounts to the clerical world-view, to a finality impatient of qualitative and thus of political distinctions along the way. In the *Convivio*, this declericalization of the moral and intellectual life takes the form of an attempt to identify a species of human happiness appropriate to, and realizable by, those 'many men and women in this language of ours ... bowed down by domestic and civic care'.[22] In the *Monarchia* it

---

[20] P. Brezzi, 'Dante e la Chiesa del suo tempo', in *Dante e Roma: atti del convegno di studi, Roma 8-9-10 aprile, 1965* (Florence: Le Monnier, 1965), pp. 97-113 (with, at pp. 115-35, R. Manselli, 'Dante e l'*ecclesia spiritualis*'); idem, 'L'Italia tra Chiesa e Impero nell'età di Dante', in *Letture classensi* 16 (1987), pp. 99-118; P. Armour, *The Door of Purgatory. A Study of Multiple Symbolism in Dante's Purgatorio* (Oxford: Clarendon Press, 1983); S. Botterill, 'Not of This World: Spiritual and Temporal Powers in Dante and Bernard of Clairvaux', *Lectura Dantis* 10 (1992), 8-21; idem, 'Ideals of the Institutional Church in Dante and Bernard of Clairvaux', *Italica* 78 (2001), 3, 297-313 (subsequently in *Dante: The Critical Complex*, 8 vols, ed. R. Lansing (New York and London: Routledge, 2003), vol. 4, pp. 405-21); A. K. Cassell, '"Luna est Ecclesia": Dante and the "Two Great Lights"', *Dante Studies* 119 (2001), 1-26; C. T. Davis, 'Dante and Ecclesiastical Property', in *Dante: The Critical Complex* (above), vol. 5, pp. 294-307 (originally in *Law in Mediaeval Life and Thought*, ed. E. B. King and S. J. Ridyard (Sewanee, Tenn.: The Press of University of the South, 1990), pp. 244-57); M. S. Kempshall, 'Accidental Perfection:Ecclesiology and Political Thought in *Monarchia*', in P. Acquaviva and J. Petrie (eds), *Dante and the Church: Literary and Historical Essays* (Dublin: Four Courts Press, 2007), pp. 127-71 (also, in the same volume, pp. 93-125, P. Nasti, 'The Amorous Bride and her Lovers: Images of the Church in the Heaven of the Sun').

[21] Recently on the forms of Dantean dissent, A. Consoli, 'Dante anticlericale?', in *Dante ecumenico. Letture e postille* (Naples: Conte, 1973), pp. 20-24; A. Comollo, *Il dissenso religioso in Dante* (Florence: Olschki, 1990; Biblioteca dell'"Archivum Romanicum", 1st series, vol. 235); V. Esposito, *La 'Commedia' dantesca tre fede e dissenso* (Pescara: Tracce, 1999). The notion of Dantean dissent stands, however, to be developed in terms of what Tillich calls the protestant principle (as distinct from Protestant*ism* as but the most dramatic of its historical manifestations) everywhere at work in Christian spirituality as the guardian and guarantor of its deep substance, as that whereby the religious undertaking is protected against 'the aspiration of its own religious and secular appearances' (*Theology of Culture*, ed. R. C. Kimball (London, Oxford and New York: Oxford University Press, 1959), p. 29). For an account of Dante's restiveness as a specifically Christian thinker in terms (*a*) of his sense of the cultural encounter in general as distinct from the ecclesiastical encounter in particular as salvifically significant, and (*b*) of his commitment to the notion of episcopacy as a matter ultimately of *self*-episcopacy or *self*-oversight (this being the final cause every proper striving of the spirit in man), see pp. 155-70 above ('Dante and the Protestant Principle').

[22] *Conv.* I ix.5 and I.i.4.

takes the form of a distinction between, as Dante sees it, the *two* kinds of happiness proper to man as man, namely the happiness of the next life overseen by the pope as bridge-builder-in-chief (*pontifex maximus*) on the basis of revelation, and the happiness of this life overseen by the emperor, as assisted by the philosopher, on the basis of reason,[23] this, then, being his way of loosening the kind of theologism and ecclesiasticism whereby the Church is able to insist on its primacy in every area of the moral and political life. Here again, however, we must be careful, for not only does declericalization *not* mean detheologization, but the ferocity of his denunciation of the Church in its lovelessness is itself testimony to the strength of his commitment to the status of the Church as but the continuing presence of Christ to us, albeit of the Christ crucified afresh. To be beyond the pale of the Church, then, and of the faith she proclaims is to be cast adrift on the sea of directionlessness and of despair, at which point courage as the *courage to be as part* yet again commends itself as a principle of self-understanding and self-implementation.

4. For Dante too, then, the formal structures of being and becoming – *civitas*, *imperium* and *ecclesia* – matter, each having a part to play in the coming about of man as man; for it is by way of the city and of the unique dynamic of the city that the individual comes home to himself as a soldier or sermonizer, by way of the empire that he enjoys the peace and quiet necessary to both the collective and the individual undertaking, and by way of the Church that he knows himself even now as party to the elect. To this extent, therefore, Dante fits the bill, his too being a sense of courage as the *courage to be as part*.[24] But to live with the *Commedia* as an account of the soul's journey into God as verified at first hand by the one who says 'I' is straightaway to become aware of its character as an essay in courage, not, in fact, as the *courage to be as part*, but as the *courage to be as oneself*, in the kind of courage whereby the individual called from

---

[23] *Mon.* III.xvi.7-8: 'Duos igitur fines providentia illa inenarrabilis homini proposuit intendendos: beatitudinem scilicet huius vite, que in operatione proprie virtutis consistit et per terrestrem paradisum figuratur; et beatitudinem vite ecterne, que consistit in fruitione divini aspectus ad quam propria virtus ascendere non potest, nisi lumine divino adiuta, que per paradisum celestem intelligi datur. Ad has quidem beatitudines, velut ad diversas conclusiones, per diversa media venire oportet. Nam ad primam per phylosophica documenta venimus, dummodo illa sequamur secundum virtutes morales et intellectuales operando; ad secundam vero per documenta spiritualia que humanam rationem transcendunt, dummodo illa sequamur secundum virtutes theologicas operando, fidem spem scilicet et karitatem.'

[24] W. Kölmel, 'Chiesa, cristianità, genero umano: riflessioni sull'autocomprensione della società medievale', *Cristianesimo nella Storia. Ricerche storiche, esegetiche, teologiche* 5 (1984), 3, 507-22.

beforehand to be in God as the first and final cause of his every aspiration of the spirit seeks to lay hold of his proper humanity *from out of* that humanity, from out of the power properly his to moral and ontological determination. Indispensable, then, as city, empire and Church are as principles both of self-recognition and of self-affirmation, there can be no escaping the anxiety of existence by taking refuge in the structures of collectivity as a response to the sensation of dividedness and catastrophe; for neither the structures of local or of world citizenship (*civitas*, *imperium*) nor the communion of the faithful as those called out for God's service (*ecclesia*) can exempt the individual from the struggle *to be* by way of an act of *self-knowledge*, of *self-reconfiguration* and of *self-transcendence* as the condition of moral and ontological emergence, at which point we witness the triumph of the *courage to be as oneself* over the *courage to be as part* as a way of seeing and understanding the human predicament. Short, in other words, of courage as the *courage to be as oneself*, as the courage to engage with self from out of the power of self to self-determination, there can be no question of homecoming, for short of courage thus understood the individual is forever engaged in a process of evasion, of sidestepping what actually matters about his presence in the world as a creature of accountability.

The moral component in this situation is set out by Dante in the central cantos of the *Purgatorio*, cantos turning on a sense of the human project as a matter of affective organization. Man as man, then, knows himself in a twofold order of loving. He knows himself by way (*a*) of the kind of love given with the act itself of existence, of an 'amore naturale' predating the moral moment proper of human experience and thus governing it, and (*b*) of the kind of love generated by this or that passing object of perception, of an 'amore d'animo' or contingent loving post-dating the moral moment and thus governed by it. His proper task, therefore, when it comes to right loving, lies not so much in the denial of this or that set or sub-set of love-impulses, as in their co-ordination, in the bringing home of elective to essential loving such that each alike serves the highest good, the call to be in, through and for God as the alpha and omega of all being. This is the meaning of the 'Né creator né creatura' passage beginning at *Purg.* XVII.91, a passage placed by Dante upon the lips of Virgil but, especially as it goes on, transparent to its theological content, to the possibility of love as, withal, a principle of apostasy (the 'contra 'l fattore adovra sua fattura' moment of the last line):

> "Né creator né creatura mai",
> cominciò el, "figliuol, fu sanza amore,
> o naturale o d'animo; e tu 'l sai.

> Lo naturale è sempre sanza errore,
> ma l'altro puote errar per malo obietto
> o per troppo o per poco di vigore.
>   Mentre ch'elli è nel primo ben diretto,
> e ne' secondi sé stesso misura,
> esser non può cagion di mal diletto;
>   ma quando al mal si torce, o con più cura
> o con men che non dee corre nel bene,
> contra 'l fattore adovra sua fattura".[25]

Now in the degree to which the individual seeks to measure secondary loving up against primary loving (the 'ne' secondi sé stesso misura' of line 98) he knows himself in the consummate character of his existence as a creature in potential to God. In the degree, by contrast, to which, waylaid by proximate possibility, he falls short in this, he knows himself only in the kinds of fear, disorientation and self-inexplicability characteristic of being in its remotion. This, then, is where Dante begins. He begins with the phenomenology of dividedness, with the psychological substance of being as ranged over against itself in the forum of conscience:

> Nel mezzo del cammin di nostra vita
> mi ritrovai per una selva oscura,
> ché la diritta via era smarrita.
>   Ahi quanto a dir qual era è cosa dura
> esta selva selvaggia e aspra e forte
> che nel pensier rinova la paura! ...
>   Io non so ben ridir com' i' v'intrai,
> tant' era pien di sonno a quel punto
> che la verace via abbandonai ...
>   questa mi porse tanto di gravezza
> con la paura ch'uscìa di sua vista,
> ch'io perdei la speranza dell'altezza.
>
>   (*Inf.* I.1-6, 10-12, 52-54)[26]

---

[25] He began: "Neither Creator nor creature, my son, was ever without love, either natural or of the mind, and this you know. The natural is always without error; but the other may err either through an evil object, or through too much or too little vigour. While it is directed on the primal good, and on secondary goods observes right measure, it cannot be the cause of sinful pleasure. But when it is turned awry to evil, or speeds to good with more zeal, or with less, than it ought, against the Creator works his creature."

[26] Midway in the journey of our life I found myself in a dark wood, for the straight way was lost. Ah, how hard it is to tell how that wood was, wild, rugged, harsh; the very thought of it renews my fear ... I cannot rightly say how I entered it, I was so full of sleep at the moment I left the true way ... she put such heaviness upon me with the fear that came from the sight of her that I lost hope of the height.

And it is into this situation that courage as the courage *to be as oneself* enters as that whereby the individual embarks on the way of death and resurrection. First, then, and as sustained by a movement of grace tending from deep within it to confirm and strengthen it, comes the courage of *acknowledgement*, the courage whereby, sensitive to everything within the economy of personality making for the alternative solution, the individual commits himself to the way of descent and of disclosure, to a laying open of self in the demonic substance of self; hence, on the threshold of the text, the 'Quali fioretti dal notturno gelo' passage of *Inf*. II.121-42, superlative in its account of courage as the courage of commitment, as that whereby, secure in its sense of the providentiality of it all, of the journey as authorized from on high, the pilgrim spirit sets about the business of recognition, of contemplating as the condition of all righteousness in human experience the spectacle of *un*righteousness:

> "Dunque: che è? perché, perché restai,
> perché tanta viltà nel core allette,
> perché ardire e franchezza non hai,
>   poscia che tai tre donne benedette
> curan di te ne la corte del cielo,
> e 'l mio parlar tanto ben ti promette?".
>   Quali fioretti dal notturno gelo
> chinati e chiusi, poi che 'l sol li 'mbianca,
> si drizzan tutti aperti in loro stelo,
>   tal mi fec' io di mia virtude stanca,
> e tanto buono ardire al cor mi corse,
> ch'i' cominciai come persona franca:
>   "Oh pietosa colei che mi soccorse!
> e te cortese ch'ubidisti tosto
> a le vere parole che ti porse!
>   Tu m'hai con disiderio il cor disposto
> sì al venir con le parole tue,
> ch'i' son tornato nel primo proposto.
>   Or va, ch'un sol volere è d'ambedue:
> tu duca, tu segnore e tu maestro".
> Così li dissi; e poi che mosso fue,
>   intrai per lo cammino alto e silvestro.[27]

---

[27] "What, then, is this? Why, why do you hold back? Why do you harbour such cowardice in your heart? Why are you not bold and free, when in Heaven's court three such blessed ladies are mindful of you, and my words pledge you so great a good?" As little flowers, bent down and closed by chill of night, straighten and all unfold upon their stems when the sun brightens them, such in my faint strength did I become; and so much good courage rushed to my heart that I began, as one set free, "Oh, how compassionate

But that is not all, for following hard upon the heels of courage as the courage of acknowledgement comes the courage of *alignment*, the courage whereby, having seen and contemplated self in its destitution, but having by grace taken the guilt of this situation into itself, the soul begins now to contemplate the shape and substance of its loving, the pattern of its disorganized affectivity – the business of the purgatorial phase of its journey into God. First, then, comes the anti-purgatorial moment of the journey, the moment of spiritual readying giving way at last to the travail of the purgatorial moment proper, to the nothing if not painful fashioning from the disgregated substance of being so far something more intimately ordered, more properly transparent to the deep reasons of that being. With this, the spirit comes at last into the fullness of its proper humanity, to a now uncluttered opening out of the intentional upon the actual and a fresh equality of self to an act both of self-understanding and of world-historical understanding, each of these things, however, bereft of its power to despair and destruction. Here too, then, it is a question of courage, of the courage, not now of recognition, but of reconfiguration, of affirming self in the revised structure of self.

But even that is not all, for the courage of acknowledgement and the courage of alignment flow into the courage of *actualization*, into the courage required of the individual as, risking all for the sake of finding all, he maps his humanity onto the kind 'transhumanity' present to him as but the most immanent of his immanent possibilities; so, then, as a call to attention in respect of this, the final step along the way, these lines from Canto II of the *Paradiso*, an essay in the courage of anticipation, the courage required of the pilgrim spirit as it projects itself upon its ultimate possibility:

> O voi che siete in piccioletta barca,
> desiderosi d'ascoltar, seguiti
> dietro al mio legno che cantando varca,
>   tornate a riveder li vostri liti:
> non vi mettete in pelago, ché forse,
> perdendo me, rimarreste smarriti ...
>   Voialtri pochi che drizzaste il collo

was she who helped me, and how courteous were you, so quick to obey the true words she spoke to you! By your words you have made me so eager to come with you that I have returned to my first resolve. Now on, for a single will is in us both; you are my leader, you are my master and my teacher". So I said to him, and when he moved on, I entered along the deep and savage way. See too in respect of the *Inferno* as, whatever else it is, an essay in the rhythm of ontological courage the 'Or sie forte e ardito. Omai si scende per sì fatte scale' moment of *Inf.* XVII.81-82 and the '"Ecco Dite", dicendo, "ed ecco il loco / ove convien che di fortezza t'armi' moment of XXXIV. 20-21.

> per tempo al pan de li angeli, del quale
> vivesi qui ma non sen vien satollo,
>   metter potete ben per l'alto sale
> vostro navigio, servando mio solco
> dinanzi a l'acqua che ritorna equale.
>
> (*Par.* II.1-6, 10-15)[28]

while as registering the triumph of the individual as he comes into the presence of the One who *is* as of the essence, these lines from Canto XXXIII of the *Paradiso*, an essay now in the courage of accomplishment, the courage of the pilgrim spirit as it rejoices at last in a consummate act of understanding:

> E' mi ricorda ch'io fui pió ardito
> per questo a sostener, tanto ch'i' giunsi
> l'aspetto mio col valore infinito.
>   Oh abbondante grazia ond' io presunsi
> ficcar lo viso per la luce etterna,
> tanto che la veduta vi consunsi!
>   Nel suo profondo vidi che s'interna,
> legato con amore in un volume,
> ciï che per l'universo si squaderna:
>   sustanze e accidenti e lor costume
> quasi conflati insieme, per tal modo
> che ciï ch'i' dico ä un semplice lume.
>   La forma universal di questo nodo
> credo ch'i' vidi, perchÇ pió di largo,
> dicendo questo, mi sento ch'i' godo.
>
> (Par. XXXIII.79-93)[29]

---

[28] O you that are in your little bark, eager to hear, following behind my ship that singing makes her way, turn back to see again your shores. Do not commit yourselves to the open sea, for perchance, if you lost me, you would remain astray ... You other few who lifted up your necks betimes for bread of angels, on which men here subsist but never become sated of it, you may indeed commit your vessel to the deep brine, holding to my furrow ahead of the water that turns smooth again.

[29] I remember that on this account I was the bolder to sustain it, until I united my gaze with the infinite goodness. Oh abounding grace whereby I presumed to fix my look through the eternal light so far that all my sight was spent therein. In its depth I saw ingathered, bound by love in one single volume, that which is dispersed in leaves throughout the universe: substances and accidents and their relations, as though fused together in such a way that what I tell is but a simple light. The universal form of this knot I believe that I saw, because, in telling this, I feel my joy increase.

To embark on the way of transhumanity, Dante suggests, is to embark on the way, not merely of recognition and of reconfiguration (each alike preliminary in respect of what comes next), but of a positive redefining of self on the planes both of knowing and of loving, of a re-dimensioning of cognitive and affective selfhood. With this, then, with what amounts to a hymn to courage as the virtue *par excellence* of being in its 'outstandingness' (*ex-sistere*), we are in a position both to commend and to qualify Tillich's account of courage at least as far as Dante is concerned; for if on the one hand Dante's is indeed a commitment to the notion of courage as the *courage to be as part, civitas, imperium* and *ecclesia* entering properly into the soteriological scheme, courage thus understood stands even so to be taken up as far as the *Commedia* is concerned in the *courage to be as oneself*, in the kind of courage born not of allegiance, but of actuality, of knowing self in the *thereness* of self.

5. Put thus, Dante's, for all his commitment in the *Commedia* to the notion of grace as the ground and guarantee of every significant inflexion of the spirit in man, is nonetheless a heroic spirituality, heroic in its commitment to courage under both kinds – but above all as the *courage to be as oneself* – as the *prius* of everything that ultimately matters in human experience, of every reaching out of the creature towards the creator. But there is more, for the courage he commends as a disposition of the spirit in its seeking out of God as the beginning and end of all seeking in human experience is the courage he himself lived out as poet and prophet of the pilgrim way. Deriving, in other words, comfort and encouragement from all those of his *auctores* to whom he was most indebted and of whom he was most enamoured (from Thomas, Albert, Bonaventure, Bernard, Boethius and from the cloud of witnesses among whom he himself now numbers), he nonetheless fashioned a theology quite other than anything he discovered in his texts; for his, wedded as it was to the idea pure and simple in all the exquisite purity of the idea, was an exploration of the theological issue by way not, in fact, of the idea *tout court*, but of the drama of being and becoming as lived out at first hand by the one who says 'I'. Responsive in the highest degree to the contents of dogmatic awareness, his was an account of the religious situation by way of its inner agony, of the pain of knowing self in the inexplicability of self and of this as the condition of new life. The courage to be, therefore, fully thematicized in the text and commended there as an object of contemplation, at every point transcends its merely textual elaboration to subsist as its encompassing – an instance, we might say, of *metalettarietà* at its most sublime.

Afterword

> 'Al Padre, al Figlio, a lo Spirito Santo',
> cominciò, 'gloria!', tutto 'l paradiso,
> sì che m'inebrïava il dolce canto.
> Ciò ch'io vedeva mi sembiava un riso
> de l'universo; per che mia ebbrezza
> intrava per l'udire e per lo viso.
> Oh gioia! oh ineffabile allegrezza!
> oh vita intègra d'amore e di pace!
> oh sanza brama sicura ricchezza!
>
> (*Par.* XXVII.1-9)[1]

Conversation with Kenelm always was, and still is, a privilege, for his was a seasoned spirituality, full of – by the time, at any rate, that I knew him – years and wisdom. Yet it generated a strange paradox, for whereas, as heir to the rich humanity of Thomism, one might have expected him to delight in the rich humanity of Dante, of a Dante attuned to the part played by man in the working out of his own destiny, Kenelm's instead was a sense ultimately of the defectiveness of it all, of Dante's falling short as a theological spirit. This, at least, is where his lifelong meditation on the poet comes to rest. It comes to rest with a sense (*a*) of the mutual far-offness, even in the *Commedia*, of grace and nature within the economy of human activity as a whole; (*b*) of Dante's somehow managing to separate out in the *Commedia* virtue as a matter of right doing and charity as a matter of right loving; (*c*) of Dante's less than deft management of his cultural premises; and (*d*) of all this as cause for misgiving. The key passage once again:

> From all the above, in any event, we may conclude, I think, that Dante shows a marked tendency, through the *Convivio* and the *Monarchia*

---

[1] "Glory be to the Father, to the Son, and to the Holy Spirit!" all Paradise began, so that the sweet song held me rapt. What I saw seemed to me a smile of the universe, so that my rapture entered both by hearing and by sight. O joy! O ineffable gladness! O life entire of love and of peace! O wealth secure without longing!

and even in the *Comedy*, to reduce to a minimum the conceivable contacts between human nature and divine grace; even if we are persuaded, by the evidence adduced in the last few pages, or on other grounds, that he did allow a bare possibility of such contact for *all* adult human beings. And that tendency, with its consequences, is what I have taken as characteristic of the 'other', the *second* Dante implied in the title of this essay. And perhaps it reveals an important defect, from the Christian point of view, in this great Christian's thinking about man: an over-readiness to conceive of moral virtue in isolation from Charity, the 'first and greatest commandment'. After all, a certain practice and cult of moral virtue is quite compatible with the radical perversity of indifference to God. But Christianity requires that the moral virtues themselves be offered to God as a way – as *the* way – of cooperating with his grace. In this perspective the natural virtues themselves, ordered under Charity ('the mother of the virtues'), become as it were organs of grace, are no longer just humanly 'acquired' but divinely 'infused'. Guided by this insight St Thomas could take over the whole achievement of Aristotle, as a philosophical moralist, while giving it an entirely new setting and direction. In Dantean terms this means the difference between Limbo and the *Purgatorio*; in which we see repentant man recovering, under grace, the lost or diminished natural virtues, but only in preparation for something that is utterly beyond their range, a love-union with the Infinite. In the *Purgatorio* Aristotelianism is integrated into Christianity; in the Dantean Limbo it is not.[2]

But this sense of Dante's falling short as a specifically Christian thinker is itself a cause for misgiving; for even taking on board the problems engendered by his particular kind of biculturalism (in truth no more acute than those of Christian Peripateticism in any of its manifestations), there is at work here something more exquisite, namely a sense of how it is that, in consequence of the original and abiding *let it be* of the Pentateuch, and irrespective of the catastrophe of Eden, man may even so be said to co-operate with God at the point of ultimate concern, to enter by way of his proper power to moral and ontological determination into the presence of his maker. Now this requires careful statement, for as far as the *Commedia* is concerned there can be no sidestepping the indispensability of grace, and above all of the grace made known to man in Christ, as the ground and guarantee of every significant movement of the mind and of the will. On the contrary, it is by way of that grace that man as man is made equal to his

---

[2] Kenelm Foster, O.P., *The Two Dantes* (London: Darton, Longman and Todd, 1977), pp. 252-53.

high calling as a creature capable of God (*capax Dei*). But that, precisely, is the point, God's undertaking in man's regard, and above all his work in and through the Christ, being for Dante but a recapacitation of human nature, a re-potentiation of man's humanity in respect of the transhumanity to which it is called from beforehand. Aristotle and Aristotelianism are there – of course they are – as an element in all this, as apt to shape and substantiate Dante's anthropology, psychology and ethic. But to suggest that the Dante of the *Commedia* was in any sense detained or waylaid by the Philosopher or at a loss as to what to do or say about him will not do. For Dante knew exactly what to do and say about Aristotle: to learn from him, to rejoice in him, and to incorporate every facet of that learning and rejoicing in a theology of love-becoming of which the Philosopher had not the least inkling.

Index of Names

Adorno, F. 3
Agresti, A. 53
Airava, E. 158
Albert the Great 2, 37-39, 217
Alessio, G. C. 127
Allan, M. 75, 127
Anselm of Canterbury 49-58, 60, 64, 116, 151
Aristotle 30, 37, 39, 108, 124-25, 130-31,133, 135, 143, 172, 180-81, 192-93
Armour, P. 81, 106, 160, 164, 183
Auer, J. 87
Auerbach, E. 78, 106, 167
Augustine 81, 97, 144, 145, 16 78, 106, 167 2
Aulén, A. G. 52
Avicenna 52

Barberi Squarotti, G. 105, 167
Barbi, M. 180
Barnes, J. C. 166
Barolini, T. 75, 78, 128, 165
Barth, K. 52
Battaglia, F. 180
Baylor, M. G. 91
Beatrice .... iii, 82-84, 97,134, 137
Bemrose, S. 16, 29-30, 35, 83
Benetollo, O. 91
Benvenuto da Imola 61
Bernard of Clairvaux 110
Biffi, I. 88
Bodei, R. 107
Boethius of Dacia 131
Boitani, P. 14, 128
Bonaventure 86
Borsellino, N. 41, 58
Botterill, S. 44, 183
Bougerol, J. -G. 90
Bouillard, H. 87
Bourke, V. J. 92
Boyde, P. 13
Brezzi, P. 183
Brown, D. 58, 153

Brugnoli, G. 165
Brunetto Latini 61
Bultmann, R. 105
Burnaby, J. 103
Busnelli, G. 2-4, 6, 78, 127, 153
Bynum, C. W. 105
Cacciaglia, N. 76, 128
Caesar, M. 155
Cambon, G. 127
Camilli, A. 127
Cannavò, G. 75
Cao, G. M. 3
Capelli, V. 44
Capéran, L. 76
Capitano, O. 3
Cardellino, L. 41, 58
Cassell, A. K. 105, 183
Castiglia, I. 158
Cattani, G. 158
Cavalcoli, G. 91
Cessario, R. 52
Charity, A. C. .... iv, 106
Cherchi, P. 89
Chiampi, J. T. 89
Chiarenza, M. M. 107
Chiavacci Leonardi, A. M. 72, 128
Chydenius, J. 106
Ciccarese, M. P. 105
Cicero 173
Clogan, P. M. 165
Cogan, M. 2
Colish, M. L. 78, 90, 128
Comollo, A. 158, 183
Comparetti, D. 78
Consoli, A. 183
Consoli, D. 78
Corti, M. 2, 132
Costanzo, N. 167
Cremascoli, G. 128
Cross, R. 47, 152
Crouse, R. D. 2
Crowe, M. B. 92
Crupi, V. 153

D'Entrèves, A. P. 180
Da Carbonara, M. 90
Dales R. C. 107
Daniélou, J. 106
Davies, B. 53
Davis, C. T. 105, 180, 183
De Blic, J. 91

De Lubac, H. 106
Deneffe, A. 47, 152
Di Giannatale, G. 83
Di Scipio, G. 75
Dillistone, F. W. 52
Dionysius the Areopagite 68
Duhem, P. 106
Dunning, T. P. 76

Elders, L. 91
Enright, N. 158
Ercole, F. 180
Ermatinger, C. I. 132
Ernst, C., O.P. 81
Esposito, V. 183
Evans, G. R. 53

Fallani, G. 53, 153
Fiddes, P. S. 152
Filosa, C. 127
Flick, M. 41, 87
Forti, F. 127
Fortin, J. R. 53
Foster, K. .... i-iii, 2, 13-14, 16-18, 31, 44, 77-78, 121-40, 145, 158, 191-92
Franks, R. S. 52
Freccero, J. 81
Frezza, M. 76, 128

Gagliardi, A. 2
Garin, E. 3
Garrigou-Lagrange, R. 86
Gemeinhardt, P. 151
Getto, G. 89
Giacalone, G. 107
Giardinazzo, F. 127
Gilbert, A. H. 180
Gilson, E. .... iii, 2, 7-13, 16, 44, 122-23, 132-33
Gleason, R. W. 87
Godenzi, G. 89
Grabher, C. 127
Grabmann, M. .... ii, 132
Gragnolati, M. 83, 106
Gray, C. B. 53
Greene, R. A. 92
Gregory Nazianzen 47, 152
Gregory, T. 3
Gunton, C. 152
Guthmüller, B. 44

Hahn, T. O'H. 75, 127
Harent, S. 76

Harnack, A. 58, 102-103
Hawkins, P. S. 74
Hayes, Z. 105
Hilary 152
Hollander, R. 75, 78
Holmes, G. 180
Honess, C. 180
Hugh of St Victor 63
Hyde, J. K. 180

Iannucci, A. A. 2, 78, 127
Iliescu, N. 75, 127
Imbach, R. 158
Inglese, G. 76, 78, 128

James of Pistoia 132
Jaspers, Karl 94, 108
John of Damascus 47, 152
Jones, P. 180
Jori, G. 44

Kallendorf, C. 165
Kallendorf, H. 165
Keen, C. 180
Kelly, J. N. D. 106, 152
Kempshall, M. 183
Kierkegaard, Søren 93, 108
Kneale, M. 107
Kneale, W. 107
Kölmel, W. 184
Kors, J. B. 41, 58
Köster, H. M. 41, 59
Kretzmann, N. 107
Kristeller, P. O. 132

La Favia, L. M. 2, 60
Lampe, G. W. H. 106
Lanza, A. 76, 158
Leftow, B. 53, 107
Livi, F. 106, 124
Lonergan, B. J. F. 87
Lottin, O. 91
Luther, Martin 174

Maccarrone, M. 180
Macquarrie, J. 152
Maier, A. 132
Mancusi-Ungaro, D. 180
Mangieri, C. A. 41, 58
Manselli, R. 20
Marshall, W. W. 41, 58

Index of Names

Martinelli, B. 76, 128
Martinez, A. L. 166
Martorelli Vico, R. 41, 59
Masciandaro, F. 107
Mason, H. A. 77
Mastrobuono, A. C. .... iii, 2, 81-89, 95
May, Rollo 108
Mazzantini, P. 3
Mazzeo, J. A. 30, 74
Mazzoni, F. 3
Mazzotta, G. 3, 81
McGrath, A. 52, 116
McIntyre, J. 52-53, 58
McMahon 53
Mellone, A. 16, 29
Metz, W. 2
Miethe, T. L. 92
Migliorini Fissi, R. 167
Minio Paluello, L. 180
Moltmann, J. 105
Montanari, F. 127
Montanari, G. 153
Moore, E. 30, 155
Morghen, R. 75, 127
Muresu, G. 53, 76, 128

Nardi, B. .... iii, 2-7, 16, 29, 35, 38, 58, 83, 122, 133, 145, 180
Nardi, T. 3
Nasti, P. 183
Ngien, D. 151
Nygren, A. 103

O'Connell Baur, C. 76, 128
O'Keeffe, D. 29
Orestano, F. 3

Padgett, A. G. 107
Padoan, G. 78, 106, 127
Palacios, M. A. 106
Palgen, R. 105
Panvini, B. 2, 89
Papio, M. 90
Paul the Apostle 74, 103, 140-42, 147
Perotti, P. A. 167
Peter (the Apostle) 158-60
Peter Lombard 89-90, 110
Peters, E. 180
Petrocchi, G. 3, 75
Picone, M. 75, 77
Plato 17, 31, 33-34, 172
Potts, T. 91

Pretto, L. ... 97
Priest, P. ... 153
Pseudo-Cyril ... 152

Quilici, B. ... 72, 127

Rashdall, H. ... 52
Ratzinger, J. ... 105
Riaud, A. ... 151
Rizzo, G. ... 77, 127
Robinson, J. A. T. ... 105
Roddewig, M. ... 14, 97
Rogers, K. A. ... 107
Rondet, H. ... 41, 58
Ross, C. ... 160
Rossi, S. ... 88
Ruffini, F. ... 75, 127
Ryan, C. ... 14, 53, 66, 81, 88

Salm, P. ... 107
Salsano, F. ... 167
Schiaffini, A. ... 3
Schildgen, B. D. ... 74, 75, 128
Schmitt, F. S. ... 53
Sciuto, I. ... 92, 107
Scorrano, L. ... 89
Scrivano, R. ... 167
Seneca ... 173
Shook, L. K. ... 8
Simmons, E. L. ... 152
Simon, R. ... 151
Singleton, C. S. ... iii, 81-88
Smalley, B. ... 106
Sorabji, R. ... 107
Southern, R. W. ... 53
Spicq, C. ... 106
Statius ... 165
Stocchi, M. P. ... 127
Stramara, D. F. Jr. ... 47, 152
Stump, E. ... 2, 107

Tateo, F. ... 127
Teselle, E. ... 120
Thomas Aquinas ... ii-iii, vi, 1-47, 65-69, 131-33, 145, 149, 151-52, 172, 174, 181, 192
Thompson, D. ... 77
Tillich, P. ... v-vi, 108, 124, 155-57, 171-78, 173, 190
Tondelli, L. ... 153
Took, J. ... 161-82
Torrance, T. F. ... 152
Toussaint, S. ... 7
Trabant, J. ... 89

Index of Names

Travi, E. 97
Turner, R. V. 76, 128

Valensin, A. 155
Vallone, A. 3, 167
Vasoli, C. 3
Vazzana, S. 114
Verbeke, W. 105
Vettori, V. 2
Virgil 78, 82-83, 87-88, 93, 95, 97, 122, 126-37, 164
Vitto, C. L. 76, 78
Von Leyden, W. 107

Waley, D. 180
Watson, N. 76
Wawrykow, J. P. 87
Wehbrink, P. 87
Weithman, P. J. 41, 59
Whatley, G. 76, 129
Wicksteed, P. H. 2
William of Ockham 129
Williams, G. H. 53
Williams, N. P. 41, 87
Wilson, W. 14
Wippel, J. F. 87
Woollcombe, K. J. 106

Yarnold, E. 41